D0083430

Foreign Policy and the
Bureaucratic Process

Foreign Policy and the Bureaucratic Process

The State Department's Country Director System

William I. Bacchus

Princeton University Press, Princeton, New Jersey

Copyright © 1974 by Princeton University Press
All Rights Reserved
LCC: 73-16759
ISBN: 0-691-07565-4

Library of Congress Cataloging in Publication data
will be found on the last printed page of this book

This book has been composed in Linotype Caledonia

Printed in the United States of America
by Princeton University Press,
Princeton, New Jersey

JX
1706
A4
B3

For

FRITZ MOSHER *and* JIM FESLER

Teachers, Colleagues—
and Good Friends

Contents

CONTENTS

Appendices

Tables

Charts

Abbreviations

ACORD   *Action for Organizational Development, a State Department program for human relations training and organizational change*

AF   *Bureau of African Affairs, Department of State*

AID   *Agency for International Development*

ARA-LA   *Merged Bureau for Inter-American Affairs, Department of State, and Bureau for Latin American Affairs, Agency for International Development*

BOB   *Bureau of the Budget*

CASP   *Country Analysis and Strategy Paper, a programming system used in ARA-LA*

CD   *Country Director*

CU   *Bureau of Educational and Cultural Affairs, Department of State*

DAS   *Deputy Assistant Secretary*

DCM   *Deputy Chief of Mission, the second in command in overseas embassies*

DOM   *Identifying symbol in text for interviewees from domestic agencies*

E   *Bureau of Economic Affairs, Department of State*

EA   *Bureau of East Asian and Pacific Affairs, Department of State*

EUR   *Bureau of European Affairs, Department of State*

FAMC   *Foreign Affairs Manual Circular, the State Department method for issuing and maintaining official administrative pronouncements*

IG   *Interdepartmental Group, a component of the NSC system after 1969, chaired by assistant secretaries of state*

IRG   *Interdepartmental Regional Group, a component of the NSAM 341 system from 1966 to 1969, chaired by geographic assistant secretaries of state*

NEA   *Bureau of Near Eastern and South Asian Affairs, Department of State*

xii

NPP	*National Policy Paper, prepared by W. W. Rostow's planning staff with the aid of operating officials for individual countries, during the Johnson and Kennedy administrations*
NSAM	*National Security Action Memorandum, a directive of the president in the national security area, Kennedy and Johnson administrations*
NSDM	*National Security Decision Memorandum, a directive of the president in the national security area, Nixon administration, outlining a decision made by the president*
NSSM	*National Security Study Memorandum, a paper prepared by or for the National Security Council Staff, Nixon administration, for the guidance of the president, NSC, and other officials in making decisions*
OD	*Office Director*
PARA	*Policy Analysis and Resource Allocation, a programming system used in the Nixon administration which served basically the same function as the CASP in other areas of the world*
INR	*Bureau of Intelligence and Research, Department of State*
ISA	*International Security Affairs, a section of the Office of the Secretary of Defense, headed by an assistant secretary of defense*
RPE	*Office of Regional Economic Affairs, Bureau of European Affairs, Department of State*
RPM	*Office of Regional Politico-Military Affairs, Bureau of European Affairs, Department of State*
SIG	*Senior Interdepartmental Group, created by NSAM 341 and chaired by the Under Secretary of State*
USIA	*United States Information Agency*

Acknowledgments

I owe numerous debts of thanks to the many people who helped in one way or another to make this book a reality. Without their assistance the task would have been very much harder, if not impossible.

Personal financial support during the initial period of the study was provided by a Yale University Graduate Fellowship in 1968-1969, and by an American Political Science Association Congressional Fellowship in 1969-1970. Research-related expenses have been defrayed in part by the Department of Political Science, and by the Council on International Relations, both of Yale. The Department of Government and Foreign Affairs of the University of Virginia provided some assistance in meeting typing expenses.

An earlier version of this study benefited in fundamental ways from the efforts of James W. Fesler and Charles E. Lindblom, and particularly from those of my primary dissertation advisor, H. Bradford Westerfield. Later drafts were subjected to searching critiques by my colleague at Virginia, Frederick C. Mosher, who made many important suggestions. The comments of the two readers of the Princeton University Press were also very useful, especially those of I. M. Destler, whose recommendations helped in a major way to solve some problems of organization. Sanford G. Thatcher, Princeton's editor, was a source of continuing support and commonsense advice. Marilyn Grosenick provided her usual impeccable typing skills on the later drafts, and served as *de facto* editor much of the time. What the reader finds good in this study is in large measure attributable to these individuals; its errors and less luminous contributions are entirely my own.

I also owe much to many people in the Department of State and elsewhere in government who encouraged the project and made it possible for the interviews to be conducted, most particularly Pio Uliassi and Joan Seasword, both of the Office of External Research, Bureau of Intelligence and Research, Department of State; and Mr. John E. Crump, formerly of the Bureau of European Affairs. Those who gave their time and cooperation in the interviews cannot be mentioned by name, but I am especially grateful to them. I was impressed by the dedication and competence of most of the individuals who devote their careers to conducting the nation's foreign relations.

My wife Mary survived the demands of this project with unfailing good humor, and contributed to its completion in ways she cannot know.

Finally, it should be noted that the manuscript for this book was completed, except for minor updating, prior to my joining the staff of the Commission on the Organization of the Government for the Conduct of Foreign Policy, and in no way reflects any official positions of the commission.

W.I.B.
Falls Church, Va.
October 1973

Foreign Policy and the
Bureaucratic Process

Introduction

In the 1970s, it is hardly necessary to emphasize the profound changes that have occurred in the nature and conduct of American foreign policy since World War II. The United States has experienced great difficulties, substantively and organizationally, in coping with the fundamental transformations of our foreign relations in a rapidly changing postwar (and cold-war) and increasingly postcolonial world. Surveys of these trends have been presented to the point of exhaustion elsewhere,[1] but a brief recital of their impact on the Department of State perhaps will serve to indicate the magnitude of the challenges State has faced in this period, and to suggest why it has had major problems in adapting itself to new responsibilities and patterns of operation. It is against this background that we must view the attempted organizational changes beginning in 1966 which are of primary concern for this study.

[1] An often cited general survey of these trends is found in John W. Spanier, *American Foreign Policy Since World War II*, 5th rev. ed. (New York: Praeger, 1973). A shorter discussion is provided by a distinguished diplomat, Charles E. Bohlen, in his *The Transformation of American Foreign Policy* (New York: W. W. Norton, 1969); while a still shorter one appears as the first chapter in the report of the Herter Committee, published as a report of the Committee on Foreign Affairs Personnel, *Personnel for the New Diplomacy* (New York: Carnegie Endowment for International Peace, 1962). Among the legion of critics of the form taken by American reaction to the new conditions are Eugene McCarthy, *The Limits of Power* (New York: Random House, 1971); and Edmund Stillman and William Pfaff, *Power and Impotence* (New York: Random House, 1967). The recent writings of Gabriel Kolko, Theodore Draper, and Senator William Fulbright are also applicable here. No serious student of this period should miss the account of the beginnings of these trends in Dean Acheson, *Present at the Creation* (New York: W. W. Norton, 1969).

3

In 1939 the United States had diplomatic relations with 62 states, managed almost entirely by four small geographic divisions of State. By 1950 the number had risen to 79 and by 1960 to 87. The 1960s saw an unprecedented number of countries gain independence, and by February 1973 the United States had formal relations with 135 national units.[2] But numerical proliferation alone does not begin to illustrate the scope of change. Before World War II, U.S. relations with other nations were confined almost entirely to the traditional functions of representation and reporting, and aiding individual Americans. These duties fell almost completely to State, although for a time Commerce and Agriculture had their own attachés abroad (as the latter still does). With the problems of postwar recovery, new alliance structures, economic development, and a huge growth in interchange of people from one country to another, many additional units of government began programs and responsibilities that ranged beyond the domestic sphere. By 1963 it was estimated that twenty-five agencies and units were involved in foreign educational and cultural affairs alone, and more than fifty agencies and departments had personnel serving abroad.[3] The number of persons required to carry out the "New Diplomacy"[4] also multiplied. The Department of State itself expanded from a total of 4,021 employees in all categories, including a tight circle of 833 Foreign Service officers in 1939, to 25,583 employees and

[2] Figures are derived from U.S. Department of State, *Foreign Service List* (Washington, D.C.: GPO, October 1, 1939; January 1, 1950; January 1, 1960; and February 1, 1973).

[3] Policy Review and Research Staff, Bureau of Educational and Cultural Affairs, U.S. Department of State, "Some U.S. Government Agencies Engaged in International Activities," November 1963, mimeographed.

[4] The source of the widely used term "New Diplomacy" to describe the greatly expanded international involvements of the United States is unclear, but the idea dates at least to a speech given by then Secretary of State Dean Acheson to the Advertising Council on March 9, 1950, on the subject of a "Total Diplomacy Policy," *New York Times*, March 10, 1950.

3,500 FSOs by the late 1960s.[5] It is almost impossible to estimate the total number of government employees whose primary functions deal with foreign relations, but by 1964 there were 23,350 U.S. civilians representing agencies and departments other than State abroad,[6] not including foreign nationals employed overseas, or the substantial support base in Washington.

The net effect of all this was to bring to the fore many competitors for control of American foreign policy. State could no longer expect to carry out the nation's relations with other states in splendid isolation, answerable only to the president and relinquishing the policy-making role only to him and only in those instances when he chose to take direct command. Aggressive and increasingly strong new foreign affairs agencies, most particularly Defense and the CIA, quickly moved to assert their organizational right to carry out their responsibilities with only minimal policy guidance from State. Many in State were ambivalent about these developments, at times attempting to reaffirm the department's authority, and at others retreating into the fiction that they could retain control of policy while leaving operational details to the other agencies.[7] State's lack of cre-

[5] Figures for 1939 from William Barnes and John Heath Morgen, *The Foreign Service of the United States: Origin, Development, Functions* (Washington, D.C.: Department of State, Historical Office, Bureau of Public Affairs, 1961), p. 242. Figures for the later period are taken from U.S. Senate Committee on Government Operations, "Organization of Federal Executive Departments and Agencies," chart to accompany Committee Report No. 27 (Washington, D.C.: GPO, 1967). Figures are as of January 1, 1967. By 1973 the number of Foreign Service Officers had declined through attrition because of imposed personnel reductions to slightly under 3,000 (interview).

[6] U.S. Civil Service Commission, "Paid Civilian Employment of the Federal Government by Agency and Citizenship, in Foreign Countries, June 30, 1964," in *Annual Salary and Wage Survey*, June 1964 (Washington, D.C.: GPO, 1964), reported in Burton M. Sapin, *The Making of United States Foreign Policy* (New York: Praeger, 1966), pp. 402-409.

[7] For evidence of the Kennedy administration's intentions to elim-

ative response[8] left the way open to others, and exasperated a series of presidents at least initially inclined to rely upon it as the central element in foreign affairs government.[9] But if State would not lead, other more specialized line agencies could not, except in their own specific areas of responsibility. The response of presidents faced with a need to bring order to foreign relations was uniform, although the methods chosen showed considerable variety. In each case more direct responsibility was undertaken by the White House, usually employing the National Security Council staff as a mechanism. Increasingly the head of this staff began to wield responsibilities which in earlier years were undertaken by the secretary of state. Yet the sheer size of the foreign affairs establishment and the vast number of issues that required attention meant that the White House could not hope to watch over more than a small percentage of the total spectrum of problems and programs.[10] So the

---

inate the operations/policy dichotomy, see McGeorge Bundy, letter to Senator Henry M. Jackson, September 4, 1961; reported in U.S. Congress, Senate Subcommittee on National Security Staffing and Operations of the Committee on Government Operations, "Basic Issues," in *Administration of National Security: Staff Reports and Hearings* (Washington, D.C.: GPO, 1965), p. 12. This volume cited hereafter as "Jackson Subcommittee," after its chairman.

[8] This failure of creative thinking was officially acknowledged by Deputy Under Secretary of State for Administration William B. Macomber, Jr., in a speech on January 14, 1970, introducing a new management reform program for State. One of the thirteen task forces named to develop this program was specifically assigned to investigate ways of improving the department's creative processes. Chapter VIII details some aspects of this program as it pertained to country directors. Macomber's speech and the task force reports are published in *Diplomacy for the 70's: A Program of Management Reform for the Department of State*, U.S. Department of State Publication 8551, Department and Foreign Service Series, 143 (Washington, D.C.: GPO, 1970).

[9] Most notably this was true for the Kennedy administration. See Roger Hilsman, *To Move A Nation* (Garden City, N.Y.: Doubleday, 1967), pp. 17-25.

[10] See I. M. Destler, *Presidents, Bureaucrats, and Foreign Policy*

answer to the question, "Who is in charge of U.S. policy?" has often been, "No one," at least in any simple command and control conceptualization.

This drastically simplified account ignores many complexities important for understanding how foreign affairs management has evolved since 1945, but hopefully it serves to suggest some of the difficulties underlying the continuing attempts at reform in this area, including those of major interest to this study.

On March 4, 1966, the White House announced a series of new procedures for "modernizing and streamlining the executive branch of government in the conduct of foreign affairs,"[11] which had been developed by Gen. Maxwell Taylor at the behest of President Johnson and ratified by the National Security Council as NSAM (National Security Action Memorandum) 341, from which the system took its name. The secretary of state "received formal and specific overall directive authority from the president," to replace the more informal coordinating responsibilities previously his with respect to the programs and activities of other agencies and departments directed abroad. While the details will be discussed later, the primary devices created to assist the secretary in these endeavors were a Senior Interdepartmental Group (SIG) at the under secretary level, led by the under secretary of state, and five Interdepartmental Regional Groups (IRGs) chaired by the five assistant secretaries of state who headed the department's geographic bureaus. Concurrently, State created new "country direc-

---

(Princeton, N.J.: Princeton University Press, 1971), pp. 256-257, passim.

[11] "White House Announcement of New Procedures for Overseas Interdepartmental Matters," March 4, 1966. Reprinted in Jackson Subcommittee (National Security and International Operations), *The Secretary of State and the Problem of Coordination* (Washington, D.C.: GPO, 1966), which also contains the text of several other relevant documents; and in *Weekly Compilation of Presidential Documents* 2 (March 7, 1966).

tor" positions under the five geographic assistant secretaries, replacing office directors and officers-in-charge.[12] The developing role and performance of these country directors, who were to have both staff responsibilities in supporting the NSAM 341 system and line responsibilities within State, are the primary focal point of this study.

On the surface these changes presaged a considerable enhancement of the secretary of state's control of American foreign relations and, by extension, an improvement in the status and influence of his subordinates in their working relationships with other parts of government. Their emphases were on leadership by State and on more efficient coordination throughout the entire foreign affairs establishment. It was hoped that better resource use in foreign operations and greater consistency of goals and objectives among international programs would result. While the occasionally heard argument that the NSAM 341 system represented State's last real chance to assume control of foreign policy was perhaps overstated, there can be little doubt that had the system worked as apparently intended, State's overall influence would have been substantially increased.

Taken literally, for example, the responsibilities of even those at the lowest rung of the new system, the country directors, were to be far-reaching, as the secretary of state suggested:

> I look to the Country Directors to assume full responsibility, under their Assistant Secretaries, for all activities in the country or countries assigned to them, and to

[12] Foreign Affairs Manual Circular (FAMC) 385 of March 4, 1966. This is the State Department document that placed NSAM 341 into effect in State and which repeated its text. The previously cited White House announcement of the same date has a slightly different wording, but the same meaning, except that FAMC 385 includes instructions regarding the country director system which do not appear in the former. FAMC 385 is reprinted in Jackson Subcommittee, *The Secretary of State and the Problem of Coordination*, and in *Department of State Bulletin*, 54 (March 28, 1966).

be single focal points in Washington to serve our Ambassadors.[13]

This official description survived basically intact more than seven years later,[14] but it does not capture the subtle details of the role country directors came to play. While they did have strong potential for exerting considerable influence in the policy process in spite of their relatively low-level positions, many factors limited their ability to be "single focal points" for their assigned countries of responsibility. This book attempts to discover the actual place of the country director in the foreign affairs community, and in doing so, to gain insights into the policy-making process as a whole. While the record of the country director system is important and interesting in itself, there are additional advantages in adopting this focus.

For example, an investigation of the role of one class of officials in the foreign affairs bureaucracy makes it possible to begin to bridge one existing gap in the burgeoning literature dealing with foreign policy making. Comprehensive studies of foreign policy processes have been abstract and theoretical rather than detailed and specific, in part because of the impossibility of exploring empirically the entire foreign policy apparatus in any depth.[15] One way out of this

[13] Dean Rusk, "Message to His Colleagues in the Department of State," March 4, 1966, reported in *Department of State News Letter*, No. 59 (March 1966), 3.

[14] Currently, the official description states that assistant secretaries are assisted in their duties by "Directors within their bureau, who are responsible for overall guidance and interdepartmental coordination with respect to their assigned countries. These directors are the single focal point in Washington for serving the needs of U.S. Ambassadors. They work closely with 'country teams' at our missions abroad to insure that all elements of a mission in a given country jointly pursue U.S. foreign policy directives." *United States Government Organization Manual 1972/73* (Washington, D.C.: GPO, 1972), p. 322.

[15] For example, see Richard C. Snyder, H. W. Bruck, and Burton Sapin, eds., *Foreign Policy Decision Making* (New York: Free Press, 1962); Joseph Frankel, *The Making of Foreign Policy* (London: Ox-

difficulty has been the case study of particular episodes or crises, using in some instances conceptual frameworks derived from the large-scale theoretical efforts.[16] Another has been the memoir or set of reflections of individual participants.[17] Such projects provide invaluable depth analysis of past events or of how foreign policy making looks and feels to those intimately involved in it, but do so by sacrificing breadth of coverage. Of necessity, they deal only with those parts of government directly involved in the situation being examined, or observed firsthand by the memorialist or participant.

This study is intended to complement rather than to replace these approaches. It attempts a broader view than one individual's recollection of his experiences or the usual case study, while retaining manageability and the opportunity to flesh out understanding of the foreign policy process by analysis in depth of one position or stratum of the foreign affairs bureaucracy. The range of impressions and evaluations reported is hopefully more comprehensive because many individuals have contributed their observations and opinions. It also is concerned in large measure with "normal" procedures. When counterpoised with case studies and personal histories that focus on crises and major personalities, knowledge of such practices may help illuminate what

---

ford, 1963); Kurt London, *The Making of Foreign Policy: East and West* (Philadelphia: Lippincott-Preceptor, 1965); Sapin, *The Making of United States Foreign Policy*; and Roger Hilsman, *The Politics of Policy Making in Defense and Foreign Affairs* (New York: Harper and Row, 1971).

[16] See as an example of a basically descriptive case study, Joseph Marion Jones, *The Fifteen Weeks*, 2nd ed. (New York: Harcourt, Brace and World, 1964); and for one based on a larger analytic scheme, Glenn D. Paige, *The Korean Decision* (New York: Free Press, 1968).

[17] Two of the most important examples of this type of memoir are Acheson, *Present at the Creation*; and the two volumes by George F. Kennan, *Memoirs, 1925-1950* (Boston: Little, Brown, 1967), and *Memoirs, 1950-1963* (Boston: Little, Brown, 1972).

lies behind crisis-handling procedures, why they seem necessary, and to explore the milieu in which the most prominent foreign policy actors must function. There are several reasons for directing attention to State's country directors in this kind of inquiry. The working level in the foreign affairs bureaucracy is usually slighted or ignored, even in studies concerned with intragovernmental and/or bureaucratic politics as a major factor in policy-making.[18] Yet officials of this level do make key decisions, and by virtue of their specific expertise, may often be the source of policy alternatives that are refined and ultimately selected much higher up. They are also likely to be involved intimately with carrying out the decisions of government, wherever made, an essential part of the conduct of effective relations with other states. Chapter I presents a general view of the policy-making process, as a means of delineating the parameters of the world in which the country director operated and suggesting the general nature of the relationships between various actors in it. The final part of Chapter I carries the argument to the more specific question of the role individual working-level actors can be expected to play in the larger process.

Another point of interest in the country director arrangement arises because the country director was a new position, established to help correct perceived weaknesses in the management of foreign affairs. Along with the NSAM 341 mechanism it held the possibility of having a major impact on the consistency of foreign policy and on bureaucratic power relationships. Chapter II discusses the new system and why it was felt necessary to install it, and describes the mechanics of bringing it into existence.

The next chapters are primarily concerned with the way

[18] This is true whether one considers popular treatments that rely on a bureaucratic politics interpretation, such as David Halberstam, *The Best and The Brightest* (New York: Random House, 1972); or more academic discussions; for example, the various treatments of Graham Allison cited in Chapter I.

11

the country director system actually functioned. Chapter III explores how new organizational roles develop around newly created positions, and discusses several of the important role elements associated with the country director positions. Chapter IV takes up the very important question of interaction patterns in which the country director was a participant, including those within State, the intragovernmental arena of contention and coordination, and the relationships between country directors and American field posts on one hand and the Washington representatives of their assigned countries on the other. Chapter V, building on previous chapters, presents a more analytic view of selected aspects of the larger policy process such as problem definition, control of information, and adjustment and analytic techniques, with specific attention to the impact country directors had in these areas.

Any such examination would be incomplete if it did not also devote attention to the individuals who held the country director jobs. Their abilities, backgrounds, operating styles, and other characteristics are the subject of Chapter VI. This discussion also considers one of the major areas of interest of organizational life, the interplay between personnel problems and resources and an organization's ability to define and meet its objectives.[19]

Chapter VII shifts the focus to the important question of carrying out change in organizations; this of course is intimately related to the development of new organizational roles discussed in the earlier chapters. The problem of innovation in bureaucracy[20] is critical in a period when adap-

[19] See Douglas McGregor, *The Human Side of Enterprise* (New York: McGraw-Hill, 1960), for a modern classic on the interrelationship of individual and organization.

[20] Innovation has been defined as "the successful introduction into existing functional relationships of an applied situation of means or ends that are new to that situation," by Robert S. Friedman, Lawrence B. Mohr, and Robert M. Northrup in their "Innovation in State and Local Bureaucracies" (unpublished paper delivered at the Annual Meeting of the American Political Science Association, New York,

tation to new needs and demands seems required of all social institutions, and the record of the country director experiment is used to suggest generalizations that may have wider applicability. The final substantive chapter, VIII, provides an evaluation of the country director system from the viewpoint of those most intimately involved with it, and discusses its prospects for the future. Chapter IX, by way of conclusion, summarizes previous material under the rubric of the role strength of the country directors, and takes up the larger question of the possibilities of and limits on providing government-wide coordination and leadership at the working level.

The data for this study are derived from three related sets of interviews conducted by the author, primarily in late 1968 and early 1969, with periodic reinterviewing until mid-1973. Together, these interviews represent an attempt to gain a wide range of opinion about the country director system from those with intimate knowledge of it. Thus, the first group of interviews was conducted in 1968-1969 with forty-six of the incumbent forty-nine country directors with several being reinterviewed subsequently in order to trace changes in the way the system worked over time. They provide most of the information about country director attitudes, role conceptions, and problems cited throughout the study. A second group of interviews, totaling fifty-four in all, was with opposite numbers elsewhere in government

---

1969), mimeographed, p. 3. Their concept of "innovation" is analogous to "implementation" as used in this study, while "introduced" is similar to "instituted" as used here. In this sense it is unclear whether the CD change represents a true innovation, but the sequence of events leading to the creation of the CD positions presents some of the more substantial problems associated with attempts to innovate in large organizations. Among the more prominent of a large group of recent studies of innovation are Anthony Downs, *Inside Bureaucracy* (Boston: Little, Brown, 1967); Michel Crozier, *The Bureaucratic Phenomenon* (Chicago: University of Chicago Press, 1964); and Louis C. Gawthrop, *Bureaucratic Behavior in the Executive Branch: An Analysis of Organizational Change* (New York: Free Press, 1969).

who worked directly with the country directors, and they are particularly important in assessing the interaction patterns of which country directors were a part. Finally, approximately forty interviews were conducted to obtain details of specific events relevant to the study, such as how the country director system came into being and why it evolved as it did. In the case, individuals with specific knowledge were sought out, rather than persons holding certain positions. Full details about the interviewing procedures, including the questionnaires used, may be found in Appendix C. The notations used to identify specific interviews are presented at the point in Chapter I where the first interview material appears.

Hopefully, the end product of this examination will be a more comprehensive understanding of the complex patterns by which national foreign policy emerges, with particular emphasis on the supporting yet at times critical part played by middle-level officials such as State's country directors. In some measure, the story told in the following chapters also reveals the extreme difficulties encountered in attempting reform in large organizations and particularly in government, suggests reasons why this is so, and clarifies some of the factors that influence such attempts at change. In order to begin this investigation, it is first necessary in Chapter I to consider the elusive nature of the foreign policy process.

Chapter One

The Context of Foreign
Policy Making

There will always be the dark and tangled stretches in the decision-making process—mysterious even to those who may be most intimately involved. JOHN F. KENNEDY

THE new trends and complexities confronting American foreign policy makers and executors since World War II discussed earlier imply what is perhaps the fundamental feature of current policy making in foreign affairs: It is a shared prerogative of a great number of individuals and organizations standing in uncertain relationship to each other. Policy making can thus be viewed as a complicated process by which these actors work with and against each other to evolve and carry out proposed courses of action. Since the primary focus here is the role played by one group of individual actors, the overall characteristics of this policy process need to be examined in some detail. This chapter is devoted to that task, so that those that follow can more intelligibly illuminate the place of the country director (CD) within the larger process.

POLICY MAKING, DECISION MAKING,
AND PROBLEM SOLVING

A first concern must be concept clarification, for the terms policy making, decision making, and problem solving are frequently used indiscriminately. The most common definition of policy links goals and desired outcomes. In this usage, "policy operates in the future," defining a nation's interests, objectives, or responsibilities, or, more bluntly, asking the question, "What difference does it make to us?"[1]

[1] Dean Rusk, "The Anatomy of Foreign Policy Decisions," speech to American Political Science Association, Washington, D.C., Septem-

15

Built on broad goals (e.g., a world of independent nations, a world free of aggression, a world where personal freedoms are secured, a world of equal rights and opportunities),[2] policy is seen as "any governing principle, plans, or course of action"[3] designed to achieve such goals. Similarly, policy may be more specific (e.g., to improve the nation's balance-of-payments position), without distorting the future orientation or linkage of goals and guiding principles. More formally, policy might be seen as "an authoritative government decision to seek X or do Y."[4]

A number of practitioners and scholars, however, find such a definition too limited, arguing it implies too direct a link between intention and action. For them, a particular policy can only be determined by looking back on a whole series of related decisions and actions which together define a nation's approach to a particular geographic or substantive area. (CD #1)[5] This interpretation allows policy to be conceptualized as the result of action taken by a number of individuals and organizations, rather than as a single pronouncement or decision. Thus, Braybrooke and Lindblom

---

ber 7, 1965, reprinted in *Department of State News Letter*, No. 54 (October 1965), 4.

[2] Listing taken from U.S. Department of State, *How Foreign Policy is Made*, U.S. Department of State Publication 7705, General Foreign Policy Series, 195 (Washington, D.C.: GPO, 1966), 20.

[3] This definition from Webster parallels most usage of the term.

[4] This usage was suggested by Morton Halperin.

[5] Throughout this study, information from interviews will be identified by an abbreviation indicating the agency or department of the source, followed by a number assigned to the individual. Abbreviations not self-explanatory are contained in the list of abbreviations following the table of contents. Quotations for country directors (CDs) are verbatim comments from tape-recorded interviews unless followed by the word "paraphrase," in which case they are close reconstructions taken from notes made during the interview. All other cited interview responses, including those from CDs not set off as quotations and/or identified as "paraphrase," reflect the thrust of what was said, but not necessarily the precise wording.

have suggested that decision making and policy making can be differentiated in that

the latter term encompasses both decision making and the course that policies take as a result of interrelations among decisions and/or in which the latter term incorporates certain political processes, in addition to analytical processes, into the determination of courses of action.[6]

Unfortunately, this interpretation deprives us of the primary usage of practitioners, who constantly refer to the existence or absence of a "policy" for a particular situation or nation. The incompleteness of either of these approaches suggests a combination usage is needed. Snyder, Bruck, and Sapin argue that two components are involved: *action* (past, current, or projected), and *rules* to guide action (which may outline the substance of response to some future situation, the occasion or conditions under which a particular response will be made, or an interpretation which will be placed on some future event). Thus,

policy can be anticipatory, cumulative, specific, and general. "To have a policy" means action and/or rules with respect to a problem, contingency or event which has occurred, is occurring, or is expected to occur.[7]

In other words, policy making is the most general of these terms. The term "policy-making process" will be used to label the entire pattern of complex interactions between officials and organizations which result in decisions and in specific courses of action.

At the other extreme, problems and problem solving refer to the occasion for action or decisional situation,[8] the stimu-

[6] David Braybrooke and Charles E. Lindblom, *A Strategy of Decision: Policy Evaluation as a Social Process* (New York: Free Press, 1963), p. 249.

[7] Snyder, Bruck, and Sapin, *Foreign Policy Decision Making*, p. 85. Emphasis in original.

[8] The terminology is that of James A. Robinson and Richard C.

17

lus that leads one or more officials to reexamine a situation with a view toward action or preparation of guidance for future action. The problem can be viewed as a threat or as an opportunity, in that innovations as well as reactions can result from the same sorts of circumstances.[9] The advantage of this usage is that it parallels that of most officials, including the country directors interviewed for this study.[10]

The third term, perhaps most frequently used by students of foreign policy, is decision making, but it differs conceptually from the other two. While decisions (choices among alternatives) play a part in both policy making and problem solving, they can be differentiated from the former in that they are limited in time (when a decision is "made" or becomes official), while policy is ongoing and composed of a series of decisions and actions. Similarly, decision making can be distinguished from problem solving:

> Decision making is that thinking which results in the choice among alternative courses of action; problem solving is that thinking which results in the solution of problems.[11]

While a choice among alternatives may be an important element in confronting a problem, the two concepts are sep-

---

Snyder, "Decision-Making in International Politics," in Herbert C. Kelman, ed., *International Behavior: A Social-Psychological Analysis* (New York: Holt, Rinehart and Winston, 1965), p. 440.

[9] This distinction was suggested by Arnold Kanter.

[10] Dean Pruitt found that most State Department officials he interviewed said that they did not make decisions, they solved problems. Most CDs interviewed did not object when the term "decision" was used in a question, but tended to use the term "problem" in framing their responses. See Dean G. Pruitt, *Problem Solving in the Department of State*, Social Science Foundation and International Relations Department, Monograph Series in World Affairs, 2 (Denver: University of Denver, 1965).

[11] Donald W. Taylor, "Decision Making and Problem Solving," in James G. March, ed., *Handbook of Organizations* (Chicago: Rand McNally), p. 48.

arable in theory and practice. Much activity is reactive, and in such situations little if any choice among alternatives may be involved. Once a problem is defined, a decision often exists only in the sense of "making up one's mind" to take or refrain from taking a particular action. This is analogous to Simon's "programmed decision," where action follows from an established routine once a problem is assigned to a particular category.[12] Even if a problem is not routine, constraints may be such that to speak of meaningful alternatives is misleading. As a former ambassador once explained,

a foreign policy problem is like a boulder rolling down a hill. If you try to get under it and hold it back, you'll get crushed; but if you can put a small stick or stone in its path, you may be able to influence where the boulder finally comes to rest. (CD #2—paraphrase)

Concepts of Choice:
Rationality vs. "Muddling Through"

At times, of course, choice among alternatives in solving problems or setting policies is possible, and it is to these instances that rational models of decision making, generally derived from economic theory, have been applied. Lindblom has suggested (without subscribing to) a picture of "rational" decision making which is representative of many such models:

1. Faced with a given problem,
2. a rational man first clarifies his goals, values, or objectives, and then ranks or otherwise organizes them in his mind;
3. he then lists all important possible ways of—policies for—achieving his goals
4. and investigates all the important consequences that would follow from each of the alternative policies,

[12] Herbert A. Simon, *The New Science of Management Decision* (New York: Harper and Row, 1960), pp. 5-6.

19

5. at which point he is in a position to compare consequences of each policy with goals
6. and so chooses the policy with consequences most closely matching his goals.[13]

This describes the process by which an individual rational man reaches a decision (makes a choice). Only minor variations are suggested by those who subscribe to the rational approach in cases where a decision is made by a collective process. One recent presidential aide, well aware of the differences between ideal and practice, puts the rational approach into the context of national security policy:

Theoretically, it would be desirable to undertake, for each important decision, a series of carefully measured, carefully spaced steps, including ideally the following:

First: agreement on the facts;
Second: agreement on the overall policy objective;
Third: a precise definition of the problem;
Fourth: a canvassing of all possible solutions, with all their shades and variations;
Fifth: a list of all possible consequences that would flow from each solution;
Sixth: a recommendation and final choice of one alternative;
Seventh: the communication of that selection;
Eighth: provision for its execution.[14]

[13] Charles E. Lindblom, *The Policy-Making Process* (Englewood Cliffs, N.J.: Prentice-Hall, 1968), p. 13. His critique of the rational model appears in Braybrooke and Lindblom, and in Lindblom, *Intelligence of Democracy* (New York: Free Press, 1965).

[14] Theodore C. Sorensen, *Decision-Making in the White House* (New York: Columbia University Press, 1963), pp. 18-19. Similarly, Harold Lasswell has identified seven stages or functions of any decision which follow the thrust of the sequences suggested in the text above. His formulation appears in several places, particularly in his *The Decision Process: Seven Categories of Functional Analysis*, Bureau of Governmental Research, Studies in Government (College Park: University of Maryland, 1956). An adapted version appears in

20

The numerous critics of rational models can be divided, broadly speaking, into two schools: those who would modify the model to account for lack of certainty, incomplete information, and other unrealistic assumptions; and those who suggest that even the modified rational model is neither descriptively accurate nor prescriptively desired. Most prominent of the first school are Herbert Simon and his associates. Their two principal alterations of the classical rational models are the ideas of "bounded rationality" and "satisficing."[15] The major elements of their modifications are:

1. Optimizing is replaced by satisficing—the requirement that satisfactory levels of the criterion variables be attained.
2. Alternatives of action and consequences of action are discovered sequentially through search processes.
3. Repertoires of action programs are developed by organizations and individuals, and these serve as the alternatives of choice in recurrent situations.
4. Each specific action program deals with a restricted range of consequences.
5. Each action program is capable of being executed in semi-independence of the others—they are only loosely coupled together.[16]

The other school, represented by Lindblom, agrees with Simon that the rational-deductive model is incapable of be-

---

Lasswell and Daniel Lerner, *World Revolutionary Elites* (Cambridge: M.I.T. Press, 1965), pp. 10-12.

[15] As noted in Taylor, "Decision Making," p. 60, the bounded rationality idea was first presented in Herbert A. Simon, *Administrative Behavior* (New York: Free Press, 1947), while the satisficing concept comes from his "A Behavioral Model of Rational Choice," *Quarterly Journal of Economics*, 69 (February 1955). Most of the discussion of Simon in this section, however, is taken from the developed version of his thinking in March and Simon, *Organizations* (New York: John Wiley & Sons, 1957).

[16] March and Simon, *Organizations*, p. 169.

ing fully realized, but goes even further to argue that it is "in most circumstances and most connections, fruitless and unhelpful as [an] ideal."[17] A further complication is that subscribers to the rational model assert policy analysis or problem solving is comprehensive or synoptic,[18] not surprising in view of the rational model's use of deductive propositions which logically should cover all situations. Unfortunately (in Lindblom's view), the synoptic ideal has a number of weaknesses: It is not adapted to man's limited problem-solving capabilities, to inadequacy of information, to the costliness of analysis, to failures in constructing a satisfactory evaluative method, to the closeness of observed relationships between fact and value in decision making, to the openness of the systems of variables with which it contends, to the analyst's needs for strategic sequences of analytical moves, or to the diverse forms in which policy problems actually rise.[19] While this critique parallels that of Simon in many ways, it does not lead to a modified rational model, but instead to an approach which is in some senses nonrational, and certainly noncomprehensive. This strategy—disjointed incrementalism—has the following characteristics:

1. The analyst compares and evaluates only policies differing marginally from existing policies (margin-dependent choice).
2. A restricted number or variety of alternatives are considered.
3. Only a restricted number of important consequences are considered for any given alternative.
4. The problem is continually redefined, with ends adjusted to means as well as the other way around—this is a means of simplification, since the incremental approach allows for countless adjustments of both kinds, making the problem more manageable.

[17] Braybrooke and Lindblom, p. 16.
[18] Ibid., p. 37.   [19] Ibid., pp. 48-57.

5. Serial analyses and evaluations are possible, meaning that there is no one correct solution for all time, but that any problem is subject to a never-ending series of attacks.

6. As a consequence, disjointed incrementalism has a remedial orientation, which is geared more to alleviation of present, concrete imperfections than to promotion of future goals.[20]

Thus far, we have been dealing with individuals, and with "intellectual factors"[21] which come into play in arriving at a decision. Once the restriction that a decision is made by a single official is dropped, however, it is necessary to come to terms with the complications introduced by multiple participants.

One approach, associated with the rational-deductive school, is to posit essentially the same process for groups and individuals. Downs, for example, suggests that an individual decision maker, faced with a perceived need for new action, goes through a series of steps related to formulation, analysis, and evaluation of alternatives, development of a strategy of action, action impact, feedback of results, and performance reassessment.[22] While the terminology differs somewhat, the model is still one of rationality. He argues that organizational decision making varies from this model because of the involvement of many individuals, with the following consequences:

—the various steps in the decision and action cycle are carried out by different persons.

[20] These characteristics are presented in considerable detail in Braybrooke and Lindblom, pp. 83-106, and summarized in Lindblom, *Intelligence*, pp. 143-147. The list in the text is paraphrased, drawing on both sources. The term, "muddling through," was used earlier by Lindblom to describe these features in his "The Science of Muddling Through," *Public Administration Review*, 19 (Spring 1957), 79-88.

[21] This term is used by Robinson and Snyder, loc. cit.

[22] Anthony Downs, *Inside Bureaucracy*, pp. 175-176.

—an organization must generate numerous conflict-controlling and consensus-creating mechanisms because its members have widely varying perception apparatuses, memories, images of the world, and goals.

—organizational decision making involves the following significant costs of internal communications that have no analogs within an individual:

    a. losses of utility due to errors of transmission
    b. losses of utility (for the ultimate uses of the data) due to distortion
    c. resources (especially time) absorbed in internal communications
    d. losses of utility due to overloading communications channels in the short run.[23]

The steps of the rational model still exist, although performed by different individuals within the organization.

But if actions taken and problems solved are the topics of interest, it may be very misleading to concentrate on the cognitive/emotional elements of the individual decision process as generalized to a group context. These outputs may emerge as much by social processes of accommodation and adjustment as they do from rational (ends-means) analysis.[24]

In addition to substituting disjointed incrementalism for rationalism in characterizing cognitive aspects of individual decision making, Lindblom has suggested that social processes of policy making can be positioned on a continuum from complete centralization (the group analog to individual rationality) to total absence of central coordination. Outcomes result from "partisan mutual adjustment"

[23] Ibid., p. 178.

[24] One excellent case study which reaches similar conclusions about the importance of social processes as determinants of outcomes, with respect to trade policy, may be found in Raymond A. Bauer, Ithiel de Sola Pool, and Lewis Anthony Dexter, *American Business and Public Policy* (New York: Atherton, 1967).

(PMA), in which a multiplicity of interdependent decision makers each pursues his own rather than generally shared goals, except as controlled by other decision makers ("partisans") or by central supervision.[25] The end result, descriptively, is incremental policy change, brought about by application of one or more techniques of adaptive and manipulative adjustment.[26] Thus PMA is the collective counterpart of the individual strategy suggested by Lindblom and Braybrooke discussed earlier. Real life situations, according to Lindblom, exhibit a mixture of central coordination and partisan mutual adjustment, and "which of the two alternatives is more suitable varies from circumstance to circumstance."[27]

Without duplicating Lindblom's several discussions, two points are of particular importance here. First, partisan mutual adjustment may be more desirable than central coordination, because it avoids centralization of power and may be more efficient:

> Central coordination may impose analytic and regulatory tasks on a central authority beyond its capacities. . . . Each limit [on man's analytic capacities][28] *is also a limit on a central coordinator's capacity to analyze the desired relations among subordinate policy makers and to regulate them.*[29]

This preference for PMA directly opposes the argument that a totally rational policy-making process, while unattainable, should still remain the goal.

Second, rational policy analysis, however extended,[30] is

[25] Lindblom, *Intelligence*, pp. 28-29, passim.
[26] Ibid., pp. 35-84.
[27] Lindblom, *Policy Making Process*, p. 82.
[28] These limits are outlined in the text above, identified by note 19.
[29] Lindblom, *Policy Making Process.* Emphasis in original.
[30] Lindblom discusses strategies or dodges used by policy analysts to overcome the limits on rationality in several places, most succinctly ibid., pp. 24-27.

inadequate in collective, group, or systemic applications because it is impossible "through analysis to find policies that are everywhere accepted because proven to be correct."[31] Yet problems must be solved, decisions made, and policies developed for society. This is done by the "play of power." Since power[32] is always held by many individuals, "policy is made through the complex processes by which these persons exert power or influence over each other,"[33] such activity being part of the overall process of partisan mutual adjustment. While the "play of power" features cooperation among specialists and proceeds according to rules, a third characteristic is most important here:

> The play of power is not a substitute for policy analysis, simply resolving those issues left unsettled by analysis. Instead, policy analysis is incorporated as an instrument or weapon into the play of power, changing the character of analysis as well.[34]

Thus any model that merely carries over individual decision processes, rational or otherwise, into a group context is likely to be incomplete and incorrect, because analyses of policy by individuals will differ from that by collectivities.

In short, any description of the policy process must account both for the limits of rationality faced by the individual and for the social and political aspects of complex col-

[31] Ibid., p. 28.

[32] There is of course much disagreement about the meaning of power, and Lindblom himself chooses explicitly not to define it, but for present purposes a general usage, incorporating meanings given to power, influence, authority, force, and manipulation is adequate. Cf. Peter Bachrach and Morton S. Baratz, "Decisions and Nondecisions: An Analytical Framework," *American Political Science Review*, 57 (September 1965), 632-642; and Robert A. Dahl, *Modern Political Analysis* (Englewood Cliffs, N.J.: Prentice-Hall, 1963), pp. 39-54.

[33] Lindblom, *Policy Making Process*, p. 29.

[34] Ibid., p. 30.

lective interactions. As Bauer argues, policy making must be conceived of as "a social process in which an intellectual process is embedded."[35] Because of this social and intellectual intermingling, the rational and mutual adjustment models can be visualized as ideal types near the extremes of a continuum, with real world situations tending toward one or the other.

In summary, one can say that rational models of decision making are most applicable when

- —goals can be clarified and ranked in a way acceptable to relevant participants in the process;
- —real choices among alternatives are possible, in that resources and circumstances would permit any of several courses of action to be followed;
- —information available is complete or nearly so in relevant categories;
- —sufficient certainty exists to predict consequences of each alternative with some accuracy;
- —utility calculations can be made to facilitate choice;
- —the problem is the primary responsibility of an official or agency whose interests are generally accepted as approximating the national interest on the issue in question;
- —there is an acknowledged higher authority to whom other actors defer in cases of conflict.

When all of these requirements cannot be substantially met, the process is more likely to be disjointed and incremental. In contrast, when decision making is disjointed and incremental, the more fragmented will be the control of resources and other sources of power and the more likely that resolution will come about through partisan mutual adjustment rather than through central coordination.

[35] Raymond F. Bauer, "The Study of Policy Formation: An Introduction," in Bauer and Kenneth J. Gergen, eds., *The Study of Policy Formulation* (New York: Free Press, 1968), p. 5.

THE POLICY PROCESS: A SIMPLE MODEL

A variety of approaches to the policy-making process (of which decision making is a part) have also been suggested by scholars.

Much as rational models posit clearly separable sequential steps in decision making, analysts of policy processes tend to partition them into discrete steps. London argues that "the normal process of policy formulation in foreign offices has four phases: recommendation, modification, crystallization, and final decision."[36] Pruitt uses a model in his study of one pre-1966 geographic office of State which asserts that "most problems pass through five phases: (a) initiation; (b) assignment to a coordinator; (c) development of a proposed solution; (d) validation of the proposed solution; and (e) action."[37] David Vital, in his study of the British foreign policy process, develops a similar, if somewhat more complex list.[38] While such exercises may be analytically useful, there is a danger of confusing a model with actual phenomena; specifically, that one will assume that real-world processes can be neatly factored into separate components. Such schemes may also imply clear-cut beginnings and endings to policy episodes, rather than visualizing them as part of a continuing chain of related events. Finally, they tend to suggest that problems move through the policy process immutably, each participant performing certain operations. This does not allow for the merger of seemingly unrelated problems into complex groupings, or

[36] London, *Making of Foreign Policy*, p. 210.

[37] Pruitt, *Problem Solving*, p. 9. He credits the last three phases to analysis by Paul Nitze for the Jackson Subcommittee in 1961.

[38] David Vital, *The Making of British Foreign Policy* (New York: Praeger, 1968), pp. 105-106. He lists the major steps as reporting from the field; collation, consulation, and assessment by recipients of reports; coordination of assessments; formulation of policy proposals; coordination of foreign policy with policy in other areas; decision; instruction of those who are to carry out the decision; secondary reporting and feedback; and so on, *ad infinitum*.

for the dissolution of problems due to the passage of time or changed circumstances.

In examining policy processes, it is also essential to specify explicitly the more general conceptual models to be employed, since one's conclusions depend directly upon this choice. In his analysis of the Cuban missile crisis, Graham Allison has shown the importance of the model used to the explanation one achieves. He uses three different paradigms.[39] The first, which Allison argues has been predominant, views policy as national choice and is a rational model focusing on the nation as the actor. The second visualizes policy as organizational output, moving the unit of analysis down to organizations as actors within a national government. The third suggests that policy is the political outcome of bureaucratic politics engaged in by individual players in positions which are critical in a given situation. The three are not mutually exclusive: "Each concentrates on one class of variables, in effect, relegating other important factors to a *ceteris paribus* clause."[40]

Model I is inappropriate if one is interested in the policy process in an individual state, although it may serve the purposes of students of international politics if its limitations are remembered. Model II is particularly important for its assumption that available organizational routines act as constraints on the range of possible actions, and the assumption of incremental decision processes. However, it

[39] Graham T. Allison, "Conceptual Models and the Cuban Missile Crisis," *American Political Science Review*, 63 (September 1969), 689-718; and Allison, *Essence of Decision: Explaining the Cuban Missile Crisis* (Boston: Little, Brown & Co., 1971). The importance of the conceptual framework chosen received earlier attention in J. David Singer, "The Level of Analysis Problem in International Relations," in Klaus Knorr and Sidney Verba, eds., *The International System: Theoretical Essays* (Princeton, N.J.: Princeton University Press, 1961), pp. 77-92; and more obliquely, in Sidney Verba, "Assumptions of Rationality and Non-Rationality in Models of the International System," also in Knorr and Verba, pp. 93-117.

[40] Allison, "Conceptual Models," p. 716.

underweights individual factors, and fails to account for those innovative decisions and solutions which occasionally do occur or to realize that outcomes are social as well as intellectual. Model III is important because of its emphasis on role playing ("players in critical positions"), but suffers from possible distortion if its primary focus on individuals results in undue concentration of personality to the exclusion of the organizations of which the players are a part. The analysis that follows, therefore, employs a framework lying between Allison's second and third models, retaining an emphasis on both the role of the individual and on the organizations of which they are a part and which define much of what they do.[41] This is somewhat untidy, but provides a better generalized picture of the "normal" policy-making processes. Vital to this concept is the assumption that the policy process consists of many units, techniques, subprocesses and interaction dyads, not all of which come into play in the resolution of a given problem or the determination of a particular policy,[42] but all of which are part of the available repertoire.

Process Characteristics

With these introductory warnings in mind, the next step is to examine the characteristics of the foreign policy process

[41] In a later treatment, Morton Halperin joins Allison in modifying model III by adding some components from model II, along the lines suggested in the text, but in much greater detail. See Allison and Halperin, "Bureaucratic Politics: A Paradigm and Some Policy Implications," *World Politics*, 24 (Spring 1972, Supplement), 40-79. This section and the remainder of this chapter were drafted prior to the appearance of this article.

[42] This is at variance with Robinson and Snyder, "Decision Making," p. 439, who suggest instead a typology of separate processes. To claim the existence of separate and parallel processes is to invite the same distortion involved in classifying a process into phases or stages, namely the failure to recognize that they may merge into hybrid varieties, and are in fact most frequently encountered in that form.

more directly. Briefly, it is *collective* and *continuous*. It has *open-system attributes*, since it cannot be isolated from the external environment. It is set in motion by *dissatisfaction* with existing performance, because of new circumstances (problems or opportunities) or reanalysis. There is a constant *interplay* between the *organization* and the *individual*. *Complexity* is the norm, due to the many ramifications of problems faced and the multiplicity of participants confronting them. It functions primarily in *reaction* to perceived problems, rather than by designing programs to attain abstract goals. Finally, process outputs tend to be *disjointed* and *incremental*, rather than synoptic and innovative. Let us now consider these features in greater detail.

First, this process is clearly collective, involving officials in many agencies and departments, as well as outsiders. The wide-ranging interactions of the country directors to be discussed later attest to this, for their purpose was to solve current problems or to provide shared background and personal relationships which could be exploited later. A collective process should not be confused with a consensual one, however, since consensus formation is only one of many ways by which a group or organization makes decisions or finds solutions to problems. Consensus may be sought to build support, but conflicts referred to an accepted "central coordinator" may be at least as frequent.[43]

Second, the process is continuous. For analysis, it may be desirable to look at individual episodes, but each relies heavily on what has gone before, and in turn influences future episodes. One CD, for example, said that

> many of the decisions that I would take on my own authority flow from a larger decision that was taken some time ago. I know, in view of the broader decision, that I can clear off a number of subordinate, sequential decisions which flow from it. (CD #3)

[43] The term in quotation marks is Lindblom's.

The progression, however, is not necessarily from major decisions to sequential minor ones. De Rivera suggests that early, low-cost decisions build up a momentum that makes later higher cost decisions much easier to make. While experimental evidence is lacking, it would seem that a costly decision is much more apt to be made if a less costly decision (based on the same premises) is made at an earlier date.[44]

Both the reliance on precedent, and the great concern of practitioners for whether a proposed action is consistent with "policy" affirm the plausibility of this "continuous web" interpretation.

Third, the process has open-system characteristics since the making of policy is intimately bound up with an uncertain and indeterminate environment. This can lead to ambiguous problem formulation, as well as to inability to foresee all alternative solutions or many consequences of any visible potential solution.[45] Vital captures this feature in his discussion of foreign policy making in Britain:

The body of men who are responsible for the formulation and implementation of foreign policy are concerned, in practice, with matters over which their control is severely

[44] Joseph de Rivera, *The Psychological Dimension of Foreign Policy* (Columbus, Ohio: Charles E. Merrill, 1968), p. 139. Francis E. Rourke argues that the momentum of previous decisions calls into question Lindblom and Braybrooke's assertion that the process "is protected from irrationality by the fact that it moves in one sequential step after another," permitting "discontinuance of effort or the reversal of direction at any point at which each is considered desirable." Rourke, *Bureaucracy and Foreign Policy* (Baltimore: The Johns Hopkins Press, 1972), p. 54. This is a justifiable position, but does not invalidate the descriptive aspects of their argument. If anything, it reinforces the incremental interpretation which is the central feature of the Lindblom and Braybrooke analysis.

[45] This interpretation follows James D. Thompson, *Organizations in Action: Social Science Bases of Administrative Theory* (New York: John Wiley & Sons, 1967), pp. 6-10, passim.

32

restricted, of which their knowledge can never be better than imperfect and which they must generally approach without the tactical and intellectual advantages of unambiguous and wholly appropriate goals.[46]

A variety of constraints result from the permeability of the process, which taken together limit the range of possible actions.

Fourth, the precipitator of action is dissatisfaction, created by pressures that build until a problem is perceived to exist and some action must be considered. The source may be external—from the foreign or domestic environment; or internal—when one actor decides what is happening is not desirable or when conflict develops between organizational units or individuals with differing goals. Efforts to reduce these tensions by arriving at acceptable solutions constitute the problem-solving and policy-making process. Many scholars suggest ways conflict can be managed, such as the following:

> Resolution may be achieved by persuasion, by "clearance" procedures, by voting, by bargaining, and by high authority.[47]

> An organization reacts to conflict by four major processes: (1) problem solving, (2) persuasion, (3) bargaining, and (4) "politics."[48]

Most comprehensive is the description of Lindblom, who posits "central coordination" and "partisan mutual adjustment" as basic procedures, and outlines many forms of the latter which parallel and expand upon the techniques listed above.[49] At times, of course, adjustment techniques may eliminate conflict entirely, if a common objective emerges at some point.[50] Occasionally the key to problem solution

---

[46] Vital, p. 13.   [47] Robinson and Snyder, p. 450.
[48] March and Simon, p. 129.
[49] Lindblom, *Intelligence*, passim.
[50] Ibid., p. 69.

is not coping with conflict at all, but rather supplying relevant information to all concerned parties.

Fifth, there is constant interplay between organization and individual, or bureaucratic and personal factors. Sometimes hierarchical authority and agency prerogative largely determine outcomes, while at others personal relationships and individual skill, talent, and power predominate. What one CD called "institutionalized personal power" (which accrues to an individual because of his relationship to other individuals but must be exerted in "legitimate" ways) is often applied. At times a CD could prevail by threatening to take a problem to high levels, if all involved were aware that the outcome would affirm the CD's position because of his close ties with the assistant secretary. (CD #4) Another said that State was "in some respects very bureaucratic and in some respects very personal," since one had to work through channels, but nevertheless at times, "one could get to see the secretary . . . without having to go through the assistant secretary, without having to go through the deputy assistants." (CD #5) The premium CDs placed on knowing how to be effective in Washington indicated that pure rationality or expertise was insufficient to guarantee success.

Sixth, the nature of the problems faced and the multiplicity of participants result in great complexity. There is a great need for adjustment among participants, substantiating the contention that the process is social as well as intellectual. As one CD argued, in explaining differences of perspective between Washington and the field,

> What you're more conscious of is the complexity of the decision-making process back here; the number of often conflicting interests from various parts of our government that have to be resolved. Problems sometimes look so clear from abroad, the answer seems so obvious that our government ought tomorrow to do such and such. Back here, you find it isn't that simple. There may be other considerations of one kind and another. . . . (CD #6)

One by-product of complexity is that many problems are forced upward, because those at lower levels are reluctant to make decisions (CD #5), or because those higher up want to make their agency's case personally. (AID #1)[51] At the same time complexity necessitates reliance upon experts and specialists, and cooperation among them.[52] This introduces a possible pathology, since those who make the decisions do not have "time to reflect very much on the philosophy of the programs [they're] pursuing," (CD #7) with the result that when problems become critical and complex and are escalated for resolution,

> One would tend to feel that sometimes people on high get too involved in some of these things without adequate knowledge of the area, and without really having had enough background.... (CD #8)

A less charitable opinion was that as the system and problems became more complex, there were more "buttinsky" interpretations at the assistant secretary level in all departments, with half-formed experts dealing with marginalia, citing their long experience as justification. (CD #9) In short, complexity is one source of the tension commented

[51] This has received considerable attention. The Jackson Subcommittee warned against premature compromise in 1960, in U.S. Congress, Senate Subcommittee on National Security Staffing and Operations of the Committee on Government Operations, *Organizing for National Security* (Washington, D.C.: GPO, 1960); and Sorensen, *Decision-Making*, pp. 3-4, argues that machinery and procedures at lower levels should not dictate decisions, and includes lower level compromise as one way the president's hand can be forced. Henry Kissinger, as the assistant to the president for national security affairs under President Nixon, apparently shared the same concern with his frequent references to the need to present the president with real options for future courses of action.

[52] As noted earlier, Lindblom sees cooperation among specialists as one of the three major characteristics of the American policy-making process in general. See his *Policy Making Process*, pp. 28-32; and also Harold L. Wilensky, *Organizational Intelligence: Knowledge and Policy in Government and Industry* (New York: Basic Books, 1967), passim.

upon earlier, because it leads to the need for both narrow experts who can analyze problems and broader gauged senior officials who can accommodate these analyses and make the adjustments necessary to produce action.

Seventh, the process in large measure reacts to perceived problems. It is attuned more to facts, circumstances, or perceptions of situations than to goals. As Vital notes, "It is the external event . . . which tends to dominate thinking, rather than the goal or purpose which the [government] itself wishes to pursue."[53] This conception of "what the process does" as problem solving (specific response to specific stimuli) rather than as decision making (choice among alternatives, implying freedom of action) may in most instances be more accurate. We shall see that country directors view themselves as operators rather than as long-range planners. This is a more general phenomenon, judging from the numerous attempts to improve policy planning in foreign affairs.[54] The unplanned nature of most foreign relations activity is an additional source for suspicion that rational models are rather imperfect for explaining or predicting actual outcomes and the process that produced them.

A final major feature of the process is that outputs tend to be disjointed and incremental, rather than synoptic and novel. This characteristic is intimately related to the others. The collective nature of the process, and its complexity, mean actors are likely to have different goals and values and, as we have seen, very different perspectives.[55] If this is true, agreement on grand schemes is likely to be either nonexistent, or so hedged, as was the case with most Na-

[53] Vital, p. 99.

[54] Three of the most recent of which were the Kissinger revitalization of the N.S.C. system; the reorganization of the Policy Planning Council in 1969, when it was broadened to become the Planning and Coordination Staff; and, turning full circle, the early 1974 reversion of this latter unit to its first (1947) name, the Policy Planning Staff.

[55] But, "Those who espouse the synoptic ideal assume that those whose values are to count agree," Lindblom, *Intelligence*, p. 140.

tional Policy Papers (NPPs) of the Kennedy and Johnson administrations and some National Security Study Memoranda (NSSMs) of the Nixon administration, that the agreement is almost worthless. Related to this is the likelihood that any agreement or adjustment is likely to differ only marginally from what has been agreed to before, unless the stimulus is so overwhelming that all important actors are convinced that only substantial change can produce successful outcomes.

The open-system nature of the process, with its accompanying uncertainty and limits on rationality has somewhat the same result: different actors will interpret the situation and appropriate responses differently, again forcing lowest-common-denominator solutions likely to diverge only incrementally from previous policy and programs (unless a dominant actor imposes his desires). Its reactive emphasis militates against comprehensive planning and encourages disjointed actions. The interplay between personal and organizational factors also has a conservative impact. The dependence of a CD on his immediate superiors and on his close working relationship with the American ambassador in the field, for example, may lead him to place a premium on support for their proposals, rather than on critical evaluation of them. Argyris has commented on the low risk taking, interpersonal style of State Department and Foreign Service Officers (FSOs),[56] and Wilensky has generalized the same argument with specific reference to administrative leaders who are frequently rotated from post to post (as is the case with FSOs).[57] Deutsch calls attention to the importance of precedent and tradition in State, which help to form a shared understanding of what constitute acceptable and unacceptable recommendations. A tendency thus exists

[56] Chris Argyris, *Some Causes of Organizational Ineffectiveness Within the Department of State*, Center for International Systems Research, Department of State, Occasional Paper, 2 (Washington, D.C.: GPO, 1967): 15-22, and esp. p. 16.

[57] Wilensky, p. 87.

to submit only those recommendations likely to be approved, providing some consistency but making major changes unlikely.[58] Finally, Jones argues that a superior must be consistent in his actions if he wants good staff work, but such consistency also inhibits innovation.[59] All this acts to affirm an incremental output interpretation as best describing the policy process under normal conditions.

In short, participants in the policy-making process do not inhabit a neatly defined and regularized world, although much of what they do is determined and channeled by bureaucratic norms and operating patterns. The characteristics of this complex and untidy process define the context in which each participant functions, acting at times as severe constraints and at others as the source of opportunities that can be exploited to further individual and personal goals.

THE INDIVIDUAL ACTOR

When the focus shifts from the policy process as a whole to the individuals in it, one must ask whether it is reasonable to assume that someone like the country director, buried in but one of the many organizations involved in foreign affairs, can play a significant or even distinguishable role. There is considerable support for a viewpoint asserting not only that it is possible to specify the part played by working level officials, but that it is vital to do so. Acheson, for example, observed that:

> To be sure, great decisions are, for the most part, made at the top, when they are not made by events. But, as for policy—the sum total of many decisions—it must be said, as it has been said of sovereignty, that its real sources

[58] Karl W. Deutsch, *The Analysis of International Relations* (Englewood Cliffs, N.J.: Prentice-Hall, 1968), p. 24.

[59] William Jones, *On Decision-Making in Large Organizations*, RAND Memorandum RM-3968-PR (Santa Monica, Calif.: RAND Corporation, 1964), 12.

are undiscoverable. One fact, however, is clear to anyone with experience in government: the springs of policy bubble up; they do not trickle down.[60]

In part, this is because the springs in question usually flow in response to specific problems, and not in search of abstract goals. Working level officials are likely to know more both causes of and possible responses to such problems, since they "have direct control over specialized operations [and] detailed information about these operations, coupled with a strong influence over the amount and form in which this information is available to others."[61] In these circumstances, the working level official is likely to make the initial proposals about what should be done: "As the drafting officer who usually is first to put policy ideas on paper, the desk man is in a sense the initiator of American policy toward his assigned country."[62] Defining or structuring a question or problem is crucial, although frequently it is taken as a given. Yet as Rusk has commented, "In many situations the very framing of the question strongly affects the answer."[63] This "ability of career officials to mold the views of other participants"[64] leads us directly to the CD as a potentially important participant in the policy process.

Investigation of organizational activity in other contexts provides further support. In a study of two municipal administrative hierarchies, Walter found that not only were subordinates relatively more influential than their superiors in the formulation and execution of novel decisions, but also

[60] Dean Acheson, "Some Thoughts About Thought in High Places," *New York Times Magazine*, October 11, 1959, pp. 86-87.

[61] Destler, *Presidents, Bureaucrats*, p. 290.

[62] Robert Ellsworth Elder, *The Policy Machine: The Department of State and American Foreign Policy* (Syracuse: Syracuse University Press, 1960), p. 22. Elder was writing well over a decade ago, but his statement is still applicable, with the substitution of "country officer" or "country director" for "desk man."

[63] Rusk, "Anatomy of Foreign Policy Decisions," p. 4.

[64] Rourke, *Bureaucracy and Foreign Policy*, p. 18.

that (unexpectedly) they were somewhat more influential in getting programmed premises accepted (that is, in defining a problem as fitting a particular programmed routine of the organization).[65] Gross has attacked much of the conventional wisdom about large organizations, arguing that assertions such as "the manager is the man on top" and "power and authority flow down from the top" are fallacious.[66] With respect to the first, he notes that three sets of facts confront any manager: there is always someone on top of him; he is hemmed in and pressured on all sides; and he is subjected to a constant bombardment from below in the form of requests for action, messages for study, and subtle attempts to direct him.[67] On the fallacy of visualizing power and authority as flowing exclusively downward, he finds that many positions carry their own authority, and that, in any event,

> it is impossible to delegate power beyond that small portion of power which is embodied in formal authority. The formal authority is merely a license an administrator can use in mobilizing the power he needs to do his job.[68]

Granted that organization charts are unlikely to accurately reflect complex patterns of authority and influence, is it still not possible that country directors and others at the senior working level are administrators and operators, but not policy makers? Such a distinction would not correspond with most recent public administration findings rejecting the separation between political and administrative realms introduced by Wilson, Taylor, and Goodnow.[69] It is falla-

[65] Benjamin Walter, "Internal Control Relations in Administrative Hierarchies," *Administrative Science Quarterly*, 11 (September 1966), 179-206.

[66] Bertram M. Gross, *Organizations and Their Managing* (New York: Free Press, 1964), p. 105.

[67] Ibid., pp. 102-103.   [68] Ibid., pp. 104-105.

[69] The classic expositions of the separation of policy and administration are Woodrow Wilson, "The Study of Public Administration," reported in many places, including *Political Science Quarterly*, 56 (De-

cious, according to Gross, to say that "administrators should execute policy, not make it," because

> the making and execution of policy are inseparably intertwined. Genuine policy—as distinguished from meaningless generalizations—comes into being through the activities of an entire organization.[70]

More directly for foreign policy making, one mid-career FSO concludes that

> in our country the line between policy maker and policy implementer has become very hard to draw, and most Foreign Service Officers find themselves on both sides of the line successively or simultaneously.[71]

If one grants the likelihood that country directors can influence policy, it is still true that some officials are more influential than others. A systematic way of establishing which ones are more so is necessary. Emmette Redford has suggested one approach compatible with a collective policy process, summarized by the statement, "Influence on decisions gets allocated to positions within organizations, which I shall refer to as *strategic positions (or locations)*."[72] He argues that those who gain greater influence (i.e., occupy the strategic positions) may do so by

> (1) delegation of authority to the position they hold, (2) practice within the organization affecting potential influ-

---

cember 1941); and Frank Goodnow, *Politics and Administration* (New York: Macmillan, 1900). Among the many critiques of this now discarded idea is that of Simon, *Administrative Behavior*, pp. 52-60.

[70] Gross, p. 107.

[71] Jack Perry, "Sorensen and Schlesinger," *Foreign Service Journal*, 43 (May 1966), 29.

[72] Emmette S. Redford, *Democracy in the Administrative State* (New York: Oxford University Press, 1969), p. 41. Emphasis in original.

ence of positions or (3) technical competence or personal qualities that give them special status.[73]

Redford continues by asserting that "policy making is achieved by focusing the action of men through strategic positions in organizations," and that "policy results from the *interaction of actors occupying strategic positions,* rather than from the behavior of a single person."[74]

Obviously, not all working-level officials occupy strategic positions. Influence is largely a function of the role associated with a position, and the way a role develops determines whether the position is strategic or not. Redford's third point (technical competence or personal qualities) helps account for the idiosyncratic and circumstantial factors making some incumbents of a given position or similar positions more strategic than others.

Our central point of inquiry is now clear: how strategic and influential has the country director become in the foreign affairs community? But before the strengths and weaknesses of his role can be assessed, it is first necessary to explore the circumstances that led to his arrival as a participant in the policy process, starting with the organization of State prior to creation of the country director position.

[73] Ibid., pp. 40-41.
[74] Ibid., pp. 42-43. Emphasis in original.

Chapter Two

The Country Director Idea: Origins and Development

We must be willing to change, to have an understanding of the past, to have a mastery of the present, but, above all, we must have a vision for the future. And it is the future that we must have in mind when we are developing and revising administrative policies and philosophies.

WILLIAM J. CROCKETT

THE ORGANIZATIONAL MILIEU: STATE'S GEOGRAPHIC BUREAUS

DEVOLUTION of responsibility into functional and geographic segments is the central element of State Department organization.[1] The boundary between them is frequently contested in border skirmishing, but the general division of labor is accepted by almost all participants. Yet it did not exist for the first eighty years of the department's life and State began to resemble its current form only after World War II. Chart II-1 summarizes the earlier patterns of organization.

The current era began in 1949 when the Hoover Commission recommended widespread changes in the department. Subordinate to the secretary, the under secretary, and two new deputy under secretaries, there were to be eleven officers of assistant secretary rank and three others of coordinate rank. Five of the assistant secretaries were to be placed

[1] Details on development of organization patterns in State, especially for the period prior to 1940, can be found in Elmer Plischke, *The Conduct of American Diplomacy*, 3rd ed. (Princeton, N.J.: Van Nostrand, 1967); Gailland Hunt, *The Department of State: A History of Its Organization, Procedure and Personnel* (New York: Macmillan, 1949); Warren Ilchman, *Professional Diplomacy in the United States, 1779-1939* (Chicago: University of Chicago Press, 1961); and for the period up to 1960, in Barnes and Morgen, *Foreign Service.*

CHART II-1
Department of State Division of Geographic Responsibility

To 1833	1833-1870	1870-1909	1908/9-1937	1937	1944	Hoover Commission	1950s	1959-
All duties *ad hoc*	7 Bureaus: Diplomatic, Consular, 5 Admin.	1st Diplomatic Bureau: Western Europe	Division of Far Eastern Affairs (1908)	Division of Far Eastern Affairs	Office of Far Eastern Affairs	Bureau of Far Eastern Affairs	Bureau of Far Eastern Affairs	Bureau of Far Eastern Affairs (later East Asia & Pacific Affairs)
		China						
		Japan	Division of W. European & Near Eastern Affairs (1909)	Division of N. Eastern & African Affairs	Office of N. Eastern & African Affairs	Bureau of N. Eastern & African Affairs		Bureau of Near Eastern & So. Asian Affairs
	°							
	In Diplomatic Bureau:	2nd Diplomatic Bureau: Rest of World						Bureau of African Affairs
	1 clerk– England France Holland	°	Division of Russian Affairs (1919) (Eastern European Affairs after 1922)	Division of European Affairs	Office of European Affairs	Bureau of European Affairs	Bureau of European Affairs	Bureau of European Affairs
	1 clerk– Europe Asia Africa	Parallel 1st & 2nd Consular Bureaus					Bureau of German Affairs	
	1 clerk– North & South America	°	Division of Latin American Affairs (1909)	Division of American Republic Affairs	Office of American Republic Affairs	Bureau of American Republic Affairs		Bureau of Inter-American Affairs (merged with AID/LA in 1964)
		1st Bureaus headed by 1 Asst Secy; 2nd Bureaus by another.	Division of Mexican Affairs (1915)		°	°		
			(Outlines of Modern Arrangement)	1 AS heads first three; 1 AS the last	For 1st time 1 AS per bureau		

in charge of the line units (four geographic and one for international organization affairs) in which there was one important change:

> Both the regional and international organization Assistant Secretaries would *at the action level* be responsible for and be equipped, in terms of personnel, to deal with not solely "political" aspects of foreign affairs, as is the basic conception of the duties of the existing geographic office directors, but for all aspects, whether they be political, economic, public opinion, intelligence, or administration.[2]

It fell to Dean Acheson as secretary to implement these recommendations. Since he had served as vice-chairman of the Hoover Commission, their path was considerably eased. There was substantial delay, however, due to the need for enabling legislation and to a fear of offending some of the incumbent ranking officials, but the substance of the recommendations had been carried out by the time Acheson departed from office in January 1953. The central element of the "new" department consisted of the five line bureaus, each headed by an assistant secretary. Personnel administration and many other activities of the former functional offices were transferred to them. Some of the remaining offices (economic affairs, public affairs, legal affairs, intelligence, and press relations) were grouped under one deputy under secretary, while most administrative functions became the responsibility of the deputy under secretary for administration.

Since this reorganization, the basic structure has remained intact. Many units subsequently became bureaus, including Economic (later Economic and Business) Affairs, Intelligence and Research, Public Affairs, and Educational and Cultural Affairs. For a short period in the 1950s, there was also a Bureau of German Affairs, headed by a director

[2] U.S. Commission on Organization of the Executive Branch of Government, *Foreign Affairs: A Report to the Congress* (Washington, D.C.: GPO, 1949), p. 40. Emphasis in original.

of assistant secretary rank. It was eventually incorporated as an element of the Bureau of European Affairs. Finally, reflecting the increased importance of Africa, the Bureau of African Affairs was split off from the former Bureau of Near Eastern, South Asian, and African Affairs in 1959. Since that time there have been five geographic bureaus, responsible for European Affairs (EUR), Near Eastern and South Asian Affairs (NEA), Inter-American Affairs (ARA), African Affairs (AF), and Far Eastern (later East Asian and Pacific) Affairs (EA).

Between the mid-1950s and 1966, all geographic bureaus were organized in similar fashion. Each was headed by an assistant secretary appointed by the president and confirmed by the Senate. He was aided at the "sixth floor" (the location of the geographic assistant secretaries' offices in the new State Department building) or "front office" level by one to three deputy assistant secretaries (DAS), who were almost always career Foreign Service Officers (FSOs) of Class-One or Career Minister rank. If there were two or more DASs, their responsibilities were divided on either a geographic (subareas of the total area covered by the bureau) or functional (e.g., economic) basis. When there was only one, he acted as an alternate to the assistant secretary; while in the bureaus with more than one, the most senior assumed this duty along with his other responsibilities. Below this level, the substantive work of the bureau was carried on in several offices (usually four or five), each of which had responsibility for a portion of the assigned area. There was also an office for regional affairs, that is, for multilateral affairs for the entire area covered by the bureau, and in the Bureau of European Affairs there were separate offices for regional political and regional economic affairs. Each of the area offices was headed by an office director (OD) and a deputy office director, who in some cases functioned as an alter ego to the OD and in others assumed a large measure of independent responsibility for a portion of the office's area. Below the office director and deputy were the officers-in-charge (O-in-C), each responsible for one or more countries. Finally, at the bottom of the structure were the desk officers, who dealt with day-to-day problems arising out of U.S. relations with one or two countries.

Relationships between desk officer, officer-in-charge, and office director could be distinguished on two dimensions. First, the desk officer concerned himself primarily with routine problems, with the higher levels attempting to have a successively broader view and concentrating on the more important and difficult issues. Second, each level, starting with the desk officer and working up, usually was charged with following the affairs of more countries. This was not always true, since in some instances there might be desk officers, officers-in-charge, and an office director all responsible for one country, in which case there was generally a functional division (e.g., OD for Germany, O-in-C for German Political Affairs, O-in-C for German Economic Affairs, and desk officers under the latter O-in-C for trade relations and for agricultural matters). Thus the more general distinction among the three levels was one of specificity of the work undertaken, rather than the geographic areas of responsibility.[3] It was the bureau structure below the assistant secretary level that was modified by creation of the country director positions in 1966. How this change came about and why it was considered necessary strongly influenced the role the country directors came to play, and it is to these factors that one must turn next.

THE COUNTRY DIRECTOR SYSTEM: ANTECEDENTS

In broad terms, the country director idea was but one of a stream of attempted organizational reforms, each of which

[3] For short descriptions of the duties of office directors and desk officers through the years, see James L. McCamy, *The Administration of American Foreign Affairs* (New York: Knopf, 1952), pp. 41-84; Elder, *Policy Machine*, pp. 19-48; and Sapin, *Making of United States Foreign Policy*, pp. 117-122.

was seen in the eye of its creators as a means of coming to grips with some of the severe problems of coordination, control, and program management accompanying the massive enlargement of the American world role after World War II. Such steps as the uneven trend toward integration of previously separated responsibilities into single units, most particularly the geographic bureaus of State after the initial Hoover Commission recommendations,[4] and the continuing efforts of every president since Truman to buttress the position of ambassadors abroad vis-à-vis representatives of other parts of government fall clearly in this category.[5]

At the working level in Washington, problems of control and coordination, if anything, proved to be even more difficult than in the field, as the Jackson Subcommittee intimated:

> In Washington the decision-making process is, so to speak, vertical—up departmental lines which converge only at the Presidential level. In the field, coordination is horizontal, with differences being resolved and policies harmonized by the ambassador.[6]

It is thus not surprising that proposals and programs would at some point begin to appear directed toward im-

---

[4] Sapin, *Making of U.S. Foreign Policy*, p. 120.

[5] See the comments on Truman's efforts in this area in Jackson Subcommittee, p. 16. President Kennedy's letter of May 29, 1961, explicitly designating the ambassador as the central figure and supervisor at missions abroad is the most remembered of these attempts. It is reprinted in many places, including Jackson Subcommittee, pp. 15-16. For a skeptical view of the efficacy of Kennedy's letter, see John P. Leacacos, *Fires in the In-Basket: The ABC's of the State Department* (Cleveland: World Publishing, 1968), p. 301; and for a more positive one from a former ambassador, Ellis Briggs, *Anatomy of Diplomacy: The Origin and Execution of American Foreign Policy* (New York: David McKay, 1968), p. 22, n. 10.

[6] Jackson Subcommittee, p. 17. The quotation, however, probably overestimates the degree of success of field coordination, but the comparison is still valid.

proving the functioning of the working level officials in State in Washington. Of course, the specific details of plans directed toward this general objective reflected the particular organizational and political environment of the times, and the perceptions of the individuals involved. In the case of the country director system, the total pattern of antecedents was quite complex, but certain important strands can be rather easily identified. The experiences and preferences of Secretary Rusk, and a growing interest in management techniques in State, personified by Deputy Under Secretary for Management William J. Crockett, kept the idea alive and helped give it form. A 1964 experiment in merging the responsibilities of State and AID with respect to Latin America indicated one possible path of change. Even so, the work of a presidential task force in late 1965 and early 1966, under the direction of Maxwell Taylor, was necessary to give this reorganization its final impetus.

The Secretary

As part of the inquiry of the Jackson Subcommittee into "the Administration of National Security," Secretary Rusk's testimony on December 11, 1963, provided considerable insight into his thinking about State's organization. He asserted that "inside of the department our principal problem is layering,"[7] that is, an excessive number of hierarchical levels through which any given telegram or proposed action was filtered, and he traced possible improvements which resembled the CD change of two and one-half years later:

> I think we do need to do something about layering, and one of the ways to do this is to upgrade the desk officer level. It seems to me that the man in Washington who spends all of his time brooding about a country like Brazil ought to be a man comparable in competence to the man who is Ambassador to Brazil. We then clear the way

[7] "Hearings: Part 6," in Jackson Subcommittee, p. 397.

49

for him to get quickly to the Assistant Secretary or the Secretary.[8]

This caught the attention of Senator Jackson, who pursued the point by asking how such an upgrading of desk officers would help. Rusk then amplified his statement:

It may be possible to eliminate the office level and have the desk officer not only report directly to the Assistant Secretary, but also to have the Assistant Secretary staffed to provide that desk officer with a good deal of the specialized advice that he needs and which we can't afford country by country.[9]

Rusk also suggested that instead of class three or four FSOs manning the desks—the existing pattern—FSO-1s or career ministers might be assigned to them to "see what the effect would be on the quality of the job done."[10] He also noted that some tentative steps had already been taken toward upgrading the desk officers, but did not elaborate. Presumably, he was referring to an experiment begun for Brazil, in which a more senior man had been appointed and given both State and AID responsibilities.[11]

Thus, the secretary's acceptance and espousal of something resembling the CD idea was clear. Apparently his concern predated his term as secretary, originating in his earlier experiences as deputy under secretary and then assistant secretary.[12] The question thus arises why changes had not been made at the time of the hearings, almost three years after Rusk became secretary, and why nothing was

[8] Ibid.   [9] Ibid., p. 400.   [10] Ibid., p. 403.

[11] Ibid., p. 398. The Brazil experiment is referred to in "ARA and AID/LA Are Joined: Combined Operations for a Total U.S. Program in Latin America," *Department of State News Letter*, No. 36 (April 1964), 6.

[12] Rusk served in these positions between 1949 and late 1951. Some substantiation for this interpretation is found in his frequent reference to the earlier period in his testimony at this hearing, in Jackson Subcommittee, "Hearings: Part 6," pp. 385-412, passim.

50

done for nearly two and one-half additional years. There are probably two basic reasons. First, organizational change was not high on Rusk's personal priority list. At the session of the Jackson hearings cited above, he prefaced his remarks with some reservations about its efficacy, arguing that one might strive for steady improvements, but should not expect "miraculous differences."[13] One of the chronic obstacles to improving State's organization has been that those at the top with the power to impose changes involve themselves so deeply in current policy questions personally, rather than supervising the way others handle them, that they can give only infrequent attention to administrative matters.[14]

A second possible reason was opposition in the department. It was clear from the way the secretary's idea emerged—in response to questions in a congressional hearing rather than through a directive to the department—that it was not a high priority item. One interviewee recalls that when the idea was first "floated out by Rusk" at the hearings, a deputy assistant secretary dutifully canvassed senior officers in one geographic bureau and found a generally negative reaction. He remembers that the incumbent assistant secretary complained that he already had too many immediate subordinates, and that elimination of the office level would just increase his problems by tripling the number reporting directly to him. (STATE #1)

[13] Ibid., p. 386.

[14] In this vein, one seventh-floor staff assistant (i.e., assistant to one of the senior officials of the department) reported that Nicholas Katzenbach, under secretary at the close of the Johnson administration, wrote a memo to his successor strongly urging him to take a close look at the organization and the people of State during his first six weeks on the job, since after that time he would be immersed in policy problems and would have neither the time nor the desire to consider problems of organization. While the danger he warned against has usually been present, Under Secretary Richardson in the Nixon administration did manage to maintain a continuing interest in organizational problems during his seventeen months at State.

Given such opposition in the department and a lack of clear direction, it is not surprising that the idea was not pursued in late 1963 and early 1964. But it ultimately re-emerged under different circumstances with greatly increased support.

An Emphasis on Management: William J. Crockett

One reason the CD idea was not extinguished was that it paralleled a general drive toward managerial improvement championed and in part implemented by William J. Crockett during his tenure as assistant secretary (1961-1963) and deputy under secretary for administration (1963-January 1967). There is little doubt that Crockett was the most controversial senior officer in the department, the secretary not excepted. He was viewed by some as a "brilliant empire builder," who moved into a leadership vacuum, giving the administrators too much say in the way State was run;[15] by others as an enthusiastic but limited individual whose abilities did not provide him with the base from which to successfully carry out his plans. (STATE #18)[16] Still others saw him as an effective innovator who "lit fires all over the State Department as he experimented vigorously to develop the new foreign affairs program manager concept," in the process of which he "conceived and put into effect a series of commonsense administrative improvements."[17]

Crockett had much more experience in State than his immediate predecessors, but he was not a traditional Foreign Service officer. He had entered as a Wristonee,[18] and had

[15] Stewart Alsop, *The Center* (New York: Popular Library, 1968), pp. 105, 110, 112.

[16] This officer was serving in the "O" or administrative area of the department during a portion of Crockett's tenure in office.

[17] Leacacos, p. 358.

[18] "Wristonization" was a large-scale program of lateral entry of civil servants, Foreign Service staff officers, and others who did not take the traditional examination path into the Foreign Service between

spent his entire career in the field of administration, held in low esteem by most substantively oriented FSOs.[19] Coupled with this lack of proper "old-boy" ties, two other factors caused him to be viewed with suspicion: He was thought to have been promoted to deputy under secretary in large measure because of his ability to get along with Congressman John J. Rooney (D-N.Y.), chairman of the House Appropriations Subcommittee passing on State's budget and the *bête noire* of the department; and his reputation as an innovator with a great interest in "new-fangled" management techniques suggested by outside consultants.[20]

Paradoxically, Crockett's interest in management and in reducing layering kept change at the working level in the geographic bureaus an open possibility, but by association with some of his other programs, the CD idea became labeled as one of many "Crockettisms," reducing its impact.[21]

It is impossible to give a complete history of Crockett's efforts, but several require mention.[22] The bulk of the pub-

---

1954 and 1958. Many of the older officers felt swamped by the influx of 1,500 Wristonees, and through the years there have been charges and countercharges about the wisdom of the program and the ability of the new group of officers. The program was named after Henry M. Wriston, then president of Brown University and chairman of a committee which recommended this and other changes. See Sapin, pp. 127-128 for more details.

[19] See Argyris, *Some Causes*, pp. 10-11, for a discussion of this point.

[20] John Ensor Harr, *The Professional Diplomat* (Princeton, N.J.: Princeton University Press, 1969), p. 83.

[21] For an example of opponents' reactions to Crockett and his innovations, see Thomas A. Donovan's savage little piece, "An Evolving Profession: Managerial Diplomacy," *Foreign Service Journal*, 43 (October, 1966), 23. See also the section on organizational climate in Chapter VII below.

[22] A short summary of these is contained in Alfred J. Marrow, "Managerial Revolution in the State Department," *Department of State News Letter*, No. 68 (December, 1966), 34-37. More detail is found in a 106-page pamphlet put out by Crockett's office in August 1966,

licity went to the ACORD (Action for Organizational Development) program, which attempted to "install and sustain a less bureaucratic and more participative managerial approach."[23] It featured "management by objectives," through creation of independent and autonomous "program managers."[24] In simpler terms, the result was a flattening of the administrative or "O" area of State's hierarchy, with a large number of officials reporting directly to Crockett, rather than to intervening layers as formerly.[25] This paralleled the country director change with regard to lines of authority, if not in responsibilities of individual jobholders.

Another major but less successful effort of Crockett and his team was the attempt to introduce program budgeting and systems analysis to the department.[26] There was a potentially close relationship between the Planning-Programming-Budgeting System (PPBS) idea and the country director concept, in that the conception of Crockett and Richard Barrett (who was directly in charge of the program) was that the basic program unit should be the individual foreign country, rather than the agency budget as argued by the Bureau of the Budget.[27] Since the country director was charged with overall responsibility for U.S. government activities relating to his assigned country, a programming system, if it could be developed on a country base, would be of considerable value as an element of con-

---

entitled "A Management Program for the Department of State," printed for internal circulation.

[23] Marrow, p. 34.   [24] Ibid., p. 35.

[25] In one case, it was claimed that six layers were cut out by a reorganization of functions, so that the chief of the Employment Division reported directly to Crockett, rather than through six intervening officials. "A Management Program," p. 85.

[26] See Frederick C. Mosher and John E. Harr, *Programming Systems and Foreign Affairs Leadership: An Attempted Innovation* (New York: Oxford University Press, 1970), passim, for a dramatic account of this episode.

[27] This information comes from several interviewees in both State and the (then) Bureau of the Budget.

trol. Ultimately, the PPBS program failed, and this resource was lost to the country directors.[28]

Some less widely known projects were even more directly related to the CD change. For example, a study prepared by the Office of Management, then headed by Ralph Roberts, entitled "Organizing for Action in the Regional Bureaus: A Study of the Role of the Country Desk Officer" concluded that the desk officer at that time (March 1963) was too low in the organization, too limited in authority and responsibility, and too junior grade to assume a major role in foreign policy. It recommended that

> to reverse this trend the country officer—the proposed Principal Policy Officer—must embody the concept of an active unifying and directive force for all United States relations with another country.[29]

With the substitution of "country director" for "principal policy officer," this phrase could stand as a summary description of the responsibilities ultimately given the CD. While it can be misleading to attempt to identify precisely the origin of specific ideas in a complex bureaucracy, Crockett has said that "I am certain that this study did play an important role in the final development of the concept," although he was "reluctant to say categorically that the concept of the Country Director originated only with [it]."[30] Even so, the recommendations of this study were quite similar to what emerged three years later. It advocated that action and leadership responsibilities be concentrated in the

[28] This argument was not accepted by many country directors. See Chapter V for more discussion. The case for the argument is most clearly presented in Glynn R. Mays, Jr., "Companion Tools for Foreign Affairs Management: The PPBS and the SIG/IRG System," *Foreign Service Journal*, 43 (September and October 1966), 16-18 [September] and 25-26 [October].

[29] Office of Management, U.S. Department of State, "Organizing for Action in the Regional Bureaus: A Study of the Role of the Country Desk Officer," Privately circulated report, March 6, 1963, p. 4.

[30] William J. Crockett, letter to W.I.B., July 22, 1969.

principle policy officer (PPO) positions, located organizationally directly below the assistant secretary; that those
filling them should have major responsibility for one or a
group of related countries; and that they should be given
the freedom to organize and use their staffs as they felt necessary. A policy for making the transition to the new system
was suggested, as were devices to prevent others, particularly deputy assistant secretaries, from impinging on the
authority of the PPOs. Also, functional specialists were to
be assigned advisory roles outside the chain of command.[31]
Although the PPO was to be given a strong role for "all
United States relations," the thrust was directed more toward the internal organization of the Department of State
than to interagency coordination. Chart II-2 summarizes
the organizational patterns existing in the five geographic
bureaus at the time of this report, along with the proposed
pattern.

Shared Responsibilities: The "Merged Bureau" for Latin America

The recommendations of the Office of Management report
were not immediately followed, but they did have some
impact on parallel developments. In late 1963 the Brazil
desk of State's Bureau of Inter-American Affairs, which had
been one of five country desks in the Office of East Coast
Affairs, was taken out of that office, and "the Brazil desk
was taken out of the corresponding operation on the AID
side, and the two merged under one director." In part because of the strong qualifications of the officer chosen for
this job, who had had a wide range of experience both in
State and with assistance programs, this experiment worked
out very well, particularly from the viewpoint of those in
the field. In effect, it became a prototype for a broader
change the next year which affected the whole bureau.
(CD #10)

---

[31] "Organizing for Action," p. 3.

CHART II-2

Proposed Changes in Geographic Bureau Organization
Office of Management—March 1963

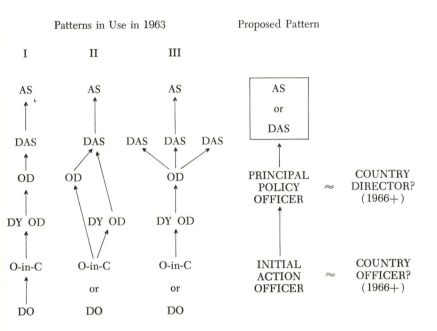

Patterns in Use in 1963   Proposed Pattern

Legend:

AS	=	Assistant Secretary
DAS	=	Deputy Assistant Secretary
OD	=	Office Director
DY OD	=	Deputy Office Director
O-in-C	=	Officer-in-Charge
DO	=	Desk Officer

The box around AS or DAS in the proposed pattern column indicates that in the study, it was proposed that there be only one DAS
in each bureau to act as an *alter ego* for the Assistant Secretary. This,
it was argued, should lead to the two operating as one unit or level,
rather than as two, as was charged to be the case under the existing
patterns.

The sign (≈) indicates the similarity between positions proposed in
the study and those ultimately created in 1966, suggesting a close
relationship between the 1963 study and the later change.

Between 1961 and 1964 a number of factors combined to make U.S. policy and operations in Latin America disjointed and forever in flux. These included the new programs of the Alliance for Progress, the delicate state of relations with Latin America generally resulting from the advent of the Castro government in Cuba, divided lines of responsibility, and short tenures for senior officials. President Johnson therefore decided to place one individual in charge of all aspects of U.S. policy in the region. His choice was Thomas C. Mann, who had begun a second tour as assistant secretary of state for Inter-American Affairs in December 1963.[32] The response to the president's call for a "total U.S. program in Latin America," as worked out by Mann and by then Administrator of the Agency for International Development David E. Bell, was the "merged bureau." Mann retained his title as Assistant Secretary, was designated Assistant Administrator of AID for Latin America, and was given the new title of U.S. Coordinator of the Alliance for Progress. With this personal mandate, Mann integrated the State and AID Latin American bureaus. Basically, the geographic offices of both were reorganized and amalgamated into nine new geographical groupings, each headed by one officer responsible for overall policy recommendations for one or two countries. The larger number of offices was explicitly intended to permit the new office directors to focus on their countries in greater depth.[33]

The job description accompanying the merged bureau change clearly showed linkage between the 1963 report and the Brazil experience on one hand,[34] and the subsequent country director change in the other four bureaus on the other. The head of the merged country units, called "Direc-

[32] "ARA and AID/LA Are Joined," p. 6.
[33] Ibid.
[34] CD #10, who was connected with Brazilian Affairs at the time, affirmed this interpretation. He stated that the merged bureau idea was "in part based on the successful experience of the previous year with Brazil."

tor of Country Affairs," was visualized as having enlarged responsibilities when compared with either State or AID desk officers under the previous system:

He is the focal point for Washington direction of the total United States foreign affairs program in his particular countries. He is concerned with the policies and operation of all U.S. governmental and quasi-governmental agencies operating abroad, as well as with the policies and activities of international agencies and foreign governments toward his countries. He is responsible for seeing to it that individual agency policies and operations have been coordinated with overall objectives and for fostering cooperation and consistency in operations.[35]

Here the ideal of control and supervision of all U.S. operations and policies for given countries received even greater emphasis than in the 1963 Office of Management report, and was extended beyond the confines of State, with the explicit inclusion of AID responsibilities. The increased number of offices with smaller areas of responsibility directly paralleled the CD change, while merger of development and political/diplomatic functions foreshadowed the later emphasis on leadership and coordination.

Reactions to the merged bureau were mixed. Bell had little choice but to accept the merger, although one inevitable consequence was that the AID Administrator had less authority over AID programs in Latin America than for those elsewhere. For this reason, his successor, William Gaud, was strongly against the idea; which may be one reason that the pattern was not repeated in other areas when the country director change was initiated.[36] It is not even clear that the change was completely welcomed by State personnel. Ten years earlier Henry F. Holland, Assistant Secretary of State for Latin America between 1954 and 1956, had pro-

[35] "ARA and AID/LA Are Joined," pp. 6-7.
[36] Interview, AID #2 and several others.

59

posed a very similar amalgamation, which was quashed by Herbert C. Hoover, Jr., then under secretary of state, on grounds that State would be blamed for everything that AID did that was unpopular.[37] Some reluctance to become too intimately involved with nondiplomatic affairs persists to the present, and consequently stands in the way of State's asserting itself in overall policy matters. Opinions about this specific change varied from Gaud's negative reaction and those of critics cited by Yager who held that it "confused lines of authority, suppressed a useful adversary relationship between the two agencies, and imposed an impossible administrative burden on the head of the combined staffs,"[38] to the assertion of Leacacos that the "bureau's effectiveness in handling complex political-economic factors can be attributed in part to [this] experiment."[39]

One additional development was also directed toward consolidation of working-level management on a country basis. In 1965 a special office for Canadian affairs was established within the Bureau of European Affairs. Prior to that time, Canadian affairs had been a typical desk operation within the Office of British Commonwealth and Northern European Affairs. The group recommending this step, headed by Ambassador Livingston Merchant, believed that the level at which relations with Canada were dealt with should be upgraded. A new official, the Coordinator of Canadian Affairs, was to have the rank of office director, instead of officer-in-charge, as previously. In addition to the new title, the change meant a direct channel to the assistant secretary; placed a considerably more senior officer in charge of Canadian affairs; and provided a stronger sup-

[37] Interview, CD #11, who was present at the meeting.

[38] Joseph A. Yager, "The Department of State: Its Structure and Role in 1968," in Keith C. Clark and Laurence J. Legere, eds., *The President and the Management of National Security* (New York: Praeger, 1969), p. 137.

[39] Leacacos, p. 64.

60

porting staff.[40] However, by the time the officer designated took up his duties in April 1966, the country director system had been installed in all geographic bureaus, and his title was changed to country director for Canada.

By late 1965, then, there had been considerable movement toward something like the CD system. But one final development was needed to bring it into existence.

General Taylor and NSAM 341

The immediate sequence of events leading to creation of the country director positions began in August 1965. President Johnson asked Gen. Maxwell Taylor, lately returned from his tour as ambassador to South Vietnam, to "review all of the activities of our Government in the Counter-Insurgency field, both at home and abroad, and to make appropriate recommendations."[41] After his own inquiries and those of four interagency task forces appointed to assist him, Taylor concluded that this mandate was too restricted. First, to deal only with insurgency would perpetuate an essentially defensive role for the United States; therefore, activities abroad that might help deter as well as combat insurgency —most notably developmental aid and other financial assistance—should also be included in the recommendations. Second, since the new procedures would presumably deal with most nations—Taylor estimated that some ninety were potential targets for insurgency—it would be logical to include U.S. activities in all countries, rather than having two sets of organizational devices and procedures. Third, since programs run by different parts of government often operated at cross-purposes, all U.S. government programs

[40] Details were provided by an FSO interviewee familiar with the Canadian change.

[41] Gen. Maxwell D. Taylor, "Speech to American Foreign Service Association," March 31, 1966, reprinted in *Foreign Service Journal*, 43 (May 1966): 34-36. The development of Taylor's thinking summarized in the following paragraphs is taken from this speech, except as otherwise noted. Cf. also my "Obstacles to Reform in Foreign Affairs: the case of NSAM 341, *Orbis*, 18 (Spring 1974).

should be coordinated from a central point. Fourth, this locus should be in Washington, since individual agency policies were developed there, and only there was a global perspective possible. In short, what began as an effort to bring consistency to a narrow range of programs in one group of countries grew into an attempt to improve coordination of all official U.S. activities anywhere abroad.

At this point, the question of the organizational devices that would be needed assumed importance. Taylor and his colleagues discarded the ideas of revitalizing the National Security Council (NSC) and of creating a cumbersome White House organization of some other type to fill the void, in each case because their investigations revealed an almost universal lack of enthusiasm. They then turned to the secretary of state as the logical central figure. When President Kennedy abolished the Operations Coordinating Board (OCB) of the Eisenhower NSC system, he said he "would look to the Department of State to assume the coordination function"; but the task forces could find no formal document specifically giving the secretary this authority. Viewing the lack of coordination and consistency that prompted his own assignment, Taylor decided something more was needed. At the same time, he believed that for maximum effectiveness, the product of his review should be a short memorandum to the president, affecting the overall organization of the foreign affairs community, rather than a bulky report that would be a collection of odds and ends about various programs. It should, in his view, concentrate on buttressing the secretary of state, rather than on a postmortem of previous failings.

Once this thrust had been decided upon, Taylor began to show a draft of his proposals, which ultimately became NSAM (National Security Action Memorandum) 341, to carefully selected individuals. This was done very discreetly, and even department heads were not given copies to keep, in order to avoid leaks, nitpicking, and suggested modifications resulting from circulation at subordinate levels. Later, Taylor assured himself of presidential support in at least two meetings; and a "supercabinet meeting," some thirty-five or forty key individuals attending, was also held. The president asked each participant how he felt about the ideas, "and of course everybody said it was okay," given what appeared to be obvious presidential desires.[42] Shortly thereafter, NSAM 341 was placed into effect on March 4, 1966.

Even so, Taylor's intention to give the secretary of state clear authority and the means to manage all foreign affairs programs was compromised even before NSAM 341 was announced. A comprehensive programming system suggested as one of several tools needed to support the interdepartmental groups created in the proposal was ultimately omitted, either because Taylor's task forces did not want to overload the NSAM 341 system at the beginning and held that the programming system could be added later,[43] or, according to other sources, because of the opposition of Henry Rowen and the Bureau of the Budget who saw such a programming system as a potential threat to their own PPBS programs.[44]

A second limiting modification came about because the legality of the NSAM 341 system was questioned by some of those consulted. According to some, the draft proposal assigned "to the Secretary of State authority and responsibility for the overall direction, coordination, and supervi-

[42] Interview (NSAM #1). Taylor task-force member later associated with the Senior Interdepartmental Group.

[43] Gen. Maxwell D. Taylor, interview August 13, 1969.

[44] Mosher and Harr, pp. 123-126. As they suggest, Taylor's commitment to the idea of programming was never in doubt. He later participated in the work of the Hitch Committee, which conducted a review of programming efforts in 1966 and 1967. For details about this committee, see U.S. Congress, Senate Subcommittee on National Security and International Operations, Committee on Government Operations, Planning-Programming-Budgeting (Washington, D.C.: GPO, 1967-1969), especially Mosher's testimony of November 27, 1968. The subcommittee listed is the Jackson Subcommittee with an altered name.

sion of interdepartmental activities of the United States government overseas."[45] The critics, primarily from Budget, argued that in view of legislative mandates given other executive departments, such a definitive delegation to the secretary of state was of doubtful legality. Although supporters of the NSAM 341 countered that it merely formalized existing authority of the secretary and in any event was a response to clear presidential intentions, the final version of the secretary's mandate included the phrase "to the full extent permitted by law."[46] The net effect was to introduce ambiguity about the strength of the secretary's position, in view of the very explicit legislative authority given to Agriculture, AID, and other agencies for certain programs. Another source for similar arguments was the passage in NSAM 341 that defined interdepartmental activities which were subject to the new procedures to exclude those that remained the responsibility of one organization and that did not *significantly* affect the overall U.S. program in a country or region.[47] The failure to provide a significance test or to indicate who was to decide how significant a particular issue was made it almost certain, given the nature of the policy process, that such issues would be bargained over exactly as before.

To enable the secretary to carry out his new duties, two types of permanent interdepartmental committees were created. One was a Senior Interdepartmental Group (SIG), headed by the under secretary of state as executive chair-

[45] Mosher and Harr, pp. 123-126.

[46] Again there is some dispute over what happened. General Taylor says he decided to include the quoted phrase so that congressional approval would not be required, and not because of any opposition (interview August 13, 1969). Mosher and Harr argue that the change was made at the insistence of Budget (pp. 125-126). The full wording was ". . . authority and responsibility *to the full extent permitted by law* for the overall direction. . . ." (Emphasis added.) This is the wording as it appeared in Foreign Affairs Manual Circular (FAMC) 385.

[47] FAMC 385, paragraph 3.

man and having as members the deputy secretary of Defense, the AID administrator, the director of the CIA, the chairman of the Joint Chiefs of Staff, the director of USIA, and the special assistant to the president for National Security Affairs. Below this level there were five Interdepartmental Regional Groups (IRGs), each with the assistant secretary heading the appropriate geographic bureau of State as executive chairman and with membership at the regional level parallel to that of the SIG. The SIG was to aid the secretary by resolving interdepartmental problems that could not be handled lower in the hierarchy, or for which existing procedures were inadequate. It was to do this by attending to important foreign policy issues as early as possible, by dealing with topics referred by its members or the assistant secretaries of state, by insuring consistent use of United States resources, by absorbing reponsibilities formerly held by the Special Group (counterinsurgency), and by periodically investigating the effectiveness of overseas activities and programs. The IRGs were to insure the adequacy of policies for countries in their regions, and of the necessary means for implementing them. They were also to isolate potentially critical situations and to make recommendations to higher officials.

A key feature was the executive-chairman concept. At each level, they were to have "full powers of decision on all matters within their purview," unless an appeal was requested to the next higher level. This provision was intended to strengthen State and to force decisions down the hierarchy, since this was more authority than could be mustered by chairmen of most interagency committees who are forced to seek consensus.[48]

Formally, then, State had been given an opportunity to exert a significantly enhanced influence in interagency deliberations, and to recoup a preeminent position in the con-

---

[48] Details in this and the preceding paragraph summarized from FAMC 385.

duct of foreign affairs. NASM 341 also provided the final impetus for the creation of the country director system.

The Country Director System: Beginnings

Senior officials in State realized that alterations would be needed in the department to achieve compatibility with NSAM 341 and began to plan accordingly. Coordination between Taylor's group and State was primarily effected through U. Alexis Johnson, then deputy under secretary for Political Affairs. Deputy Under Secretary Crockett was also involved almost from the beginning, and supervised drafting of the State documents along with Johnson. It was done almost entirely by Mrs. Gladys P. Rogers, a career Foreign Service officer and director of the Office of Organizational Studies and Procedures.[49]

As consideration progressed, it was decided that successful functioning of the SIG and IRGs would require another, supporting, level beneath the IRGs. In the course of the review, Crockett apparently remembered the principal policy officer study he had commissioned three years earlier.[50] Mrs. Rogers may have been instrumental in reminding him about it, since she had been working for Ralph Roberts at the time it was written. Apparently the PPO, renamed the country director, struck those in State as the answer to the problem of levels below the IRG or assistant secretary. According to one source, however, the idea was incorporated only a day or two prior to the announcement of the SIG/IRGs system.[51]

Rusk had been following the developments and gave his approval to the idea of adding the country director to the devices developed by the Taylor group. (STATE #2) But the CD change was never discussed by Taylor's task forces, and no thought was given to incorporating it in NSAM

[49] Interview, officer formerly serving in this office (STATE #2).

[50] William J. Crockett, letter to W.I.B., July 22, 1969.

[51] Interview, officer formerly serving on management staff (STATE #3).

341.[52] This omission was one cause of future difficulty, since the CD's place in the new arrangements was somewhat ambiguous from the very beginning. This sequence of events, while underlining the linkage between NSAM 341 and the CD system, also indicates the latter's independent origins. Later developments showed that the CD idea was a viable organizational arrangement within State, with or without the existence of the SIG and IRGs.

It is important to note that the geographic assistant secretaries, whose bureaus were to be reorganized by the CD change, had little input into the decision process. U. Alexis Johnson apparently did consult them, but only after he and Crockett had worked out the basic proposal, and the considerable opposition encountered was essentially ignored. (STATE #4) Thus those most affected by the change and most directly in a position to influence its success, with the possible exception of the CDs themselves, had little personal stake in the idea, and in some cases actually opposed it. This, too, did not bode well for the CDs' ability to play the role apparently envisioned by those who designed the system.

In any event, State was prepared to release Foreign Affairs Manual Circular (FAMC) 385 on the same day as NSAM 341. It repeated much of the latter's language, spoke directly to State's new responsibilities, and created the position of country director. It was accompanied by a message from Secretary Rusk "to his colleagues in the Department of State and abroad," expressing his strong desire that State move quickly to assume the leadership role assigned to it.

The intended goal of the country director change was apparent from the secretary's comments:

> I look to the Country Directors to assume full responsibility, under their Assistant Secretaries, for all activities in the country or countries assigned to them, and to be

[52] Gen. Maxwell D. Taylor, letter to W.I.B., July 10, 1969.

single focal points in Washington to serve our Ambassadors.[53]

They were directed to develop necessary channels, contacts, and mechanisms "appropriate to and necessary for full interdepartmental leadership on country matters"; to raise specific matters for consideration by the IRGs when necessary and to bring detailed knowledge to them when requested to do so; and to serve as the basis for crisis task force operations when required.[54]

The first task facing State was to determine how many CDs were to be appointed and to fill these positions. The responsibility for developing the changes required by FAMC 385 fell to the Office of Organizational Studies and Procedures, working under Crockett and headed by Mrs. Gladys Rogers. Members of this office worked out the details with the executive directors in each of the four affected geographic bureaus (ARA being omitted because of its already functioning merged bureau operation with AID/LA). Each participant reported back to his superior (to Crockett for the administrative side, and to the several assistant secretaries for the geographic bureaus). There was considerable horse trading, the usual pattern being that the executive directors proposed arrangements which deviated as little as possible from the existing pattern. This was in part because the incumbent office directors, some of whom were to become country directors, did not like the idea of having fewer countries than before the change. Eventually Crockett prevailed and there were more country directors than the bureaus originally desired.[55] While some executive directors interviewed said that there was no real difficulty in working out these arrangements, Crockett demurred and argued that

[53] Rusk, "Message to His Colleagues in the Department of State," March 4, 1966.

[54] FAMC 385, paragraph 7.

[55] Interview, officer serving in this office at the time. (STATE #2) Source for whole paragraph.

the simple, most difficult problem was one of management style . . . i.e., the number of people a man felt that he could have reporting directly to him. To reduce layers one must *increase* the numbers of people for which he is directly responsible.[56]

In addition to disagreement over the number of country directors, there was some opposition to the basic concept, attributable both to tradition and to concern with the span of control. Given the secretary's avowed support there could hardly be a frontal assault on the idea, but some resistance nevertheless was felt:

> The chief opposition was covert rather than overt and took the form of cynical depreciation of the idea rather than direct opposition. Thus we faced the task of trying to make enthusiastic supporters and operators out of officers who quite cynically thought of it as being a gimmicky new name for the same old function.[57]

The time required for these discussions and negotiations led to a period in limbo, from the time of the announcement in early March until late April and early May when the CD areas of responsibility were announced.[58] The assignments took even longer, with a complete list not being published until September,[59] by which time most of the appointees were on the job.

Organizationally, several modifications followed final resolution of these questions. First, the office director positions in the geographic bureaus were abolished, and their responsibilities given to a larger number of country directors of the same rank. In classical public administration terms,

[56] Crockett, letter to W.I.B. Emphasis in original.

[57] Ibid.

[58] Dates of announcements and the document numbers were: FE (later EA), April 21, FAMC 400; EUR, April 25, FAMC 401; NEA, April 25, FAMC 403; AF, May 13, FAMC 406.

[59] In *Department of State News Letter*, No. 65 (September 1966), 32-33, 37.

this was a change to a "flat" hierarchical structure from a "taller" one, with a consequent increase in the span of control, i.e., in this case more officials reporting directly to each assistant secretary of state.[60] According to classic theory, one could expect such a change to force some decisions downward. Chart II-3 compares the old and new structures of the Bureau of Near Eastern and South Asian Affairs, and similar changes occurred in each of the others.

Second, as a corollary to this flattening, one level was in theory eliminated between the assistant secretary and those directly responsible for relations with individual countries. However, this assumption needs closer examination before it is accepted, since several deputy assistant secretaries were appointed in each bureau. Intended to be alter egos to the assistant secretaries according to U. Alexis Johnson,[61] there was a tendency for them to assume responsibilities for a specific geographic area within the bureau. This in effect partially screened off the assistant secretary from his "direct" subordinates, the country directors.

Third, those directly responsible for relations with given countries were upgraded in rank. Formerly, these were the officers-in-charge, or in some cases the desk officers, generally class-three or -four Foreign Service officers (FSO-3

[60] Span of control is an old and frequently contested concept. One of the most interesting developments of the idea, in this case from a mathematical model, is found in V. A. Graicunas, "Relationship in Organization," in Luther Gulick and L. Urwick, eds., *Papers on the Science of Administration* (New York: Columbia University Institute for Public Administration, 1937). The classic attack on the span of control idea is Simon, *Administrative Behavior*, 2nd ed. (1965), pp. 20-44.

[61] U. Alexis Johnson, "Opportunity and Challenge," *Department of State News Letter*, No. 61 (May 1966), 6. Reprinted from *Foreign Service Journal* 43 (April 1966). There is of course the obvious question about whether it is possible to have several alter egos to a single assistant secretary. If he intended one alter ego deputy assistant secretary in each bureau, then another question is why additional ones were appointed. See Chapter IV for a fuller discussion of this problem.

CHART II-3

Bureau of Near Eastern and South Asian Affairs
Department of State
BEFORE 1966

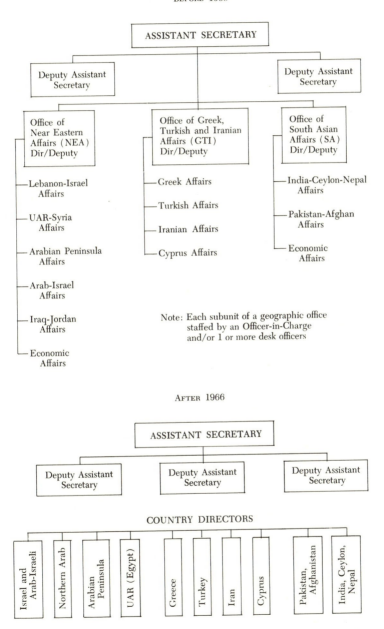

ASSISTANT SECRETARY

Deputy Assistant
Secretary

Deputy Assistant
Secretary

Office of
Near Eastern
Affairs (NEA)
Dir/Deputy

Office of Greek,
Turkish and Iranian
Affairs (GTI)
Dir/Deputy

Office of
South Asian
Affairs (SA)
Dir/Deputy

— Lebanon-Israel
Affairs

— UAR-Syria
Affairs

— Arabian Peninsula
Affairs

— Arab-Israel
Affairs

— Iraq-Jordan
Affairs

— Economic
Affairs

— Greek Affairs

— Turkish Affairs

— Iranian Affairs

— Cyprus Affairs

— India-Ceylon-Nepal
Affairs

— Pakistan-Afghan
Affairs

— Economic
Affairs

Note: Each subunit of a geographic office
staffed by an Officer-in-Charge
and/or 1 or more desk officers

AFTER 1966

ASSISTANT SECRETARY

Deputy Assistant
Secretary

Deputy Assistant
Secretary

Deputy Assistant
Secretary

COUNTRY DIRECTORS

Israel and
Arab-Israeli

Northern Arab

Arabian
Peninsula

UAR (Egypt)

Greece

Turkey

Iran

Cyprus

Pakistan,
Afghanistan

India, Ceylon,
Nepal

Note: Each Country Directorate staffed by
two or more Country Officers in
addition to Country Director

or FSO-4).[62] The country directors, with broader substantive but not geographic responsibilities, were for the most part FSO-1s, occasionally FSO-2s, or rarely, Career Ministers. Those filling the previous office director positions were of these same ranks, and in some cases moved directly from OD to CD jobs.

A fourth and related feature was a probable decline in the status of the desk officer. This position, now called country officer, was still filled by FSO-3s and FSO-4s, but they now reported to country directors rather than to office directors. Under the new arrangement, a country officer might find himself less able to play an independent role, since he might report to a CD with the same geographic responsibilities as his own, rather than to an OD with wider geographic responsibilities who was perhaps more inclined to rely upon the desk officer to conduct day-to-day relations with countries for which he held broader responsibility. This effect was not universal, however, since some desk officers had previously reported to O-in-Cs or ODs with the same area.

Finally, the country director was assigned additional formal responsibilities not held by the office director, even if his geographic span was narrower. He was given explicit instructions to coordinate all activities relating to assigned countries, a duty which was at best implicit for the OD. He was charged with supporting the NSAM 341 system, which did not exist in the time of the OD. In this context, he was to provide *staff* support for the IRG, stemming from his *line* duties in State and his coordination responsibilities.

As noted above, the mechanics of establishing the country directorates and filling the new jobs had to be carried out

[62] The Foreign Service operates on a "rank in the man" basis, like the military, but unlike the civil service, in which the rating is applied to a particular position. Foreign Service ranks range from class eight, the most junior, to class one, with two additional ranks of Career Minister and Career Ambassador available to a very few. A rule of thumb is that an FSO who reaches class one has had a successful career.

after the change was announced. General Taylor and his group held the SIG/IRG change closely in order to avoid mobilization of opposition; but for this they paid a price: There was little understanding of it when it was announced, and no commitment to it outside of the small group that designed it. Parenthetically, one informed interview source believed that the NSAM 341 change was so tied to Taylor's personal experience that even Rusk and the president did not completely understand what was implied. (STATE #5) General Taylor agreed that this was true for some participants, but believes the president did understand what he had in mind. Even so, he concluded, President Johnson did not rely on the new system because his personal style was to pick individuals for specific tasks, rather than to assign projects to organizations.[63] Since neither the NSAM 341 structure nor the ancillary CD system was operable when they were announced, there was an initial loss of momentum that diminished their impact at all levels. More importantly, it guaranteed that the nature, extent, and importance of the changes announced would in practice be determined after the system was formally adopted, by political interplay and bargaining subject to all the uncertainties and constraints on rationality that are a part of the larger policy process.

The Country Directors: A Brief Introduction

Before turning our attention to the place the country director came to occupy in the foreign affairs community, it is useful to consider the individuals who were assigned as CDs, since performance of any formal position is an amalgam of an individual's characteristics and the role he occupies. As already mentioned, the "average" CD was a career Foreign Service officer of class one or two, with previous background and experience in government covering a period of approximately two decades. He was at least a col-

[63] General Taylor, interview, August 13, 1969.

lege graduate, with over half of the forty-six CDs interviewed holding a master's degree, and six having Ph.D.'s.
Like other members of the Foreign Service, his education
was more likely than not obtained at an Eastern private
school, often Ivy League, and his major field was most likely
to have been one of the social sciences, particularly international relations, history, or political science. He usually
had a career specialty in the political field, rather than in
administrative, economic, or politico-military areas. Although his previous experience had been gained in a variety
of positions both in the field and in Washington, he was
likely to have spent a greater portion of his time abroad.
Almost certainly he had recent field experience in the area
of his responsibility, although not necessarily in one of the
countries assigned to him. His career prospects after being
a CD depended on his age. If he was in his mid- or late for-
ties, or even in some cases early fifties, he was generally in
the pool from which future higher officials of the department and ambassadors would be chosen; if he were older,
the CD was possibly the last or next-to-last position before
retirement. This was much less likely. Only ten of the 153
officers who had held a CD job as of September 1973 retired
directly upon the completion of their tour of duty, while by
that time twenty-two had already held ambassadorial posts,
including six who had held two, twelve others had been
assigned as principal officers at posts where there was no
ambassador, and almost all the rest had gone on to more
responsible positions, including forty assigned to the second-ranking position in an embassy, deputy chief of mission
(DCM), twenty-four directly after their CD tours. Still
others were assigned to positions of comparable importance
within State, including three as assistant secretaries and ten
as deputy assistant secretaries.[64]

[64] The figures in this section were compiled from a variety of State
Department sources, primarily the assignments section of the *Department of State News Letter*, the *Foreign Service List*, and the short

In short, care was given to the selection of CDs, and those chosen in most cases had been identified as superior officers. If they performed well, they were likely to advance to even greater responsibilities. Whatever the difficulties to be encountered in establishing the CD system, the individuals selected to fill the jobs were among the best in Foreign Service, at least by traditional standards.[65]

---

biographies of FSOs published annually in *The Biographic Register.* For more details see Appendix A.

[65] Whether these standards were appropriate for the tasks at hand are discussed at length in Chapter VI.

Chapter Three

The Emerging Role
of the Country Director

[Role] provides a comprehensive pattern *for behavior and attitudes; it constitutes a* strategy *for coping with a recurrent situation; it is* socially identified, *more or less clearly, as an entity; it is subject to being played recognizably by* different individuals; *and it supplies a major basis for* identifying *and* placing *persons in society.* RALPH H. TURNER

IT HAS long been realized that organizational life cannot be adequately described by examining only formal structures and procedures. As a result, concepts such as Barnard's "informal organization,"[1] distinctions between "rational" and "natural system" models of organizational activity,[2] and the notion of the "living system" of an organization[3] have been introduced in an attempt to capture reality. A divergence between what is intended and what actually happens is always present, so one should not expect official commentary about the country director system to do more than sketch some possibilities about how it might function in practice. The true place of country directors in the foreign affairs community can more nearly be understood by turning our attention to the role the individuals filling these positions played, and to how it developed

[1] Chester Barnard, *The Functions of the Executive,* 2nd ed. (Cambridge: Harvard University Press, 1962), pp. 114-123.

[2] This distinction is developed at length in Alvin W. Gouldner, "Organizational Analysis," in Robert K. Merton, ed., *Sociology Today* (New York: Basic Books, 1959).

[3] Argyris, *Some Causes,* p. 2. He defines the living system of an organization as "the way people actually behave, the way they actually think and feel, and the way they actually deal with each other. It includes both the formal and the informal activities. The living system represents how things are, not merely how they are supposed to be."

as it did. This allows one to link the individual and the organization of which he is a part, taking cognizance of both formal and informal determinants of behavior.[4]

AN OVERVIEW OF ROLE ANALYSIS

Before turning to the specifics of the country director role, a brief summation of some of the major elements of role analysis may be helpful. Role can be defined as "the behavior expected of the occupant of a given position or status."[5] Most formulations contain components of *role expectation* (beliefs and cognitions) about expected behavior, and of *role enactment* or *performance*, or actual conduct.[6] A role is associated with a social position, but, in order to avoid an undue emphasis on formal aspects, should not be seen as being synonymous with it.

Role expectations can be differentiated either by content or by who holds them. The term generally has been used to indicate standards or norms held for behavior of a role incumbent, but it also needs a nonnormative component, to indicate behavior thought likely, whether or not approved by the evaluator.[7] An expectation in the first sense can be defined as "an evaluation standard applied to an incumbent of a position," while a probability statement with respect to actual behavior can be called *role anticipation*.[8] Role expec-

[4] Most systems-oriented social scientists consider role to be the basic element of systems analysis. See Talcott Parsons, *The Social System*, 2nd ed. (New York: Free Press, 1964), pp. 58ff.

[5] Theodore R. Sarbin, "Role: Psychological Aspects," *International Encyclopedia of the Social Sciences* (New York: Macmillan and Free Press, 1968), XIII, 554.

[6] Ibid. Enactment can be equated with role performance as used by some other writers. Cf. Bruce J. Biddle and Edwin J. Thomas, "The Nature and History of Role Theory," in Biddle and Thomas, eds., *Role Theory: Concepts and Research* (New York: John Wiley & Sons, 1966), p. 10.

[7] Biddle and Thomas, pp. 10-11 (Table 3).

[8] This distinction is explicitly used by Neal Gross, Ward S. Mason, and Alexander W. McEachern in their classic role study, *Explorations*

tations can be held by both role incumbents and by others with whom they interact, so it is convenient to call standards and norms held by the former *role orientations*, reserving the term role expectations for standards and norms held by others.[9] If expectations are not met, the result may be application of *sanctions* by one actor which reward or punish another, in the context of conformity by the latter to norms or rules.[10]

Since role is a relational term, in that "persons cannot be located without describing their relationships to other individuals,"[11] some basic relational concepts should also be kept in mind. *Status* is used either as position (a person's "identity" in a social situation)[12] or as power and prestige associated with a position. While the term has been used in about equal measure each way,[13] the connotation of prestige is used here, reserving "position" to indicate locational aspects.

Role conformity is also an important concept, since it measures correspondence between actual behavior and prescriptions for that behavior. It thus links expectations and actions. *Consensus* and *role conflict*, on the other hand, do not bridge belief or cognition and conduct, but instead refer to consistency or the lack of it within one of these areas. Consensus denotes either sameness or similarity of norms and conceptions held by two or more actors; or when applied to actions, sameness of behavior in general. Role conflict is generally limited to the area of belief and cognition

---

in Role Analysis: Studies of the School Superintendency Role (New York: John Wiley & Sons, 1958), pp. 58-59.

[9] This fairly common distinction has been employed recently in Raymond F. Hopkins, "Political Roles in a New State: A Study of Politics in Tanzania" (diss. Yale 1968), p. 75.

[10] Biddle and Thomas, loc. cit.   [11] Gross, et al., loc. cit.

[12] Kingsley Davis, *Human Society* (New York: Macmillan, 1949), chapter 4. Reference taken from an extract appearing in Biddle and Thomas, p. 67.

[13] Gross, et al., loc. cit.

with few if any behavioral components. It is variously used to mean inconsistent prescriptions for a given position (whether internalized by a particular actor or between multiple actors); the attribution of such conflicting prescriptions about one's own role to others; or feelings of unease resulting from the existence or assumption of such inconsistent prescriptions or standards.[14] The more role conflict exists between a role incumbent and another person, the more likely available sanctions will be applied to each other, and the less likely one's role will be considered legitimate by the other.[15] The converse also holds: The more legitimate a role, the less likely it is that conflict will arise from behavior or performance which is consistent with that role. Once roles stabilize, there is a tendency for legitimate expectations to be assigned to them,[16] and hence for reduction of role conflict. Evaluation also plays a part in reducing conflict by increasing legitimacy: "To the extent to which alter's role is positively valued with respect to rank and favorableness, ego will translate his anticipations regarding alter's role into legitimate expectations."[17] Finally, ambiguity of role may have diverse effects. It may lead to conflict if behavior is not considered legitimate, or it may allow more freedom of action with respect to another:

In ambiguous or partially structured situations the actor may influence the role of the other by casting himself in

[14] Definitions in this paragraph follow Biddle and Thomas, p. 12.

[15] See Ralph H. Turner, "Role: Sociological Aspects," *International Encyclopedia of the Social Sciences* (New York: Macmillan and Free Press, 1968), XIII, 554, for a short consideration of role legitimation. Because a role is in part informal, legitimate here does not mean lawful, but rather in accordance with established norms and patterns. Turner notes that "there is a tendency for stabilized roles to be assigned the character of legitimate expectations, implying that deviation from expectation is a breach of rules or violation of trust." Ibid.

[16] Ibid.

[17] Ibid. Ego is sometimes used to describe a role incumbent, while alter refers to others with whom ego interacts.

one rather than another permitted role. His behavior
. . . serves as a potential constraint on the role enactment
of the other, who must also locate himself in the social
structure.[18]

All of these facets of role conflict are observable when ana-
lyzing the role of the country director.

When our attention turns to the country director, we are
confronted with the need not only to describe his role, but
also to examine how that role came into existence. When a
new position is created, the role associated with it develops
only after a period of continuing interactions between initial role incumbents and other actors. Certain role elements
may quickly stabilize, while others fluctuate for a considerable period. The point of departure for this process of role
development is of course what has gone before, particularly
when, as with the country directors, holders of new positions assume some of the functions performed by others in
old positions that have been abolished. Starting from these
residual elements, the new role is compounded from two
other basic groups of factors: the formal prescriptions and
instructions about the new positions, and the informal
norms and expectations that develop in response to the creation of the positions and the actions of those who fill them.
In the following sections, these three sets of factors are examined individually, while in the next chapter the major interaction patterns in which the CDs participated are
discussed.

RESIDUAL ROLE COMPONENTS

Some elements of the CD role after 1966 were continuations
of what officers in the geographic bureaus had been doing
since at least World War II. These activities, carried out by
office directors, officers-in-charge, and desk officers, formed
the base line against which the developing CD role could
be measured.

[18] Sarbin, p. 548.

At the heart of these continuing duties was a multifaceted interaction between an American embassy in the field and the geographic officer for that country in one of the regional bureaus. The latter was the first point of contact for the embassy on a whole range of matters, from requests for policy guidance to pleas for administrative support. Through close and continuing contact with the post, he was in the best position of anyone in Washington to give a clear picture of the embassy's problems, its staff's view of the situation in the country, and their recommendations on policy and programs. But he was more than a reporter mirroring embassy opinions. He also served as an expediter, attempting to meet embassy requests and needs, which might require considerable persuasion and coordination, both within State and elsewhere in government. It was his responsibility to support the posts in their requests when possible and to make clear to them why some could not be met.

The geographic officer's relationship with the field post was complex because he was as much the secretary of state's subordinate as the ambassador's "man in Washington." He had responsibility for insuring that instructions to the post covering all important matters were prepared, and that the post received them in time and in such a way that they could be carried out. Thus, what he sympathized with as the ambassador's representative he might have to challenge or to deny as a subordinate of the secretary of state.

One of the most important functions of the geographic officer was to act as a repository of expertise, providing current and accurate information to policy planners, other agencies, and the senior officials of State. As long as State had no effective information management and retrieval system, this was indispensable.[19] When this expertise was well

[19] This problem is generally recognized, and was frequently cited as a major difficulty by CDs interviewed. In the late sixties, State began to develop a computerized information retrieval system, but success did not come easily, owing to the inherent difficulties of the project, and in the beginning, severe limitations on funding. The system was undergoing a trial run on a limited basis in late 1972.

developed, the geographic officer had a substantial impact on policy. In most cases, he recommended steps for the approval of policy makers at higher levels, and in that way determined in part the range of possible decisions. His knowledge was also drawn upon to brief new personnel going to his countries,[20] to prepare high-ranking personnel for official visits abroad, and to provide answers to congressional inquiries.

Another major part of the geographic officer's job has always been to maintain contact with the local embassy of his country, both diplomatically and as a source of assistance. Similarly, the geographic officer would generally take charge of making arrangements for the visits of dignitaries and delegations from his countries to the United States.

All these duties were carried out primarily in response to current developments, and the heavy load of such activity was responsible for the "fires in the in-basket" syndrome which has been frequently commented upon.[21] The geographic officer also had some duties that were carried out on a more regularized basis. He participated in staff meetings at the bureau and subbureau level at which longer range trends and problems were considered. He evaluated a flood of reports, telegrams, and letters from the post; intelligence summaries; and a variety of other information, from which he distilled a picture of relations with his country. He based much of his reaction to specific problems on this image. He requested information from the post on items he felt had received insufficient coverage, periodically

[20] "His country" is used as a shorthand phrase to replace "his country of responsibility" here and throughout. Possession or patronization is not intended.

[21] John Leacacos uses this phrase in the title of his book, cited previously. Another source of detail on the routine of the desk officer is David K. Willis, *The State Department* (Boston: Christian Science Monitor, 1968). This work is a collection of eleven *Monitor* articles on State written by Willis in 1966 and 1967. Chapter 4 gives a detailed summary of the routine of a desk officer for Ecuador during a week filled with considerable activity.

reviewed the caliber and scope of reporting, and suggested changes to improve it. He was involved in whatever continuing country planning efforts were being carried out, generally in a clearing rather than a drafting capacity. He also monitored programs of other agencies in his country, and coordinated them as necessary, although this was done unevenly.

All these elements have traditionally been part of the geographic officer's job; the emphasis given to each was dependent on the country he dealt with, his own rank and experience, and his relationships with other officials. Similarly, they describe in broad terms the official prescription of the roles of the country director and his subordinates, the country officers. The CD role was intended to differ primarily in the emphasis and attention given to certain role segments, particularly leadership, breadth of substantive concern, and personal status. This overlap between old and new and the somewhat intangible nature of the changes desired made it possible for skeptics to downplay the new system.

A natural concomitant of the CD's assumption of these continuing responsibilities was the survival of earlier role orientations and expectations. But the intent of the CD change was to alter precisely these residual elements. In the absence of explicit modifications in formal prescriptions and strongly supported expectations of changed role performance by superiors, there was a danger that the old would overwhelm the new. As one would expect, old patterns were given predominance by those who did not want a stronger role for the geographic officer in State, while those who might benefit tended to emphasize the changes.

A brief exploration into what might be called the "politics of role definition" serves to indicate the effect of residual expectations. An official of the Treasury Department who dealt routinely with a State official responsible for a given area, for example, would have certain expectations that would carry over to interactions with any working-level State officer, even if that officer now was a country director rather than an office director or officer-in-charge. This presaged considerable role conflict, if current expectations of State's hierarchy and CDs themselves differed considerably from previous ones. As noted earlier, when role enactment or role behavior stabilizes, there is a tendency for actions that fit the established patterns to be anticipated and to be legitimized. Some of these residual expectations come from the preferred styles of the individuals involved, while others are a manifestation of certain problems that continually arise. For example, State officers generally expect to have more difficulty gaining agreement with domestic agencies than with other foreign affairs agencies.[22] Just as State officials were likely to feel that Treasury in its concern for balance of payments difficulties ignored foreign relations repercussions that might follow cuts in programs abroad, or that Agriculture saw Public Law 480, the "food for peace" program, primarily as a surplus disposal device rather than as a form of foreign assistance, so their opposite numbers in Treasury and Agriculture felt that State was insufficiently cognizant of domestic needs, requirements, and agency clienteles.[23] Opposite numbers in domestic agencies were therefore skeptical about the sudden emergence of a "presidential viewpoint" by FSOs simply upon being appointed country directors, and CDs were not convinced that such a viewpoint would be accepted if exhibited.

Also of considerable importance for initial expectations was the existence of the so-called policy-operations dichotomy. Beginning about the time of the creation of a separate

[22] See Chapter IV. For example, of the 46 CDs interviewed for this study, 16 listed Agriculture and 18 Treasury as the most difficult agencies to work with (multiple answers possible). Defense was listed by 16, with no other agency being mentioned in this context by more than 4 CDs.

[23] This generalization based on the whole body of interviews with CDs and their opposite numbers in Agriculture and Treasury.

intelligence service (the CIA) by the National Security Act of 1947, and given real emphasis during the Dulles period, there was a trend toward placing operational programs in other agencies, with State limiting itself primarily to providing policy guidance. In 1953 information and assistance programs were removed from State and placed in new agencies, USIA and the Foreign Operations Administration (FOA). In 1954 the Foreign Agricultural Service (FAS) was created to take over agricultural functions abroad. In part this was because State was under attack; but it pleased the White House, Secretary Dulles, and most FSOs. The latter liked this emphasis, as Harr has written, because a State Department concerned only with policy matters meshed compatibly with the traditional diplomatic role most of them preferred.[24] Coordination was of course required under this "policy only" doctrine, but it was not always carried out with verve or dispatch. In any event, the dichotomy between policy and operations was generally recognized.

The Kennedy administration attempted to end this separation,[25] but given the independence of the various departments, State was unable to regain effective policy control. This was a primary reason for creating the NSAM 341 system. Given this past history, the potential for role conflict between CDs and their opposite numbers was obvious. If a CD actively concerned himself with major operating programs of other agencies, he was likely to evoke hostility

[24] Harr, *Professional Diplomat*, pp. 23-26. Between 1930 and 1939 there had been a previous Foreign Agricultural Service as well as a Foreign Commercial Service, but in the latter year they were both incorporated into the general Foreign Service. In 1954 re-creation of the Foreign Agricultural Service was clearly a step away from the idea of State managing all of the country's foreign relations. See Lincoln Gordon, "The Growth of American Representation Overseas," in Vincent M. Barnett, Jr., ed., *The Representation of the United States Abroad*, The American Assembly (New York: Praeger, 1965), pp. 18-28, for more details.

[25] See Chapter I, n. 7.

from those accustomed to conducting their activities with minimal State Department participation and interference; if the CD did not take an interest in those activities, he was not meeting the formal requirements placed upon him. These cross-pressures and ambiguities, due in part to inconsistent responsibilities and in part to political factors, were a continuous fact of life for the country director.

FORMAL PRESCRIPTIONS AND INSTRUCTIONS

Against the background of these deeply entrenched residual role expectations, the formal instructions and responsibilities given the country directors assumed considerable importance. Strong and continuing advocacy of the CD idea would be a minimum prerequisite for success in improving country-level management and leadership. Certain parts of these statements and documents have been previously introduced, but additional details must be presented before it is possible to evaluate what was really intended.

Formal announcement of the CD system was made in two documents issued on March 4, 1966, referred to previously: State Department circular FAMC 385 and an accompanying message to the Department and the Foreign Service from Secretary Rusk. FAMC 385 stated the CD would:

a. provide continuing departmental and interdepartmental leadership in planning, coordination, and implementation of decisions;

b. raise specific matters for consideration by the IRG, and bring detailed knowledge to the IRG discussions when so requested;

c. serve as the base for crisis task force operations as necessary.[26]

It also charged CDs with organizing and developing "such contacts, channels, and mechanisms as are appropriate to

[26] FAMC 385, paragraph 7.

86

and necessary for full interdepartmental leadership on country matters, and for full support to the Assistant Secretary"; stated that one or more deputy assistant secretaries would provide guidance and direction to the CDs in each bureau under the direction of the assistant secretary; and provided for abolishment of office director and officer-in-charge positions as the CD positions were created.[27]

Although the country director's stated responsibilities seemed to require a strong emphasis on leadership and coordination both within State and government-wide, there were several obvious problems. First, as long as the department did not have firm hierarchical control over the activities of other governmental units, could such leadership ever be more than a fiction, given its lack of a natural constituency and the lingering suspicion with which it was viewed by Congress and other agencies? Second, as long as the budgetary process was based on individual agency expenditures rather than on functional/geographic programs, could all United States activities involving a given foreign country be treated in a truly integrated way? Finally, in the absence of a government-wide program budgeting system to generate comprehensive country programs, was it possible for the country director to obtain enough information about other agency activities to effectively control them? More generally, to what extent was it possible to delegate interagency authority below the political level, that is, below the assistant secretaries? None of these questions has been resolved as this passage is written, more than seven years after the CD system was born.

More specific questions arose from the instructions themselves. No mention was made of the devices or methods the CD should use in his planning, coordinating, or implementing functions; he was merely charged with doing what was necessary to obtain "full leadership on country matters." Leadership itself was left undefined. Was it to be similar to

[27] Ibid.

that exercised by the under secretary and the assistant secretaries as executive chairmen of the SIG and the IRGs— that is, including the authority to make a firm decision after taking the several agency positions into account—or was it to be more of a secretariat and monitoring function? Additionally, the relationship between the "one or more Deputy Assistant Secretaries" and the country director was unspecified, leaving for future resolution whether these officials were to be "second bosses" between the CDs and the Assistant Secretaries.[28]

Several efforts were made to clarify both the NSAM 341 system and the closely associated country director function. U. Alexis Johnson attempted to provide more information in an article in the April 1966 *Foreign Service Journal*:

> The term "Director" in the new position of "Country Director" has been used to impart the sense that these officers will be expected to be truly "Directors" of all U.S. Government activities involving the country for which they are responsible. . . . The concept is that these positions will be occupied by senior officers, to the maximum extent possible qualified to be, or having been DCM's or Ambassadors abroad. . . . It is expected that, depending on the country and the range of its problems, they will, with appropriate representatives from other departments and agencies, constitute, under the Assistant Secretary and the Interdepartmental Regional Group, "country teams" at the Washington level. They will report directly to the Assistant Secretary, thus cutting out the "Office" level now interposed between the "country desk" and the Assistant Secretary.[29]

---

[28] The term "second bosses" was used in the Report of Task Force VIII, "The Role of the Country Director," in *Diplomacy for the 70's,* p. 344. Cited hereafter as TF VIII. This report is discussed in some detail in Chapter VIII.

[29] Johnson, loc. cit. DCM is the abbreviation for deputy chief of mission, the second ranking official in an American embassy.

He also wrote that deputy assistant secretaries were not to constitute a layer between the country directors and assistant secretary, serving instead as alter egos to the latter.[30]

As the first country directors began to be appointed and to take up their duties in the late spring and early summer of 1966, however, confusion persisted. One recalled his impressions:

> I'm not at all sure that the communication . . . wasn't obliterated, obscured by a certain amount of static. I discussed this question of what the secretary really was aiming at with some of the people who were designing the country director concept, who were getting the department ready for this changeover, and I said, "It's not at all clear to me how it is reflecting a desire of the secretary. Maybe it would be a good idea to have the secretary explain this to the country directors." (CD #12)

Such a meeting was eventually held in August 1966; Secretary Rusk recalls it as being "an informal discussion, a get-acquainted session" during which he emphasized several points. The CDs should accept a full share of initiative, he said, without waiting for higher officials to tell them what they should be doing—*they* should be initiating and telling the sixth and seventh floors what they should be concerned with. Also, he was trying to get the CDs to accept complete responsibility not just for State but for all agencies.[31]

This meeting emphasized the secretary's interest without clarifying specifics, and perhaps raised expectations too high. One CD, writing of the meeting later, remembered that

> one precocious seeker after identity asked: "Just what are we?" The hearts of forty-odd fledgling Country Directors

[30] Ibid.
[31] Dean Rusk, interview August 14, 1969.

throbbed when Mr. Rusk replied: "For your country or countries, you are me!"[32]

Even with this encouragement, for many the situation remained vague: "Now, I think if you will check back on the reactions to that meeting, we didn't get a clear signal from the secretary as to how the new system was to be different from the old." (CD #12)

One other attempt was made, doubtless indicating the seventh floor had become aware that ambiguities persisted. On August 4, 1966, just prior to Rusk's meeting with the country directors, Deputy Under Secretary Crockett began a letter to them by saying, "I have been asked by many officers to make clearer what the Country Director is, what is expected of him, and how he should operate."[33] Much of this letter was couched in the same generalities as the statements which had preceded it, but at last there were more specific instructions:

The Country Director sees that the Ambassador's needs are served within the Department and government-wide. He assures that the mission is fully supported in the full range of its requirements: policy, programs, resources, operations, and administration.

For example, the Country Director must

—provide policy guidance on which operating agencies will base their programs

—insure that recommended programs of the various agencies are consistent with and support U.S. policy objectives and provide the most effective *total* use of proposed U.S. resources

—develop devices for ensuring interdepartmental imple-

[32] James W. Spain, "The Country Director: A Subjective Appraisal," *Foreign Service Journal*, 46 (March 1969), 35.

[33] William J. Crockett letter to country directors, August 4, 1966, reprinted in *Department of State News Letter*, No. 67 (November 1966), 13, 69. The longer quoted passage following is from the same source.

mentation of decisions requiring interdepartmental action

—maintain continuing purposeful contacts with other agencies' representatives, and establish channels for prompt interchange of information on policies, country developments, potential crisis situations and similar matters

—marshall his departmental team to meet IRG and SIG requests, and bring his detailed knowledge to IRG discussions when his country is concerned

—maintain constant readiness on an interdepartmental basis to anticipate and meet crises, and serve as the base for crisis task force operations when necessary.

Even with this letter, it remained for experience to establish what kinds of role performance would be considered legitimate. Whether the letter, Rusk's comments at the August meeting, or Alex Johnson's article were to be taken seriously would depend upon the form of day-to-day interactions as the system became operational. The true test would be whether the secretary and assistant secretaries handled issues differently after the reform, giving clear indications that they expected the CDs to have the strong role in country policy making that the formal statements and explanations seemed to imply.

INFORMAL ROLE ELEMENTS

As the system began to function, the norms and orientations of CDs themselves and the expectations of others began to emerge. Together, they form the other group of basic factors shaping the country director role. These can be grouped according to the types of activity seen as desirable (planning or operations, initiation or reaction), the substantive breadth of their concerns, the degree and type of leadership CDs exhibited, and the status they came to have in the foreign affairs community.

Activity Dimension 1: Planner or Operator?

If the country director was to have a broad coordinating function, it was inevitable that he engage in more planning than had office directors and officers-in-charge, for without it he would be unable to bring coherence to the activities of the many agencies.

A first question is definitional: the difference, if any, between planning and operations. For most CDs, operations had a day-to-day connotation of taking action on incoming cables, problem solving, and responding to specific requests. Planning involved thinking ahead, formally or informally, explicitly or implicitly. One European CD said that

> planning and policy have to do with the approach you take, and then devising concrete means for implementation; while the operational has a natural look about it: science exchanges, visas, exchange agreements, seizure at sea, bilateral talks on all sorts of things. (CD #13— paraphrase)

However, one-third of the CDs queried (fourteen of forty-two) did not believe it possible in practice to separate the two. For most, nevertheless, there was at least an analytic distinction, and one that divided planning into the operational sort done by CDs, and grander scale advanced thinking, carried out by planning units and higher officials. One CD distinguished the elements this way:

> There is an overall, almost esoteric policy that the U.S. government follows, which is very useful in pointing our heads in the right direction over a long period of time. Then there are your day-to-day operations. In between, there is planning for the use of our resources (AID programs and others), where it's hard to make any really advanced planning for any length of time, and that is where I would say that the people who are not in operations can't do a very effective job. (CD #14)

92

The last part of this statement touches upon the unresolved problem of how to plan effectively for the conduct of foreign policy. Within State, this has usually been considered in the context of whether or not planning should be the responsibility of a separate element in the department. At the time he resigned as the Policy Planning Council's first director, George Kennan observed that

> . . . my Planning Staff, started nearly three years ago, has simply been a failure, like all previous attempts to bring order and foresight into the designing of foreign policy by special institutional arrangements within the Department. Aside from personal shortcomings, the reason for this seems to lie largely in the impossibility of having the planning function performed outside of the line of command. The formulation of policy is the guts of the work of the department, and none of it can successfully be placed outside the hierarchy which governs operations.[34]

Twenty years later, another member of the Council, Zbigniew Brzezinski, arrived at the same conclusion:

> In practice . . . there develops an inescapable gap between the planners and the operators. The planner must "avoid trivia" in Secretary Marshall's famous injunction: the operator cannot help but find the planner's preoccupation with grand designs rather irrelevant.[35]

Country directors generally subscribed to this viewpoint, but were ambivalent about the ability of the operators to take up the planning function. Only two saw their jobs as primarily consisting of planning. The others considered it either to be mostly operations with some planning (35), or almost entirely operations (5). One of two who said his job

[34] Kennan, *Memoirs: 1925-1950*, p. 467. The passage is part of a diary entry written on November 19, 1949. The name of the Planning Staff was changed to Policy Planning Council at a later date.

[35] Zbigniew Brzezinski, "Purpose and Planning in Foreign Policy," *Public Interest*, No. 14 (Winter 1969), 61.

was primarily planning did not accept this distinction between planning and operating. To him, operations meant
large-scale activities such as military and economic assistance programs rather than the routine activity of the geographic desks of State. The other, assigned a country with
which the United States did not have relations, noted that
his major responsibility was to look toward future changes
in policy.

In short, most CDs saw themselves as operators who did,
to quote one, "a dash of forward planning." This emphasis
arose from lack of time and resources or from a general
skepticism about the worth of planning. An example of the
first view was given by a CD who tried to do major planning on the future of arms levels in his area, was unable to
staff it out, and finally concluded a CD had no hope of being able to complete a major new policy paper entirely in
his own office. It was thus necessary to work with formal
planners in the Bureau of Intelligence and Research and in
the Policy Planning Council. To make this useful, there had
to be a formal interchange: "Neither in the bureau nor in
the Policy Planning Council can you have planning types
wandering around and giving ideas." (CD #15)

The position of those skeptical of planning generally was
typified by an African CD:

> This government operates, rather than plans. I'm a victim
> of that system, I guess. I find most planning is interesting,
> but is not implemented. So there are some areas that
> spend full time in planning, but in my view have little
> effect on foreign policy. (CD #16)

A related argument was that formal planning was superflu-
ous, since the operator always had "to consider the long-
term effect of any recommended solution." (CD #17)

The tendency of CDs to rely on their own analysis rather
than formal plans was buttressed by the necessity for
agreed papers. One CD said that one of the great services
of the Policy Planning Council was to do most of the work

on National Policy Papers,[36] since the CD did not have time to do it. However,

> the great disadvantage there is that the NPP is an agreed document, a negotiated document with every agency of the government that has anything to do with that country signing off on it, and it therefore is a mass of waffles. . . . What really is an effective guide is the personal political philosophy of the man dealing with the problem—one that maybe he never puts down on paper. (CD #7)

Planning undertaken by CDs was generally operational in nature, the middle level in the three-stage classification suggested by the CD quoted earlier in this section. Included here were contingency plans dealing with possible eventualities (*coup d'état*, death of a major leader, election outcome), and what the U.S. should do about them; resource planning, generally for a period of one to three years; and AID annual program reviews in the Latin American bureau where the CDs held joint State/AID responsibilities. Some CDs did put themselves through a self-conscious review at periodic intervals:

> Consciously, three or four times a year I sit down and look through the whole bit myself. That is, I am the focal point, talking to the desk officers, my deputy, other people in the bureau, other people outside the bureau in other agencies, and even people in the academic community, the foundations and that sort of thing. I go through about fifty people every time. Then I sit down, and I may write a paper for myself, I may write a paper to send upstairs, or I may not. It's a review of where we are—what's the six-month and twelve-month future? What should we be doing that we're not doing, what

[36] The national policy papers were written, under the aegis of Walt W. Rostow, during the Kennedy and Johnson administrations. In some sense they are equivalent to some of the national security study memoranda (NSSMs) of the Nixon administration.

should we be changing that we're not changing, what should be deemphasized and so on. My planning can't very well extend beyond six or twelve months. (CD #18)

The summary of responses about planning and operations in Table III-1 clearly shows that the CD was primarily an operator. Formal planning was not highly valued, and little time was devoted to it. In this respect, the CD role had not changed appreciably. In general he was as much an operator as his predecessors had been, and planning did not serve as an element of control over the activities of others with respect to his countries. The difficulties of the CD in this area, as well as the planners quoted earlier provide support for the generalization that a natural incompatibility exists between operations and planning, and that those whose roles theoretically contain both functions are forced to emphasize one at the expense of the other. To the extent this is true, the original expectations of what the CDs might be able to accomplish was unrealistic.

TABLE III-1
PLANNING AND OPERATIONS

Planning and Operations Separable?	Primary Job Component							
	Mostly Planning		Operations Some Planning		Almost All Operations		Not Asked		Total	
	N	%	N	%	N	%	N	%	N	%
Yes	2	100.0	21	60.0	5	100.0	–	–	28	60.9
No	–	–	14	40.0	–	–	–	–	14	30.4
Not Asked	–	–	–	–	–	–	4	100.0	4	8.7
Total	2	4.3	35	76.1	5	10.9	4	8.7	46	100.0

Note: Table cell percentages based on column sums. Marginal percentages based on proportion of total N in each category.

Activity Dimension II: Initiator or Reactor?

A related question was whether the CD acted primarily in response to current developments, as opposed to initiating new activities himself. Both patterns are subtypes of the operations-oriented role described above, but the CD as initiator would have to be more concerned with planning, acting on the basis of some view of the situation at hand and what he hoped to accomplish.

Considerable unanimity emerged when thirty-eight CDs were asked about this part of their role. All but a few said that as operating officers with direct contacts with field posts and foreign embassies in Washington, much of their work was necessarily reactive. Estimates ranged from 75 to 90 percent. In one sense, of course, foreign relations is almost all reaction, as one CD argued:

> I would say . . . everybody, including the people in the field and in the other agencies . . . are reactive, in the sense that decisions are made in the context of a continuity of events in foreign countries, or in the context of our relations with those countries, and a decision is made because something has happened, or in anticipation of something happening at this level. (CD #19)

In the eyes of many CDs, however, reacting did not have to be equated with operating, since an operating official could take either a passive or an active approach to his job. Typically, one argued that

> . . . over the years, most of the policies as they ultimately emerged, most of the really important decisions, really had their genesis . . . with the professional people in the office. (CD #20)

CDs did not see any obstacles except work load to taking the initiative. As one said, "If I decided that it would be a good idea to attempt to persuade [European neutral nation] to join NATO, I could ride that horse as far as it would carry me." (CD #21) However, one impediment was always present. Time and time again, CDs emphasized that their independence and influence depended on the trust and respect of their superiors. If so, a CD who constantly advanced radical proposals that did not fit the analyses made by others would find his position eroded, since superiors would monitor his activities more closely out of fear he might commit them to an ill-founded course of action. But as long as the CD and his superiors were in basic agreement, his initiatives were likely to receive fair consideration. This is not to accuse senior officials of having a status quo bias, but merely to suggest that they almost certainly believe in the course they are following, and therefore doubt the perspicacity of those who differ with them. To continue the example cited above, if the CD had strongly advocated persuading the neutral country to join NATO, a step almost universally deemed to be impossible and unwise, he would have undercut his position on other issues because his understanding of that country would have been suspect. Initiatives that can have this result are most unlikely, acting as a brake on precisely those new approaches needed to break impasses.

Several CDs were concerned about another limitation, the tendency of programmed (routine, reactive) work to drive out nonprogrammed (in this case, new initiatives; generally, new or unusual) work.[37] If the daily load was too heavy, there was little chance to reflect or plan:

> We've had so much stuff coming in from the field, and we've had these various [transition] papers to prepare, so that the combination of the two has left no time for taking initiative—so it's largely been reactive. (CD #22)[38]

Another said that there was great room for initiative, and asked himself if he were doing as much as he might to take

[37] See Simon, *New Science*, pp. 5-6, for the standard commentary on this problem.

[38] This interview was conducted in January 1969, just prior to the change in national administrations. Many CDs said they had spent much of their time between September 1968, and January 1969 preparing transition papers for the new leadership.

advantage of it. In order to help himself be more imagina-
tive and creative, he asked his desk officers to come up with
an agenda of relationships between countries he was responsible for, so that he might better focus advance thinking on them. He argued that this personal ordering of problems was nonreactive, and hoped that new ideas would
emerge from it. (CD #5) Others made similar arguments.

A related problem was the general scarcity of ideas. One
European CD said that "you prepare the ideas of how to
handle a negotiation, with the assistance of the bureau. . . .
But the ideas come from here. I wish they'd come more
from the embassies." (CD #20) Others chose to emphasize
the importance of taking ideas from whatever source and
turning them into realities. (CD #23) Carrying through
on an idea was often more difficult than finding it:

> Anybody can take an initiative, throw an idea in the hop-
> per. What's difficult is to follow through and see that any-
> thing is done about it. . . . You've got to come back at it
> time and time again—and of course that's true in spades
> when it's a matter of another agency program. (CD #7)

A change in program or policy was seldom an individual
effort; success generally resulted from collective action:

> Although you spend most of your time putting out fires,
> there is a tremendous latitude and scope to think ahead.
> You do this in part by carrying on a running dialogue
> with the ambassador. This is what really leads to eventual
> policy. (CD #4—paraphrase)

Of course, who initiated and who reacted often reflected
the state of relations, and specifically which side was attempting to alter an existing relationship. A country with
substantial American military presence might desire additional concessions as a price for keeping the troops there;
both sides might be pressing for alterations in trade terms;
or the United States might be attempting to gain military

concessions from another government, to mention examples given by CDs.

The CD's best opportunity to exercise initiative came from being conversant with all U.S. activities in a country. One said he and his staff constantly asked themselves, "What fields of possible cooperation are there?" with respect to a country with which relations had been strained, and argued that if one kept asking these questions with knowledge of what had gone before, one could frequently come up with new ideas. These could then be transmitted to superiors in the department, after which attempts were often made to place them into effect. (CD #13) Others cited specific examples of policy changes that had resulted from their own knowledge of the countries and U.S. programs.

It seems fair to conclude the CD role was overwhelmingly reactive to developing situations, both in the United States and abroad, but that there were few impediments to initiation of new approaches other than temporal pressures. Little change on this score was found to exist from the role played by office directors or officers-in-charge. Thus, CDs were less dominant in initiating new activities than intended, just as they failed to engage in significantly greater planning than their predecessors.

Breadth Dimension

One potentially troublesome role aspect related to the quality and thrust of the activities undertaken by the CD. Should he be concerned primarily with supporting the embassy; with managing all bilateral activities relating to his countries; or with mediating between the posts, the department, and the rest of government as necessary to harmonize conflicting positions? If all parties were agreed on policy and programs, of course, there would be no conflict between these functions, but this was seldom the case. The dilemma for the CD was real if he were forced to choose between supporting the ambassador at the risk of being considered too parochial by others in Washington, and arousing the ire of the ambassador by siding against him. One Latin American CD, with responsibilities for AID programs, explained what could happen:

> Often ambassadors, particularly those with AID programs in their countries, tend to be more liberal about what should be given to the country than the central AID officials in Washington. This is perhaps because the president of the country calls them in once a month and says, "We can't meet your conditions. We'll do our best to meet them next time, but what can you do for us right now?" The Washington AID officials, on the other hand, are likely to say, "If they don't meet the conditions, they don't get the loan." The country director has to try to fuse both sides, so that the ambassador can be constantly aware of the standards that apply. This is the real importance of the country director's job. He is always the man in the middle, and is always being blamed by somebody, either the ambassador in the field or the AID manager in Washington, who doesn't like the way things come out. Thus, the job is both threatening and difficult. (CD #4—paraphrase)

In spite of such cross pressures, very few CDs (four of forty-six) felt that they had become such partisans that embassy support was their primary responsibility.

Most chose instead to focus on managing or at least monitoring all bilateral relationships with their assigned countries. There were shadings of difference, of course, in how broadly such relations were defined. Some tended to limit their concern to State Department aspects of the relationships between Washington and the post:

> I am prepared to do battle with the deputy or the assistant secretary, if I think we're being moved in the wrong direction. I am prepared to do battle with the ambassador, if I think his recommendation isn't in our best inter-

LIBRARY
EISENHOWER COLLEGE

ests. And once we've gone through the process, I'm prepared to live with the decision that emerges. (CD #17)

Others explicitly extended their responsibilities to include other agencies as well:

> Our relations with the embassy are really a rather minor part of the job. I think . . . that there must be somewhere in the U.S. government, an office and an individual who is concerned with the overall character of our relations with his country. . . . If, for example, there is some kind of interplay between an AID program and a military assistance program, or some kind of an interplay between something that we're doing to them in the economic field and something we're doing for them in the political field, this is the only . . . place where all of these strands can be brought together and thought through, and balanced off against each other. (CD #7)

This was the modal view. Forty-two CDs saw bilateral relations as their most important charge, although the emphasis varied as sketched above. Seventeen specifically mentioned that the mediating function was necessary if the CD was to concern himself with *all* elements of bilateral relations, unless that involvement was merely pro forma. Intent did not insure success, and performance matching these expectations was not easy to achieve, as one of the more aggressive CDs explained:

> What you're really trying to do as country director is to control the bilateral relations of the U.S. government with the host government you handle—not [just] the State Department, because then you'd be just a desk officer. . . . You operate in a vacuum, because other departments are going to take you only if you can prove that you're valuable to them, unless you know more about what they are doing than they know themselves. You have to be able to give good advice, and that they appreciate. Then they accept you. (CD #20)

This emphasis on expertise was related to another component of breadth—functional competence and interest. Opinions of opposite numbers in other parts of the government with whom CDs interacted suggested that such technical expertise was critical.[39] A widely held belief was that where technical matters were involved, the CD was unlikely to be able to cope effectively. One FSO dealing with trade agreements argued that if the CD was not equipped to lead, somone else would. For example, a CD could easily arrange the visit of a foreign head of state, but was not knowledgeable enough to set U.S. policy on an automobile trade agreement with another country. (STATE #6)

The CD who aspired to an influential role had little choice except to become conversant with a wide range of matters outside the traditional political/diplomatic concerns of the FSO. If he did not, his views would not carry great weight, much less allow him to control the process.

Opinions diverged over CDs' breadth of vision as distinguished from their expertise. A significant proportion of the opposite numbers said that CDs were usually cooperative and willing to consider the needs of others. One regional deputy director in the International Security Affairs (ISA) section of the Office of the Secretary of Defense noted that a CD had to have a comprehensive perspective, in that no one could ride roughshod over the opinions of others and still fulfill a role requiring leadership by persuasion. He said he had always received a full hearing even when the CD disagreed with the DOD/ISA position. (ISA #1)

At the same time many felt CDs were susceptible to parochialism and excessive advocacy of measures directed toward improving relations with their countries of responsibility. Some of this was expected and even supported. An official of the Department of Commerce believed that it was natural for "the man in the country and his backstopping

[39] The comments on this point and the next which quote or cite opposite numbers are intended to be indicative of broadly held opinions about the CD, but no claim is made that they are universal.

103

in Washington to take country considerations first." (DOM #1) An assistant secretary for international affairs in a major domestic department went further, saying that a really good country director would have empathy with his country, and that this happened to specialists in all fields. In the case of the CD, he continued, this did not mean that he saw himself defending the interests of country X. Rather, it meant that he felt relations with country X were important to U.S. interests. If CDs were totally neutral, as higher ranking officials were presumed to be, one could probably lose something, because one couldn't be sure that the effect of a proposed action on all the sets of bilateral relationships would receive proper attention. (DOM #2)

It was important that the effect of a proposed action on bilateral relations was considered, just as it was important that political effects of the technical programs of other agencies be scrutinized, but each of these concentrations weakened the concept of the CD role as one of "across-the-board leadership," exhibiting "presidential interest." Perceptions of such narrower emphases, real or imagined, weakened the CD's ability to lead. A number of country directors indicated there was some substance in charges of parochialism on their part. Twelve of forty-one said that there was a danger of becoming too limited in viewpoint, even to the point of becoming an advocate for "their" countries.

An experienced FSO has recently argued that the policy formulation process of the government depends on advocacy proceedings, with more senior officials judging competing advocacies within their broader levels of advocacy.[40] This pattern presented a real problem for the CD. If his legitimate concern was political and diplomatic matters because that was the realm of State, then by the logic of the argument he could not adjudicate between political interests and economic development concerns, financial policy,

[40] John W. Bowling, "How We Do Our Thing: Policy Formulation," *Foreign Service Journal,* 47 (January 1970), 19-22, 48.

or military programs. Either State would have to be legitimized as the final arbiter of all components of foreign policy, or the advocacy syndrome would have to be broken down. To this extent, the breadth-of-concern problem and possible solutions to it were out of the hands of the country director and his opposite numbers.

It was almost universally accepted that the CD should have a broad range of concerns and interests. But while role expectations of opposite numbers and role orientations of CDs were generally congruent on this point, differences arose about the ability of the CD to perform in this fashion. The difficulty lay in his immediate responsibility for relations with a small number of countries and for political and diplomatic relations, and in his lack of expertise in other fields and in evaluating global U.S. interests. In large measure, his ability to cope with these often contradictory aspects of foreign relations was derived from his own qualities and experience, from the strength of support from his superiors, and from his ability to take some risks to gain wide agreement—and not from the strength of his role.

Leadership Dimension

In spite of these limitations on their potential influence, almost all CDs thought they had considerable latitude to exert leadership. A common view of interagency dealings in government is that they are conducted in an atmosphere of controversy and struggle for power. This may approximate reality in many instances, but as Secretary Rusk testified to the Jackson Subcommittee, it is not universally true:

> There are those who think that the heart of a bureaucracy is a struggle for power. This is not the case at all. The heart of the bureaucratic problem is the inclination to avoid responsibility.
>
> One of the reasons that organization seldom gets in the way of a good man is that if a man demonstrates that he is willing to make judgments and decisions and live with

the results, power gravitates to him because other people will get out of his way.[41]

Country director opinion generally substantiated Rusk's view. One CD, generally considered to be among the most effective, explained what a CD had to do:

> My basic thesis is that even if you're not senior, act senior. People then begin to take you seriously. . . . The country director has to act senior. He has to be willing to stick his neck out and take responsibility, and sign out telegrams that are controversial. In other words, he has to be willing to put his name in the same sense that the ambassador, chargé, or [deputy chief of mission] is going to put his name down. The buck shouldn't be passed. . . . The country director has got to have a willingness to take responsibility, and deal with the problems as if he were responsible. (CD #1)

The possibilities for CD leadership can be viewed as a continuum extending from none—with all interagency differences settled and all coordination performed at higher levels, to very strong, with all matters except those of highest importance resolved at his level in the way he believed best. Neither of these poles represented the actual situations encountered by CDs. Along the continuum were the points which more nearly approximated reality. The weakest was the position of the meeting-caller and secretariat official, who insured that the necessary consultations were made but did not exert influence on the outcome. Next was the CD who brought political competence and country considerations to any particular issue, just as others brought their special interests and expertise. In this situation most difficult issues, particularly those requiring a choice between short-range political gains and longer term goals or technical efficiency, were referred to higher levels. A

[41] Dean Rusk, testimony of December 11, 1963, reprinted in Jackson Subcommittee, *Administration of National Security*, p. 403.

stronger position was that of overall coordinator, whose right to be involved in all issues relating to the country was acknowledged, and who was accorded a *primus inter pares* status because only he among the participants was charged with rationalizing activities of all agencies and departments. A still stronger position was one approximating the executive chairman concept of NSAM 341 discussed earlier, where the CD could make a firm decision over the objections of other participants, leaving them to decide whether or not to risk an appeal to higher levels.

No CD found himself occupying any of these positions at all times. Of forty-five CDs asked how they thought their opposite numbers viewed them, twenty-one felt they were seen as legitimately providing the political input in any matters affecting relations with their countries, fifteen believed they were perceived as gradually acceding to legitimized roles as overall coordinators, four chose a middle position, two said they had not been country directors long enough to know, and three gave ambiguous answers which tended toward the weak end of the continuum.

Some CDs were quite content with the strength of their leadership role:

> I think that just about every other agency looks to the State Department, to the country directors, for policy guidance. I think they really do feel that this is our job. (CD #24)

> There is not a rival, let us say, policy-making focal point in Washington, with respect to my area as a whole, or any one of my countries. (CD #19)

Others felt that although legitimate, their role was more circumscribed:

> While others see me primarily as the man who provides the political component, it is possible if necessary to block other agencies to a certain extent. In order to do something, they have to clear with the country director. If it

can't be resolved there, it has to go to a higher level, and I have usually had success gaining acceptance for my point of view in such situations. (CD #25—paraphrase)

Most other agency representatives may not be too strong for the idea of the country director at the center, but they go along. In short, they accept limited leadership, always of course *ad referendum*: "I've got to check back with my boss." (CD #26—paraphrase)

Several CDs, like the one quoted below, pointed out that the content of the leadership dimension of their role differed from issue to issue:

In dealing with some subjects, the country director's function is one of coordination. In other situations, it's one of substance. In dealing with the Department of Defense on orders, primarily a military matter, the role becomes more coordinative than substantive. On the other hand, if it's a political matter, or essentially a political matter, then it is recognized that the action starts here. (CD #17)

Some impediments to the CD's ability to lead were not attributable to the man and his experience. When legitimate interests were in conflict, an issue generally had to be resolved at the senior levels of government, and if important or intense enough, at the White House. If anything, this tendency increased during the Nixon administration. This proclivity to "escalate" a problem hamstrung the intent of the system, as one African CD strongly suggested:

I think the system will never work, and can't be expected to, as long as whenever there is any real disagreement it is not going to be resolved at the country director level. No matter how hard the country director works, or how aggressive he is, it is sheer delusion to feel that he can get closure and resolution anything like what the ambassador can get in the field. On the lesser issues, he can impose himself and give a general judgment across the board, but not on the major ones. (CD #27—paraphrase)

Much depended on whether another agency was strongly interested in a given matter. If its involvement was peripheral to its major interests, it was much more likely to defer to the country director. More simply, "when you get close to the nerve of any agency, you're going to find a feeling expressed or implied that 'this is our business.'" (CD #12)

Legal prescriptions and requirements, too, could make it difficult or impossible for the CD to exert effective control:

The other agencies, the other parts of government have statutory responsibilities, and we cannot, . . . to my mind, assert our statutory responsibilities over theirs. And there are conflicts, so you've just got to work in that framework to get the job done. (CD #14)

This problem, affecting all levels of government, was exacerbated by the decision to include the phrase "to the full extent permitted by law" in the mandate given to the secretary of state in NSAM 341. Realistically perhaps no other choice was possible, but the result was to exclude from the NSAM 341 system and from the CD's purview precisely those questions most difficult to resolve, forcing them to be fought out exactly as before.

Because of the existence of substantive, legal, and occasionally, bureaucratic conflicts, CDs frequently found that a decision or problem was appealed to a higher level. At this point, it became critically important for a CD to assure himself that his position was the one that his superiors in State would take, if he did not wish to see his authority eroded. Twenty-seven of thirty-nine CDs asked, including some of those who felt they were coming to be considered as overall coordinators, reported that at one time or another their decisions had been appealed to higher authority.

The responses of the CDs, summarized in Table III-2, make it clear that the leadership dimension of the country director's role was not as strong as intended. Nevertheless, the CD gradually gained some acceptance as at least an overall coordinator with a right to participate in activities and decisions dealing with his countries.

TABLE III-2

OPPOSITE NUMBER REACTIONS TO COUNTRY DIRECTORS
AS SEEN BY COUNTRY DIRECTORS

How Is CD Accepted by Opposite Numbers?	Are CD Decisions Appealed to Higher Officials?							
	Yes		No		Not Asked		Total	
	N	%	N	%	N	%	N	%
As overall coordinator (1)	11	40.7	6	50.0	4	57.1	21	45.7
As bringing political component (2)	8	29.6	5	41.7	2	28.6	15	32.6
Between 1 & 2 (3)	2	7.4	1	8.3	1	14.3	4	8.7
Other (4)	3	11.1	–	–	–	–	3	6.5
Can't say (5)	2	7.4	–	–	–	–	2	4.3
Not asked (6)	1	3.7	–	–	–	–	1	2.2
Total	27	58.7	12	26.1	7	15.2	46	100.0

Note: Table cell percentages based on column sums. Marginal numbers and percentages based on proportion of total N in that category.

Status Dimension

The status (power and prestige) associated with the CD's position was not sharply defined. By rank, he was equivalent to the former office director. By area of geographic responsibility, he was more equivalent to the officer-in-charge, a comparison strengthened by the larger number of CDs compared to office directors. Because the OD and O-in-C positions were eliminated and replaced with CDs, some viewed the latter as a combination of the two former positions, with a status somewhat greater than the O-in-C but less than that of the OD. This argument, as summarized in the following comment, would probably be accepted by most CDs:

> At least to my mind, what has happened is [that] the functions of the then office director have moved in both directions. They've moved up to the assistant secretary, and they've moved down to the country directors. I would think that most of them moved to the country director, rather than up to the assistant secretary. (CD #14)

The status of the CD was also poorly delineated because newer elements of his role remained obscure. It has been alleged that "one of the great weaknesses of the country director system is that there really is no prescribed range of authority." (CD #1) The lack of power and prestige of the CD was strongly emphasized by a CD who had been a deputy office director prior to the change:

> I think they look upon the country director at least in my relationships with other agencies . . . much less as somebody who can make the decisions of the type they want than [could] . . . the office director. There is a tendency to go up a step. (CD #28)

Another CD who had also been a deputy office director saw this very starkly. In this case, his office had been split, with the former OD becoming CD for one part, and his deputy the CD for the other. The result, as seen by the former deputy: "I gained, he lost." (CD #29)

At the time the system was established, much was made of the equality of country directors in Washington and ambassadors in the field, each serving as head of a country team at his location. There was almost universal agreement by country directors, higher ranking State officials, and opposite numbers that such equivalence had not been reached. Most would agree with the conclusion of one CD: "Certainly, this country director doesn't have anything re-

111

motely approaching the status of an ambassador." (CD #30) The CD was often equated with the number-two position in the field, the deputy chief of mission (DCM). This interpretation is supported by the fact that most CDs either came from DCM-level positions or were assigned to them after their CD tours.[42]

A prior question, of course, is what difference high status made for policy making and problem solving. Certainly, greater status was one of the benefits Secretary Rusk and others had in mind when they attempted to "upgrade the desk officer," and a desire to give the new position high status was a primary reason some former ambassadors were appointed in the first group of country directors.[43] For State, there was an advantage in having issues resolved as low as possible, in order to free higher echelon officials to concentrate on new or major issues.[44] To do this, the CD had to have the power to decide, delegated by his assistant secretary, and the prestige that would persuade others to deal with him rather than to carry an issue upward. In a bureaucracy staffed by career officials, whether FSOs or civil servants, formal rank has much to do with status, as one CD indicated:

> I think [the ability to act as overall coordinator] relates in some measure to the rank you carry on the job, which of course is one of the reasons they wanted to have . . . these jobs filled by FSO-1s, they said, or FSO-2s. My predecessor here was a two, and I am an O-3, and I think this is a factor. (CD #5)

Another said the NSAM 341 grant of authority to the secretary of state and the higher rank of the CD helped at least "marginally" in dealing with personalities and other bu-

[42] See Appendix A for details on pre- and post-CD tour assignments.
[43] Dean Rusk, interview August 14, 1969.
[44] During the Nixon administration, there was an increasing tendency as time went by for this advantage not to be accepted, due to a desire to centralize the decision process. See Chapter VIII.

reaus who were rank conscious. (CD #2) Thus the CDs and others in State, at least, did feel that it was helpful for the CD to carry high prestige in his dealings with the rest of the government.

The status dimension of the CD role was intimately related to others previously discussed. A breadth of concern for the interests of other agencies, and strong and effective leadership which took them into account could be a major force for increasing the status of the country director. Conversely, increased status would make it far easier for the CD to be an energetic leader of a Washington country team. In turn this would increase the chances that U.S. policy for an area or country would be consistent and that its diverse elements would operate in concert. When CDs rated poorly on these dimensions, as was often the case, they found it difficult to be a major force in the foreign affairs bureaucracy.

Chapter Four

One Actor among Many:
The Country Director in the Foreign
Affairs Community

The organized patterns of activities and interactions that have not—perhaps, not yet—been officially institutionalized reveal bureaucracy in the process of change. PETER M. BLAU

THE country director's role by definition involved coordination and interaction with many members of the foreign affairs community. Disputes and conflicts were inevitable, given differences of perspective and conflicting goals, but he had to seek continuing cooperative relationships which could survive disagreements on individual issues. Through these encounters residual norms and expectations carried over, and through them new ones deriving from the CD's formal responsibilities became manifest.

THE VERTICAL PATTERN: THE COUNTRY DIRECTOR AS STATE DEPARTMENT OFFICIAL

The country director's influence with field posts, other agencies, and foreign embassies was dependent upon his relationship with his superiors, most particularly the geographic assistant secretary, under secretary, and secretary. It was hoped that the CD change, by reducing hierarchical layering in State, would improve reaction time and put the individual with detailed knowledge in more direct contact with senior officials of the department.

It soon became obvious, however, that relations between the "seventh floor" (secretary and under secretaries) and the CDs were not going to be particularly close or frequent. Secretary Rusk never intended to work directly with them,

114

except in rare instances. His primary conception was that of a policy chain including the secretary, assistant secretaries, and country directors, with deputies at each level assisting when and where the principals desired.[1] More or less routine matters would be dealt with in this chain of command—that is, through the assistant secretaries—while the acknowledged expert, wherever he might be located, would be brought in on more complicated or important matters.[2] This might be a CD, a deputy assistant secretary (DAS), the assistant secretary, or some other person.

Thus, while the CD was linked to the seventh floor, the more important question became whether he could work closely with the assistant secretary, and whether the latter was therefore more effective because he received better advice and received it sooner. Assistant secretaries interviewed said this was the case, even though some of their predecessors had initially resisted the new system. Their belief was difficult for them to document conclusively, and their preference for the CD concept over the office director arrangement was mild.[3]

For their part, country directors did not find the path to the assistant secretary blocked, although ease of access varied. It depended not only upon the wishes of CDs and assistant secretaries, but also on the part played by deputy assistant secretaries. Most problems were resolved either by the CD alone or by the CD and DAS together. One CD estimated that the assistant secretary "gave" the CD 80 percent of his authority, but on 20 percent of the matters he preferred to have someone in addition to the CD check it out, and on 5 percent desired to do so himself. (CD #31)

[1] Rusk, interview August 14, 1969. Additional interviews in 1971 and 1972 suggest that much the same conception was held by Secretary Rogers in the Nixon administration.

[2] Generalization based on composite of all interviews with seventh-floor principals and special assistants.

[3] Based on interviews with three of the five geographic assistant secretaries in office during the major part of this study.

Usually the CD determined whether he could take action on his own. If he thought a problem should be considered by his superiors, he then decided who should be brought in.[4] This higher level consultation might take one of several forms. Some CDs acted in a strictly hierarchical fashion, leaving the DAS to decide whether to bring in the assistant secretary. A variation of this was also used:

> On some things, when I think it should go to the assistant secretary, I will still go to the deputy assistant secretary, but I would say "I've got an appointment with the assistant secretary on this. Do you want to go instead of me, or do you want to go along with me?" This gives the deputy a chance to interpose himself, while insuring that the assistant secretary will consider the matter. (CD #32—paraphrase)

In other cases, the CD worked with the DAS because he was more accessible:

> I go to whichever one I can get to—whichever one's available at the moment, if it's an urgent problem; and I don't particularly worry about going through one to the other. (CD #6)

When operating this way, some CDs felt they must keep the DAS cut in, while others left it to the assistant secretary and the DAS to keep each other up to date.

Many factors influenced the path a particular problem might take:

> It is difficult to say in the abstract what will be taken where. It tends to go to [the DAS] or to the assistant secretary if it is a policy matter, if it is controversial, or if you have doubts about the wisdom of your own decision. So much depends on the CD and the amount of authority he has taken for himself; on his rapport with the DAS and assistant secretary; on the amount of time the senior offi-

[4] How this decision was made is discussed in Chapter V.

cials have available, and so on. There are no hard and fast rules. Sometimes a DAS or the assistant secretary has become involved in a particular problem, so you take more to him in that area, while at others they may have neither the time nor the interest, so you do it yourself. Again, if a DAS or the assistant secretary has served in a country, he naturally takes more interest in it and again you take more to him. But if there is a crisis or a big problem where the front office has to spend most of its time, then you try to ease the burden. If this is not the case, then you take more to them. (CD #29—paraphrase)

Another CD added that the assistant secretary's confidence in his subordinates could also dictate working relationships:

At first, the assistant secretary apparently didn't have a DAS he wanted to delegate much to, so I dealt with him directly. Since Ambassador [X] has come in, this is not the case any more. (CD #27—paraphrase)

Preferences of the CDs were also important, and many tried, when possible, to work with the higher official in whom they had the greatest personal confidence. (CD #32)

Close relationships with senior officials increased the CD's potential for success in interagency dealings. Direct contact with the assistant secretary made it more likely the CD would accurately reflect the latter's preferences, and consequently less likely he would be overruled if an issue were taken higher. Easy access made for quicker reaction times, allowing State's position to be established early enough to have full weight in interagency consultations. It also enabled the strong and innovative CD to influence the thinking of his superiors. In addition, it was valuable in bringing the assistant secretary into disputes to force resolution when necessary, and it gave the assistant secretary a firm idea of the CD's abilities, allowing him greater latitude if adjudged capable.

Ties between the assistant secretary and the CD might predate their current tours of duty, since career FSOs reaching the assistant secretary level were likely to know almost all officers assigned to their bureau personally or by reputation. This opened the possibility of selecting those they already had confidence in to be CDs, since the assistant secretary had considerable voice in determining CD assignments. Generally, six to eight months before rotation was due, the front office would begin to consider possible replacements. This might be done by the assistant secretary. The executive director then negotiated with the Senior Assignments Panel and the Career Management Staff (in the Nixon administration, with the office of the deputy director of the Foreign Service for Career Counseling and Assignments, which formally made assignment decisions), and with any other bureaus that might have a claim on an officer's services. Particularly for the important countries, the assistant secretary was likely to be able to obtain his first choice. In any event, it was extremely unlikely that anyone would attempt to override his veto of a candidate.[5] This procedure was likely to build mutual confidence between an assistant secretary and his CDs.

Most of the above assumes a convergence of interests between assistant secretaries and country directors, with the latter supplying improved country-level advice and undertaking a major share of the burden of bilateral relations, but dependent upon their respective assistant secretaries for guidance and for support outside the bureau. Yet the CDs could have become threats to the assistant secretaries, if they had been able to assert as much country-level leadership or control as some thought was originally intended, or if they had developed strong and direct working relation-

---

[5] This description is based on interviews with three assistant secretaries, two bureau executive directors, and two deputy assistant secretaries who had been involved in selecting new CDs. The pattern described incorporates the principles, if not the exact procedures, followed in all five geographic bureaus.

118

ships with senior officials. Under such circumstances, the ability of assistant secretaries to set policies and programs for their regions might have been impaired. But because the CDs generally came to have access to the seventh floor only through their assistant secretary, there was little chance that the latter would or could be undercut. And as previously discussed, the CDs had considerable difficulty in developing a strong leadership position across agency and departmental lines. Thus any threat to assistant secretary authority from strong CDs was remote.

Moreover, the way the bureaus functioned after the CD change further limited the possibility of a strong and independent role for the CD. Instead of clearing the track for direct access to the assistant secretary for the individual with country expertise (formerly the O-in-C, then the CD), an avowed purpose of eliminating the office director level, new obstacles appeared. This can be seen most directly in the relationships that developed between CDs and deputy assistant secretaries, as a result of the more limited area covered by each CD as compared to the former office directors, and the increased number of DASs in each geographic bureau. The two were related:

> An Assistant Secretary . . . must have *a* deputy to whom his truly formidable and sometimes indivisible responsibility for a fifth of the world can be passed on occasion. However, the establishment of two or three deputies with sub-regional responsibilities can, if not very carefully managed, come close to reintroducing a layer of "super office directors" between the Country Directors and the Assistant Secretary.[6]

The Bureau of Near Eastern and South Asian Affairs provides a good example. In early 1966 it had three geographic offices, one regional affairs office, and two deputy assistant secretaries. In April 1966 the three geographic offices were

---

[6] Spain, p. 36. Emphasis in original.

divided into ten country directorates. The Office of Near Eastern Affairs was divided into four: three dealing with the Arab states and one with Israel and Arab-Israeli affairs. The Office of South Asian Affairs became the India-Nepal-Ceylon directorate and the Pakistan-Afghanistan directorate. The Office of Greek, Turkish and Iranian Affairs was broken into four, one each for Turkey, Greece, Cyprus, and Iran. At the same time, the number of DASs was increased to three, each with responsibility for the area covered by two to four country directorates in a pattern exactly analogous to the geographic responsibilities of the three offices under the previous system. Similar arrangements existed in the other bureaus during both the Johnson and Nixon administrations. When DASs acted as "super office directors," the thrust of the CD concept was vitiated since a layer again had been interposed between those with country expertise and the policy level.

This possibility was intensified when issues were related to multiple foreign states. Obvious examples include the continuing Cyprus question, inevitably involving Greece and Turkey as well (and therefore three CDs), or the Arab-Israeli problem, which cut across the areas of four CDs, and there were numerous others. Coordination on such matters was essential, and it was very likely to be handled by a DAS if there was one with geographic responsibilities encompassing the area in question, as in each of the examples above.

Not everyone agreed on the seriousness of this problem. Spain concludes that it had been "more apparent than real," because of the "common sense, self-restraint, and mutual respect of the men involved."[7] But a CD serving in the same bureau (NEA) at the same time argued that

> the deputy assistant secretary is acting as office director in this case, and with the disadvantage that he doesn't have a deputy. He really doesn't have the time to concen-

[7] Ibid.

trate on all the problems he should, and the great problem to me with this system is that we lack overall coordination. (CD #33)

Another qualified this position by limiting it to policy coordination, with the CD retaining control of all management and administration matters. (CD #28) Still another CD in NEA agreed the DAS was acting as office director, but felt that to "the extent that you have people operating at one level higher, it's easier to get things decided." (CD #22)[8] In other bureaus, opinion was similarly mixed. Altogether, seventeen of forty-six CDs interviewed said deputies tended to function as office directors.

Nowhere did the indeterminate (some would say anomalous) nature of the position occupied by the deputy assistant secretaries emerge so clearly as from the opinions of several of the original CD sample who later moved up to the DAS level.[9] All agreed that the DAS was able to intervene between the CD and assistant secretary, but differed in how much they attempted to do so, and in how desirable they thought this to be. One, a strong supporter of CD prerogatives when serving as a CD, held to the same position as a deputy assistant secretary, and thought the DAS should restrict himself to filling in as necessary for the assistant secretary, to shoring up weak points in the bureau, and to coordinating problems which cut across country directorate boundaries. In his mind, this could be accomplished with a smaller number of deputies than under the prevailing pattern. By contrast, another former CD, serving as a DAS in a more centralized bureau, acted as a hierarchical channel between the CDs in his subregion of the bureau and the assistant secretary. As a CD, he had preferred the former of-

---

[8] By "one level higher" he meant that CDs were being coordinated by a DAS, while under the old system officers-in-charge were coordinated by an office director, who still had a DAS between himself and the assistant secretary.

[9] A total of four former CDs falling in this category were reinterviewed, one in January 1972 and three in April 1973.

fice director system, and thus his more recent opinion was consistent. At the same time, he agreed that the CD system did have the advantages of shortening lines of communication, albeit not to the originally envisaged degree of direct CD-assistant secretary contact, since there were now only three essential levels (CD, DAS, assistant secretary) rather than four as previously (O-in-C, OD, DAS, assistant secretary). But whatever their position on the role the DAS should play, all agreed that on balance, the country directors appeared to have less latitude in the early 1970s than they themselves had had while serving in the equivalent positions in the late 1960s.

Several CDs suggested ways of bringing CDs out of the shadow of the deputy, usually in this vein:

> We have had underemployed deputies in this bureau. Now this creates problems because they don't have enough to do, and they tend to crowd the country directors too much. . . . My own view is that the deputy's level should be more functional, rather than geographical. (CD #1)

Such an emphasis would find each CD dealing with each deputy in the bureau, drawing on functional expertise applied across the entire region. Whether this would be as desirable for the front office as it seemed to this CD is questionable. It would weaken the DAS as a buffer and contribute to a span-of-control problem. The assistant secretary might benefit from opening himself up to additional considerations unfiltered by a deputy, one CD said, but there would be tremendous time constraints if the assistant secretary were to deal directly with nine or ten country directors. (CD #34)

Another way of retaining CD authority and responsibility was to resolve everything possible at their own level. The traditional bureaucratic view, of course, is that a dispute between two officials of equal rank should be resolved by their common superior, if one exists. It was exemplified by one CD who believed if he wrote and cleared a message with fellow CDs, "as a matter of form it [was] a good idea to get a higher ratification." (CD #2) However, others argued that two or more CDs could and should work out such subregional matters between themselves:

Never in two and a half years have PAF [Pakistan-Afghanistan Affairs] and INC [India-Nepal-Ceylon Affairs] had to take an issue to the Assistant Secretary for decision. This is not to say that the Assistant Secretary does not review or even reverse my colleague's and my decisions, nor that the Secretary himself does not make the important ones. We have managed, however, to spare both of them the nonsubstantitative histrionics that we go through with each other before reaching a mutually agreeable position.[10]

Interviews with others in NEA bore out this assertion, and the additional point was made that when two CDs for areas with directly conflicting interests (e.g., India and Pakistan) could agree, it was highly unlikely (although not impossible, as events during the Indo-Pakistani war of late 1971 clearly showed) that anyone higher up would challenge their joint recommendation. If they could do this, they retained more policy control than if differences forced referral to higher levels.

The need for coordination across country directorate lines is also demonstrated by the increasing number of regional and subregional problems handled recently by the regional affairs (RA) offices of the bureaus. They provided an additional forum below the AS/DAS level, at the price of jurisdictional conflicts. This was particularly true in the Bureau of European Affairs (EUR), which had two such offices, one for regional politico-economic affairs (RPE) and one for regional politico-military affairs (RPM). Some hairsplitting was required, for example, to separate French

10 Spain, p. 35.

economic affairs from Common Market affairs, although in theory the former were handled by a CD and the latter by RPE. The regional offices tended to take borderline issues away from CDs, partially as the result of staffing difficulties. In at least one case, all economic matters for one country directorate were taken over by RPE because the assistant secretary did not feel the CD's staff was competent to handle them, and returned to the country directorate only when an officer trained in economics became CD. (CD #12) Similarly, over a period of time responsibility for almost all bilateral military relations with a major NATO member was shifted to RPM, until a "peace treaty" was worked out stipulating that in the future it would revert to the CD. (STATE #7) Such occurrences reflected the location of expertise, as well as the assertiveness of the regional affairs offices, eager as "late-comers" to establish their own importance. (STATE #8)

There was disagreement about whether the rise of the regional affairs offices was due to the smaller areas covered by CDs under the new system, or to the increasing importance of multilateral policy concerns. One assistant secretary took the latter position, noting that some matters would always cross organizational lines and be pushed up or go to the regional office, however a bureau was organized. But the director of the regional office for the same bureau, having headed that unit under both systems, argued that many more matters came to him after the change.[11] He regarded the extra work as a burden, but others saw it as an opportunity. One noted that the RA role had bcome easier and probably more important, due to the increased number of CDs and the consequent debasing of the rank and prestige of the CD as compared to the OD. Since the RA director's responsibilities were unchanged, his role became somewhat more prominent. (STATE #11)

---

[11] Joint interview, geographic assistant secretary and director, Office of Regional Affairs, same bureau (STATE #9, STATE #10).

Use of these offices varied according to responsibilities of the bureaus and the location of necessary expertise. However, the CD's role as overall coordinator was diminished if issues relating to his country were managed elsewhere. Other agencies were unlikely to stand on formal principles; they would work with anyone able to meet their needs.

It was almost universally held that subordinates should be allowed enough latitude to take command of their jobs. One DAS who had previously been a country director explained why this was sometimes difficult:

> I'm sure that if the secretary passes me in the hall, he thinks of me as the country X man. As a result, he will call me directly on country X matters. This presents a problem both for me and for the country director. There is probably no way of preventing or resolving this problem, unless you go back to an assistant secretary and one alter ego DAS. I've found that if you are moved up as I was, you have to make a real effort not to take the old job with you, or you run the risk of putting yourself in as a layer between the country director and the secretary of state. (STATE #8)

Another DAS believed the solution lay in operating style:

> The DAS should not attempt to produce much on his own, but should limit himself to keeping up with the telegrams, making sure that the CDs are on top of all they should be, and meeting important visitors. (STATE #12)

Even when all were aware of such problems, correcting them was not easy. For example, the current CD for country X in the example above said that, in a way, the DAS was still acting as CD, simply because others still regarded him as the man to see. (CD #34)

A problem analogous to that faced by CDs with respect to DASs arose for the CDs' subordinates, the country officers, who often found their own latitude circumscribed. A CD who had previously served as OD related the conflicting effects of the change:

> I can read more about a smaller area [now], be perhaps a little more thoroughly informed than I would be otherwise. But by the same token I also tend to take on, perhaps, more of the chores. (CD #3)

Another CD believed that on balance this was an unfortunate development:

> If the country director is supposed to get so deeply involved in the details of his country or countries, then the usefulness of the desk officer begins to decline. (CD #18)

A related argument is that if a senior man and a more junior one have the same area of responsibility, people will work through the more senior. (CD #34) To some CDs, the reduced status of the desk officer contributed directly to the problem of getting FSOs to take responsibility, since they had little chance to prove themselves early in their careers:

> Junior officers are really staff officers until they reach class two. Before the change, they had lots of independence and responsibility. I was a desk officer as a class-five officer, and had more contact with the secretary of state than I do now as a class one. (CD #29—paraphrase)

Such dissatisfaction on the part of the CDs and country officers reflected residual expectations derived from the old system about the "proper" level at which things should be accomplished, and from their viewpoints were valid concerns. But this must be balanced by the explicit desire of senior levels to place more experienced officers in charge of bilateral relations.

The variations in these relationships among the several bureaus are more difficult to isolate than are the general patterns discussed so far. Most appeared to result more from the personalities and styles of those involved, from special circumstances affecting bureau work loads (e.g., Vietnam for East Asian and Pacific Affairs), and from the number of countries in bureau areas than from the oft-cited variations in style and outlook among the bureaus. In EA, the assistant secretary spent most of his time on Vietnam, so the DASs assumed many of his duties with respect to other countries. Several strong CDs emerged under this arrangement, since when they were working with a DAS, in effect the latter was acting as assistant secretary and not as a layer between CD and assistant secretary. In this bureau, more than any of the others except NEA, the CDs were responsible for one or perhaps two countries, allowing them to focus more directly on one or two sets of bilateral relations. Except for the special case of Latin America (discussed below), CDs in this area seemed to have more opportunity to emphasize the newer leadership and coordination aspects of their roles.

In the Bureau of African Affairs (AF) by contrast, only one CD had as few as three countries, two had four, three had five, two had six, and one had ten.[12] Since the depth and range of U.S. ties with African states was generally less than elsewhere, this made sense administratively. Less work was involved in each set of bilateral relationships, but in-depth country expertise at the CD level naturally suffered. Thus CDs tended to function somewhat as office directors had, but now had an increased number of DASs to contend with. Moreover, as time passed those assigned as CDs became more junior (usually O-2s, and several O-3s), so that they lost the advantages that more senior rank afforded. There were some outstanding CDs in AF, but the CD con-

[12] For details of countries assigned to individual country directors, see Appendix B.

cept was perhaps least well suited to the responsibilities of this bureau. In 1969 its organization reverted to a smaller number of units, usually with even more countries in each (see Chapter VIII).

The case of NEA has already been discussed, but it is worth reemphasizing that while CDs did have responsibility either for one or a small number of closely related countries, the mystique of the former office arrangement survived. A DAS had responsibility for a geographic area exactly the same as covered by each former office director. Given the traditionally "lean" organization in NEA, this was not an insurmountable obstacle to close relationships between the assistant secretary and the CDs, as some of the comments cited earlier indicate, but it did partially subvert the intent of the CD system. At the same time, after 1969 CDs in this bureau did have the advantage of serving under a dynamic assistant secretary, Joseph Sisco, who to a degree unmatched by his counterparts for other areas of the world, was able to set the tone of U.S. policy. His strong position, in part due to an informal decision by Henry Kissinger, appeared to provide advantages to his subordinates in their dealings with other parts of government.

There was more resistance to the CD change in the Bureau of European Affairs than in any other. The incumbent assistant secretary in early 1969, alone of any approached, declined to discuss the system, and both DASs interviewed preferred the previous office director pattern of organization. Span of control was seen as a problem, and the strong regional affairs offices discussed earlier tended to syphon off duties and issues that might have been assigned to country directors. An additional difficulty from the CD viewpoint was that EUR had responsibility for several major countries, in particular Germany, Britain, France, and the Soviet Union, about which major decisions were almost certainly going to be made at the top levels of government, regardless of the organizational structure of the bureau. CDs were often relegated to providing staff support for their superiors and performing the routine work. The importance of these countries made this escalation understandable, but it did vitiate the CD concept. Ultimately, in 1972, EUR like AF partially reverted to older patterns of organization (see Chapter VIII).

The merged State/AID bureau for Latin America was rather unique, although most of the general factors described were found here as well. Its hierarchy was considerably more complex than that of the other geographic bureaus. In 1969, for example, there were five officials in addition to the assistant secretary with the rank of DAS or higher: the deputy U.S. coordinator for the Alliance for Progress, with bureauwide responsibility for AID matters; a principal deputy assistant secretary who functioned as alter ego to the assistant secretary for political (i.e., Department of State) matters; a DAS for Economic Policy (State); one for Social and Civic Development (AID); and one for management (both State and AID).[13] The chain of command from CD to assistant secretary was never simple, since the CD had no single superior below the assistant secretary. An issue with both State and AID implications might follow a tortured path from the CD to one DAS, and from there to either the principal DAS or the deputy coordinator before reaching the assistant secretary. (CD #26) A question of economic development policy, for example, could result in a dispute between the DAS for Economic Policy and the DAS for Social and Civic Development, or between the deputy coordinator and the principal DAS. Such disputes could embroil the CD in a controversy between his State superiors and those on the AID side. (CD #35) If the assistant secretary was unavailable, there might be no single official in the bureau who could resolve a major disagreement. The effect varied according to the circumstances.

---

[13] In 1972 the latter position was eliminated and its duties assigned to the Office of Management, under the executive secretary of the bureau. The duties of the other four were partially realigned, but the complex working relationships remained.

Sometimes, if the multiple superiors were directly engaged in an issue, the CD was immobilized until resolution was negotiated higher up. At others, senior level disagreement, less focused or less intense, might allow the country director some latitude and flexibility to choose the course of action he personally favored.

A second difference was the existence of functional AID offices which were organizationally coequal with the country directorates. As a result, the bureau was not truly merged, except in the persons of the CDs and their staffs on one hand, and of the assistant secretary/U.S. coordinator for the Alliance for Progress on the other. There were eight offices in addition to the merged country directorates at the time of the bulk of interviews for this study, and two special missions. The amount of coordination required between the CDs and the functional offices within the bureau was considerable, and meant that a large number of problems had to be settled at higher levels in ARA-LA.

For the CD, the major difference was the inclusion of AID responsibilities in his office. Subordinates were assigned from both State and AID, and unlike other CDs, he was officially provided with a deputy director. This meant that the coordination problem between CDs and AID geographical offices faced in other bureaus was nonexistent, since these CDs combined both duties in their own person. This of course was why they occasionally found themselves caught between two superiors who did not share these merged responsibilities. However, a study made by the management office of ARA-LA in February 1969 showed that those serving in country directorates overwhelmingly preferred the merged offices, and many said that they would not continue to serve if they did not retain both responsibilities.[14]

In spite of coordination problems and the more complex hierarchy, CDs in ARA-LA were nearly alone in feeling that

[14] ARA-LA/EX internal study prepared at the request of the deputy U.S. coordinator, Alliance for Progress, dated February 10, 1969.

the CD system truly integrated the important elements of foreign policy. Only seven of the forty-six CDs volunteered this point as an advantage of the new system, and six of these were from ARA-LA and held merged responsibilities. To this extent, the Latin American CDs as a group were apparently more successful in carrying out the prescribed functions of the CD than their counterparts in the other four bureaus.

The Horizontal Pattern: The Country Director as Interagency Coordinator

While the country director made some progress in State, he was less successful elsewhere in government. His imputed leadership role was never fully accepted by other agencies. His own uncertainty about how he should function and his inexperience outside the traditional politico-diplomatic area were compounded when he came into contact with members of agencies whose backgrounds and organizational philosophies differed greatly from his own. Moreover, there was the continuing problem of how much coordination was desirable. The line between necessary coordination and undue interference was seldom located at the same point by any two participants involved in a given issue.

The SIG and the IRGs

Although, as discussed previously, the CD concept had independent origins, the designers of the country director mechanism hoped it would be an integral part of the NSAM 341 system with which it was simultaneously introduced. Just as the SIG was supposed to focus on major interdepartmental problems, and the IRGs had responsibility for their regions, so the country directors were to lead at the country level. When interagency disagreements arose, the three levels were to complement each other. While the CD was not given the formal executive chairman's authority held by assistant secretaries for the IRG and the under secretary for the SIG, he was to exercise "full interdepartmental leadership on country matters,"[15] with the expectation that disputes would be taken to the IRG, just as participants at that level could appeal to the SIG.

The CD's ability to lead was thus partially tied to his working relationship with the assistant secretary and to the latter's effectiveness as executive chairman of the IRG. If the country director's position was based on broad consideration of U.S. interests and reflected the thinking of his superiors, there would be an incentive for others to work matters out at the CD level, since the executive chairman of the IRG would be likely to ratify the CD's decision. But if carrying a problem to the IRG might lead to a more favorable outcome, there would be little reason for another agency to compromise with the CD. An agency which felt its interpretation of an issue was being slighted could hardly be faulted for selecting the forum likely to produce the most favorable result. To make the system effective, each level had to work efficiently and in tandem with the others. If each of the higher officials was the recognized leader of the relevant portion of foreign affairs community, the CD as a respected subordinate was much more likely to be accepted. However, almost all who observed the SIG/IRG system concluded it did not function well.

SIG operations got off to a slow start owing to the early departure of George Ball, the first SIG executive chairman, and the desire of his successor, Nicholas Katzenbach, to proceed cautiously.[16] Neither made a strong initial commitment to the SIG as a decision-making device. Moreover, Secretary Rusk did not lend active support, since he thought too much time in government was taken up with formal meetings, and was inclined toward use of task forces or ad hoc devices rather than formal procedures. He thus was not particularly impressed with the potential of the SIG, and commented after leaving office that "it was just as

[15] FAMC 385, paragraph 7.   [16] See Chapter VII for details.

132

well" that it did not meet as often as originally intended.[17] Since State's leadership did not emphasize the system, there was little reason for others to do so. A 1968 SIG staff study concluded that "there is little doubt that the SIG—and the IRGs and Country Directors as well—would be strengthened by a greater direct commitment and support from the Secretary of State."[18]

President Johnson, for his part, continued to use the "Tuesday Lunch" and other informal techniques for important decision making. As a politician who had little feel for organizations because "he dealt with people," he was disinclined to say, "let the SIG handle this problem." While he accepted the NSAM 341 system as something that might be useful, he did not push it once it had been created.[19] This lack of support was manifested in the way the system operated in practice.

Even when the SIG began to meet frequently in mid-1967, it was not a dominant force, although more than thirty meetings were conducted between mid-1967 and the end of 1968. A wide range of matters was considered: long-range policy guidelines, "threshold decisions" where timely SIG discussion might establish a sound base for future action, preparations for international negotiations, questions of management and personnel, legislative strategy, and specific country problems. Perhaps the most telling commentary on the SIG's importance, however, is that at no time during its existence did it deal with the fundamental foreign policy problem of its era—Vietnam. Its major success was much more mundane—deciding on reductions in personnel stationed abroad to be made by each agency under the BALPA (BALance of PAyments) program of 1967-

[17] Rusk, interview August 14, 1969.

[18] The quotation is from an unpublished study prepared by the SIG staff in November 1968.

[19] Interview August 1969, NSAM #2, former senior advisor to President Johnson.

1968.[20] Although it was operating somewhat as originally intended by the fall of 1968, its reputation, in the eyes of General Taylor, had been irrevocably tarnished by its previous difficulties.[21] The new administration, interested in reviving the National Security Council, consigned the SIG to a distinctly secondary position as the NSC Under Secretaries Committee. It emerged with essentially the same membership but with the reduced mandate of insuring execution of NSC decisions.[22]

There are a number of reasons for the ultimate failure of the SIG, in spite of its surface attractiveness. In addition to the lack of support from the top and the initial limitations placed on the authority of State discussed in Chapter III, several other weaknesses were never overcome. For one thing, the executive chairman idea failed to take root. Presiding officers at both the SIG and IRG levels frequently lapsed or were pushed into pursuit of consensus, rather than providing decisive leadership. The general weakness of State and lack of demonstrated top-level support, and a growing conviction in other agencies that the NSAM 341 system was basically an instrument of State rather than of the whole government contributed to this. Executive chairmen had little "clout" with which to impose their decisions on other departments. Even in State, the assumption was that they could not be assertive because, as one official argued, "the boys won't play the game if they feel they won't get a fair hearing in this court." (CD #29) Since the secretary of state was unwilling or unable to dominate his opposite numbers in developing policy, his subordinates could not do so.

[20] The criticisms listed to this point are summarized from the SIG staff study.

[21] Taylor, interview August 13, 1969.

[22] Details of the new system can be found in the *New York Times*, February 5, 1969, and in Edward A. Kolodziej, "The National Security Council: Innovations and Implications," *Public Administration Review*, 29 (November-December, 1969), 573-585.

Additionally, staff support was weak. Materials were seldom circulated in time to allow for completed staffing by individual agencies before meetings, and little effort was made to insure compliance with SIG decisions. These shortcomings resulted in part from the small size of the SIG staff (never more than four officers), and in part because all staffers were "users of words" from State rather than "manipulators of men" from throughout government.[23] There were no contact men or expediters who could ferret out developing problems for early SIG attention and oversee execution of SIG directives. A larger, multiagency staff had been intended, but the first staff director wished to avoid having "front-office hatchetmen" interfering with the IRG level of the system, and was uncertain of what his superiors really wanted.[24] While this caution was understandable, the result was to deprive the SIG of the advantages of a strong and active staff, respected and perhaps feared throughout the bureaucracy.

The difficulties discussed to this point might have been avoided, had there been different individuals in critical positions and perhaps a different configuration of foreign policy problems. Other, more fundamental weaknesses, however, were probably inherent in the NSAM 341 concept. It may not be possible today to delegate major foreign policy decisions to interdepartmental committees at the deputy secretary level, or even to the secretary of state. Both presidential responsibility and criticality of issues may mean that the "Tuesday Lunch," some more structured White House equivalent, or the president alone with his legal pad will invariably dominate major decisions. Any lower-level group would then play an essentially supporting role, however well it functioned.

Second, the NSAM 341 system was designed to strengthen the secretary of state, but none of its formal elements

[23] SIG staff study. Source for whole paragraph to this point.
[24] Interview, NSAM #1, Taylor task-force member later associated with SIG, January 8, 1969.

involved him personally. His enhanced position was to be arrived at only indirectly, and consequently he and those at his level had little obvious stake in the success of the system. It may be vital to insure that the advantages to be gained and the responsibility for success of any reorganization are centered in the same individual(s), if its objectives are to be met.

Third, any reorganization which from the beginning, in both concept and practice, is so obviously contrary to preferred decision-making styles of major actors is likely to find its impact diminished and its lifetime short. A system which would work well at one time with certain individuals may be ineffective at another with other players. Since President Johnson never made it clear that he expected the secretary of defense, the national security advisor, or other powerful figures to subordinate themselves to the direction of the secretary of state, there was little reason for their subordinates to defer to lesser officials in State.

Finally, because of existing vested interests in the status quo, it is possible that any change that leaves entrenched bureaucracies basically unchanged is unlikely to achieve more than a fraction of what was intended. One of those who worked closely to develop the NSAM 341 system asserted later that all that was initially hoped for was a 25 percent improvement in processes of foreign affairs management, which was all that could be expected. Even that proved to be impossible, given the handicaps confronting the few officials strongly committed to making the system work.[25]

As has been implied, all these factors vitiated the ability of the SIG, and to a certain degree the IRGs (see below) to make decisions. Their essential irrelevance was therefore compounded by a reluctance to refer problems to them. Not only did they act slowly, but meetings frequently deteriorated into briefing sessions for the principals, or at best

[25] Ibid.

into an opportunity for "exchanging views and creating a better idea of what we're trying to do." (CD #8)

While many of these problems were as obvious at the IRG level as for the SIG, the operations of these regional bodies did follow a somewhat different pattern. They were not equally active, nor given equal responsibility. The IRG for Latin America was generally considered to be the most successful, followed by the one for NEA, while that for Europe was unimportant. Those for Asia and for Africa were more active, but less highly regarded than the first two.

In the bureau of Inter-American Affairs, a Latin American Policy Committee existing before 1966 was quickly transformed into the IRG. It was strongly supported by the principal DAS, Robert Sayre, and instead of waiting for problems, it was able to undertake advance consideration of plans and programs, and the resources necessary to carry them out. Many meetings were used for two annual reviews for each country, the Country Analysis and Strategy Paper (CASP) and the annual AID program review. The CASP was an outgrowth of the first effort to apply program budgeting to the Department of State, and was unique to ARA-LA.[26] The country team in the field prepared the CASP following policy and procedural guidelines prepared by the bureau. It was intended to be a succinct statement of U.S. goals and objectives, an analysis of threats and prospects, and a detailed summary of all U.S. programs designed to achieve the basic objectives. The preparation of the CASP gave the ambassador a chance to work out differences and to articulate assumptions of the various participants. Once it was sent to Washington, the CD had primary responsibility for eliciting the opinions and recommendations of other agencies. After these had been incorporated, the CASP was taken up at an IRG meeting reserved for that one paper, modified as necessary, and then used to guide

[26] See Mosher and Harr, *Programming Systems*, passim, for details of this and other programming efforts.

agency budget submissions and operations for the next year.[27] One advantage of the CASP operation for the CD was that he was of primary importance in determining its final form, thereby enhancing his status.

The NEA IRG was also very active during the Johnson administration, holding about seventy-five meetings altogether. It was used for program reviews less formal than the CASP and, along with the other IRGs, was employed extensively in late 1968 for the preparation of contingency plans and transition papers for the new administration. Unlike ARA-LA, however, where nine of ten CDs said the IRG was useful, there were several reservations among the NEA CDs. It was criticized on grounds that meetings were sometimes held simply to justify its existence, or as one CD put it, "just to keep the animal fed." (CD #36) Some saw it as more useful to other agencies than to State and the CD, serving as a "handholding device to make others feel involved," (CD #28) but "virtually useless as a decision-making device." (CD #8)

The EUR IRG was less important, primarily because the assistant secretary and the IRG staff director thought IRG meetings had no particular educational value, and should be held only when decisions were needed.[28] The role of this IRG was also reduced since military and commercial matters, being largely multilateral, were handled by the Regional Politico-Military Affairs and Regional Politico-Economic Affairs (RPM and RPE) offices.[29]

The EA IRG was less busy than some others, in part because Assistant Secretary William Bundy preferred to deal directly with his numerous contacts, being very suspicious of the value of committees in government. It was used essentially as a sounding board for ideas, and for some con-

[27] Details of CASP preparation taken from CD interviews, and from those with IRG staff.

[28] Interviews with IRG staff director, CDs, and DASs in the Bureau of European Affairs.

[29] Ibid.

tingency planning. Even so, officers in this bureau argued that it helped standardize certain repetitive forms of decision making, such as contingency planning; that it insured that all interested parties were brought into the discussions; and that it facilitated organized consideration of a problem, even if the major decisions were ultimately made elsewhere.[30] The IRG for Africa was reasonably active and its use followed the pattern in EA, although it engaged in more formal decision making.[31]

The IRGs were not noticeably important in most crisis situations, because their membership did not contain needed country specialists. But through institutionalized contacts they did provide a mechanism for assembling and supporting crisis task forces quickly and efficiently.

With the coming of the new administration the IRGs too were transformed; they became Interdepartmental Groups (IGs) with membership similar to that of the IRGs, but with more of a study function than an operating one. The executive chairman's authority for the assistant secretary heading them was retracted.

It is obvious the SIG and IRGs were not particularly effective, although they did provide a forum for regular contact between the major foreign affairs agencies. The executive chairman's power was employed only rarely, and many important issues bypassed these bodies. As a consequence, they provided little support for the country director. When a CD was able to draw on the prestige of his assistant secretary, it was primarily due to personal competence, not institutionalized power. Only one of forty-six CDs volunteered that he had more clout because of the existence of the IRG chaired by his assistant secretary.

Twenty-eight CDs on balance saw some utility in the IRG, eleven had not found it useful, and seven did not feel

---

[30] Interviews with IRG staff directors, CDs, and DASs in the Bureau of East Asian and Pacific Affairs.

[31] Interviews with IRG staff director and CDs in the Bureau of African Affairs.

that they had had enough personal experience with it to comment. Favorable opinions, however, were mild in intensity, reflecting a general belief that these bodies did not live up to expectations. One CD said that situations where the IRG could be useful were only those which

> (a) cannot be worked out in detail at my level, and (b) where there are a number of agencies involved, because if you just have a problem with DOD, or with Commerce, you don't need the IRG. (CD #33)

Some CDs, although they felt it could be useful to have IRG discussions, doubted their ability to get clear decisions:

> In the IRG meetings I've been associated with, I've seen the assistant secretary develop a consensus of the people present, and bring people around, but if there's ever been a quite obvious division, the tendency has been not to thrash this out, but to get together bilaterally with whoever it was afterwards, or before if you knew this was going to be a problem, and try to work it out in the traditional way of one-to-one discussion. (CD #28)

Others said the IRGs failed frequently, especially when many people claimed a hearing and muddled discussion resulted. When they worked, it was because a specific problem was up for decision, and only those with a real interest played an active part. (CD #27)

Still other country directors were reluctant to suggest that problems be taken up by the IRG:

> If a matter goes to the IRG at the start, then the CD is diverted to preparing papers for it instead of actually deciding on the question. . . . As a result of all this, I try to stay away from the SIG and the IRG, because it leads to time spans of weeks, not days, and also means involvement in wider coordination and therefore education. They should be used to resolve, not to debate or to educate. (CD #15—paraphrase)

Another believed that no CD would want to say in effect, "either agree with me or take it to the IRG," because that smacked of an adversary relationship—"I'll see you in court." Rather, IRG should be reserved for those difficult substantive issues where the principals must argue it out, and not be used as a forum for bureaucratic battles. (CD #37)

How a CD reacted to the SIG and IRGs was of course primarily a result of his own experience. Usually a CD had his problems taken up by these groups only once or twice during his tour of duty. Either the CD was resolving most problems, or much of the real work of problem solving was being handled outside the NSAM 341 system. From other CD comments, it was clear that the latter was a better picture of what actually occurred.

This is not to say that the SIG and IRGs were not useful at times, for example during the BALPA exercise mentioned earlier. As one CD explained:

> It compelled organizations which it would have been very difficult to get to reduce their staffs . . . to reduce their staffs simply by pressure of, if you like, public opinion: "We're all cutting ours, what the hell is different about you guys? Why should you be exempt from this sort of operation?" So in that one case—actually it was a SIG decision—it was rammed down their throats, and in the end they had to take it and live with it, and are now in the process of implementing it. (CD #7)

One Asian CD reaffirmed that the SIG and IRG were occasionally instrumental in forcing decisions from recalcitrant agencies. It helped just to get the matter into a meeting chaired by Katzenbach or Bundy, in order to "demonstrate to them they are a minority of one," and to "force them to examine their own position harshly." Usually the end result was a settlement. (CD #38)

On balance, a majority of the CDs interviewed found the SIG and IRGs to be a mild improvement over the less struc-

141

tured methods of coordination in existence prior to creation of the NSAM 341 system, in spite of their very apparent weaknesses.

The inadequacies of the NSAM 341 system do not seem to have been fundamentally responsible for the failure of the CD system to develop fully, although the intended linkages between the SIG, IRGs, and country directors no doubt would have enhanced the power and prestige of the country director role if they had become more important. But the major problem seems to have been the futility of ascribing a government-wide role to the country directors at a time when State itself could not seriously claim such primacy at higher levels. Thus, what the CD really needed was to be part of a more powerful State Department, and this could have been achieved in a variety of ways in addition to or instead of the NSAM 341 mechanism.

The Country Level Interagency Committee

Country directors had great latitude in choosing other coordination procedures, being instructed only that they were to "organize and develop such contacts, channels, and mechanisms as are appropriate to and necessary for full interdepartmental leadership on country matters."[32] With the relative lack of importance of the SIG and IRG linkages, CDs were forced to attempt to carry out this responsibility by a variety of other, more informal devices.

Arthur Macmahon suggests four basic means of making the contact necessary for coordination to occur: person to person, through liaison officers or units, by group or committee meetings, and by circulation of materials.[33] The country directors used all these techniques, with emphasis on personal contacts and circulation of papers for clearance. Liaison usually was carried out informally. Use of for-

[32] FAMC 385, paragraph 7.

[33] Arthur Macmahon, *Administration in Foreign Affairs* (University, Ala.: University of Alabama Press, 1953), p. 167.

mal committees varied, since there was no agreement on their desirability. Thirty-two of forty-six CDs interviewed used some form of interagency committee. Twenty-three used only a general purpose group, meeting at intervals from weekly to every two to four months; five used continuing special purpose committees to consider specific problems; and four CDs had both a general purpose group and a special purpose group, usually with partially overlapping memberships. Of course, even CDs who used no formal group held ad hoc interagency meetings to work out specific problems. When a continuing group was used, its membership generally included the CD and one or more of his staff, a representative from AID if appropriate, from the Joint Chiefs and from the International Security Affairs section of the Pentagon, from USIA, from the Bureau of Intelligence and Research (INR), frequently from the CIA and the Bureau of Educational and Cultural Affairs of State (CU), and occasionally from one or more of the domestic agencies with foreign interests. Composition naturally varied according to the country and the degree of agency involvement. Table IV-1 summarizes the committees used in each of the five geographic bureaus.

There was general agreement that the main contribution of these groups was to facilitate information exchange and to educate participants. Only six of the forty-six CDs found the general purpose committee useful in decision making. Whether or not they were used therefore depended on how important the CD believed the informing function to be. As one of twenty-four supporting this use said,

> More than anything else, [these meetings] bring people together so that everybody is working from the same background, and everybody has a sense of being part of the same operation, part of the same grouping. (CD #22)

Another made the same point more explicitly:

143

TABLE IV-1
USE OF INTERAGENCY GROUPS BY BUREAU

Type of Interagency Group Used	African		Near Eastern and South Asian		East Asian and Pacific		Inter-American		European		Totals	
	N	%	N	%	N	%	N	%	N	%	N	%
General Purpose Only	6	75.0	6	60.0	5	45.5	2	20.0	4	57.1	23	50.0
Special Purpose Only	1	12.5	–	–	1	9.1	2	20.0	1	14.3	5	10.9
Both Used	–	–	–	–	2	18.2	1	10.0	1	14.3	4	8.7
None Used	1	12.5	4	40.0	3	27.3	5	50.0	1	14.3	14	30.4
Total CDs	8	17.4	10	21.7	11	23.9	10	21.7	7	15.2	46	100.00

Note: Cell percentages based on column sums. Marginal percentages based on proportion of total N in category. Does not include CDs not interviewed, so total bureau figures vary slightly (total number of CDs = 49; total N—those interviewed— = 46).

I frankly feel that they're of pretty limited utility. Now if I were looking at it from the other end, from the point of view say of the Peace Corps' [country X] desk officer, it might be very different, because they probably learn a good deal that otherwise would never come to their attention in the course of the meeting. (CD #7)

Twelve CDs of this group of twenty-four saw such meetings serving the additional purpose of enhancing the CD's role, as one explained:

As I see this, it is more a way of asserting State Department leadership, trying to keep all these people marching in the same direction, and of giving me an opportunity to bring them around to the extent they will go back to their agency to hopefully get the decision we want. (CD #39)

Sixteen CDs believed formal meetings were of limited value. Two were holding such meetings during the period of the interviews, but were considering dropping them; three were involved only in special purpose groups with more focused objectives; and eleven were holding no formal meetings. In the minds of the latter group, the disadvantages of the meetings, particularly their inability to make decisions and their inefficiency, outweighed any possible gains:

I don't [have an interagency meeting] because I think any established organization of that kind gets sterile quite quickly. . . . I know who to go to in the other agencies, and I do. (CD #14)

I'd much rather do things on an individual basis. You get a group together from the different agencies [and] they all take up the time arguing their own points of view. I actually think it's more efficient, quicker, and less wearing on the nerves to go to them separately. (CD #33)

145

Only two CDs said that such groups were useful *primarily* for decision making. One of them had only a special purpose group, and the other used no group at that moment because he felt the IRG could manage decision-making situations. Other supporters of these committees as means for making decisions still saw their primary utility as facilitating the exchange of information. One CD, whose group was acknowledged to be one of the most successful, argued that its impact on decision making might be delayed but nevertheless influential:

> The decision-making process is just that, a process. Part of the process is exchanging views, and ironing out differences, and agreeing on positions, and this is done in informal meetings. So to the extent that our [name of group] moves on these particular points, why, it is contributing to the decision-making process, so that decisions are taken more quickly and effectively by those who have the authority to decide. (CD #10)

Of the four CDs not yet mentioned, one did not call such meetings because he felt other agencies would not attend. No codable response was obtained from the others.

Two types of asymmetry were partially responsible for the weakness of these committees as decision-making devices. First, not all participants could contribute to any given decision. Second, the CD often lacked precise opposite numbers. Other agencies were not organized to the same depth as geographic bureaus of State, and the CD was often forced to choose between working with someone of roughly the same rank who had responsibility for a larger geographic area, and someone more junior with the same area of responsibility but without authority to decide. The situation facing one CD indicated the nature of the asymmetry problem:

> AID has no equivalent of the country director because the man with equivalent rank has too broad a geographic

146

territory, so a man who has part of the area comes to meetings, but this doesn't touch the major country I am responsible for, where 95 percent of the AID given in my area goes. The USIA man does have exactly the same area as I do, but he is really the only decision maker in the group, and most problems do not really involve him or USIA. So, the decisions have to be made on an ad hoc basis with the agencies involved, and at the level where you can get a decision. (CD #15—paraphrase)

One country director, who had both a special purpose group and a monthly interagency meeting, indicated why the latter was not a strong decision-making body, making the former necessary:

The interagency committee meets about once a month on a rather informal basis, but it is an information session, not a working session. . . . Part of the problem is that the people on this committee are generally of too low a level to actually make decisions. The people I get together in ad hoc working meetings are often not the same ones from their agencies who are part of the established committee. The people who can make decisions are just too burdened down to come to nonworking meetings. (CD #1—paraphrase)

Experiences of the CDs with these groups suggest that certain conditions are necessary, although not in themselves sufficient, for a committee to function effectively as a decision-making body. A majority of participants should have an action as opposed to an information interest in the specific matter at hand. The active participants should have roughly equal authority to commit their units, and this should be sufficient to allow adoption of any of the possible solutions considered (otherwise a conflict may arise between what it can do and what it deems most appropriate). Finally, the active participants should have roughly equal spheres of competence (breadth). The CDs found it diffi-

147

cult to regularly meet these conditions, which is why very few interagency committees at their level really could be called decision-making groups.

When opposite numbers in other agencies were asked about these meetings, they agreed that the major advantage was exchange of information. Unlike the CDs, however, they strongly supported them as a means for keeping current, particularly in agencies such as ISA and USIA. AID officers were less enthusiastic, but most noted that they were in frequent contact with CDs since they were physically located in the same building. Officials in domestic agencies (Agriculture, Treasury, Commerce) at times found such meetings helpful, but had a limited number of officers who could attend, and were forced to restrict their participation. This was true for ISA and USIA as well. The functional bureaus of State which were organized geographically, such as CU and INR, were generally favorable toward the meetings, but those such as the Bureau of Economic Affairs organized by subspecialties had no direct opposite numbers who could logically attend them. They dealt with CDs on an ad hoc basis as specific problems arose.

As a generalization, admittedly impressionistic because of the small percentage of opposite numbers in other agencies interviewed, it appeared that most CDs underestimated the value of interagency meetings for asserting their own influence. Almost without exception, opposite numbers who had actually attended them said they were better informed on country matters, understood the points of view of State and the other participants more clearly, and had an opportunity to make their own cases with greater effectiveness. It was to the country director's benefit to do whatever possible to improve coordination, particularly under his own auspices, but the evidence suggests the interagency committee was not always used to best advantage for this purpose. In some instances, this reflected CD orientations more attuned to the internal State Department and embassy-service dimensions of his responsibilities, rather than to providing interagency leadership.

Interagency Conflicts

It is tempting to attribute agency disputes that impede a consistent foreign policy to narrow bureaucratic interests, or to abrasive personality conflicts. If these were the only, or even the major sources of difficulty, such imbroglios would be easier to deal with than they are. It is naïve to deny the existence of real and fundamental differences in agency approach and mission, in legal requirements, in constituencies and in responsibilities. More often than not, policies are set on the basis of reaction to particular problems, rather than in the framework of one consistent grand strategy (although all participants may be guided by the national interest as they see it).

The need for coordinating devices such as the SIG, IRG, and others used by CDs are demonstrations of this inherent inconsistency. Almost all of the events, mechanisms, and conflicts described in this study can be considered as manifestations of or reactions to a basic fact of bureaucratic life: Where multiple units with differing responsibilities are involved, conflict will arise from differing conceptions of organizational goals, missions, and interests, and from different interpretations of the facts of a situation resulting from differing perceptions. In a complex policy environment, these conflicting interests are not only present but are necessary to insure that all important viewpoints are given adequate representation.

The challenge that faced the country directors was not to eliminate differences of opinion, but to manage them. As one CD stated:

Almost by definition there are going to be differences. The question is not whether there are differences, but how do people behave in the process of trying to resolve the differences that necessarily exist? (CD #2)

149

The basic sources of difficulty for CDs were the differing primary interests of the several agencies with foreign affairs involvements. Their legitimate desire to maintain harmonious relations with client countries might be directly opposed to the equally legitimate interests of other agencies to resolve particular problems or to assist domestic client groups. One CD told of this kind of difficulty:

> The Bureau of European Affairs is concerned with maintaining good relations with West Germany, "our closest ally," while Treasury, with its concern for the balance of payments deficit, is naturally antagonistic toward the Germans because of their reluctance to assume the major costs of keeping American forces there, and their lack of enthusiasm for revaluation of the mark. (CD #34—paraphrase)

Of course, differences could be carried to extreme. One CD recalled that in the course of attempting to convince a senior official of Agriculture that the domestic and international interests of the United States needed to be reconciled, he was told:

> "Look. I'm not the secretary of state; I'm not the president; I'm not the ambassador, and I don't give a good goddamn about the problems of the United States abroad with [country X]! I'm paid to look after agricultural interests, and that's going to be that." (CD #10)

Most conflicts reflected a broader vision, but diverse and opposing goals were accepted as a fact of life by most members of the foreign affairs community. Another CD, when asked if it was difficult to work with Agriculture and Treasury because their vision was filled by surplus crops and balance of payments, replied,

> Yes—but against that you have to set the fact that we undoubtedly appear just the opposite to the Treasury and Agriculture people. . . . I'm sure you get the same thing

150

from them; we aren't as aware of balance of payments problems as we should be; we aren't as concerned about disposing of surpluses as we should be. I think this is just the nature of the work, and of the individual's primary interest. (CD #22)

In some cases, the responsibilities of other agencies had been given the force of law, which might conflict directly with those of State and the CD, leading to an impasse:

> You cannot get other agencies to abdicate their responsibilities to the Department of State. They can't afford to, and it would be illegal if they did. Say, for example, the Department of Agriculture had something that they statutorily were supposed to do, and I felt that from a foreign policy point of view it was not right. Maybe we could work out something, but if I tried to tell them that the State Department had statutory responsibility for carrying out foreign policy which was contrary to the law which Congress passed for them, you can see immediately that gets right into a conflict that has to go to the highest level in the government to get resolved. (CD #14)

Organizational and technical factors also complicated working relationships. One CD argued that country-level officers in State had more authority than their counterparts in other agencies, so that any decision, however simple, took more time to make because it had to be cleared at a higher level in the other agency. (CD #29) Another said that in some agencies, an issue might have to go all the way to the top, even if State were willing to resolve it at a lower level. At times, too, this occurred because of the legal necessity for a particular official to sign certain agreements, or because technical precision was critically important. (CD #40) Sometimes, as with Defense, relations were difficult because its several parts acted as if they were independent, and the CD first had to determine the authoritative agency

151

position. Finally, a weak agency such as USIA was at times reluctant to compromise at lower levels because it was protective of its position. (CD #1)

Naturally an agency was not equally troublesome on every issue. A normally difficult one might present little or no problem if its conceived prerogatives and interests were only peripherally involved. One CD, for example, noted that since few agencies had programs in his countries, contact was primarily for information and for solving small problems, so that he had no interagency difficulties. (CD #2) On the other hand, an agency with major interests and responsibilities was expected to present more problems:

> There are certain [agencies] that are members of the IRG/SIG that have major responsibilities overseas, and naturally one would expect that they would be very deeply involved and often might think long and hard before they agreed to a certain suggested policy. Those that have a somewhat more marginal or peripheral interest, that sort of weave in and out of the picture, we would have less of a dialogue with and perhaps less of a problem. (CD #23)

The overall importance of a particular issue also influenced working relationships. One Latin American CD found that the bigger and more urgent the issue, the more reasonable other agencies became. (CD #26)[34]

Among the most difficult problems were those involving use of scarce resources. One Asian CD detailed a recent case:

> You throw a really insuperable problem at these people, and they all have the same amount of difficulty with it. A good example right now is the difficulty we're having trying to slice down what's left of the AID pie. It's so damn small, I really have a great deal of sympathy for the people who are trying to chop this up, because you're going

[34] For a general discussion of this argument, see Wilensky, pp. 75-81.

to get what you need for Thailand, over and above what they can see to give you right now. Since we're in a deficit situation, [it] is going to have to come right out of the hide of the Korea program, where we have fixed commitments, or out of the Laos program, where really everything depends on it, or from what we can do for Indonesia. That's one of the excruciating decisions you have to make. (CD #41)

The resource problem was in the minds of all those who were responsible for operating programs, and substantial support from CDs and opposite numbers was gained for the generalization that interunit conflict is minimized when adequate resources are available for the core projects of all units, but that when resources are scarce, conflict results as each unit urges that its projects be given priority. Moreover, it was often noted that at the working level, resource decisions are ultimately made by the unit controlling the resources, regardless of who sets policy. Other units may be able to veto certain projects on grounds that they are not in the larger interest, but are almost never able to force those controlling the resources to commit the latter against their will.

Certain difficulties, of course, were attributable to individuals and personalities. Some country directors said it was at times possible to tell when particular individuals had left or taken over an office, because working relationships improved or deteriorated. (CD #29) However, most CDs said the majority of problems grew from agency rather than individual factors. Specifically, thirty said they had problems traceable to specific agencies, while twelve said they had no real agency difficulties. One declined comment; two felt that the distinction was not meaningful and that the substance was the primary determinant of working difficulties; and one was not asked the question. Of the specific agencies cited, Treasury, Agriculture, and Defense were overwhelmingly held to be the most difficult. Problems with

Treasury and Agriculture usually grew from what CDs felt were narrow views on specific issues—agricultural price support and surplus crop disposition for Agriculture, and balance of payments for Treasury. With Defense, there were several general sources of difficulty. One was a difference of perspective between the military desire to prepare for the worst possible future situation and State's concern with the most likely future developments. (CD #5) This was often reflected in substantive policy disputes. Second, the large number of quasi-independent units often made it difficult and time-consuming to determine the DOD position. Finally, at times there were controversies over whether State or Defense should "control" the action, particularly in the politico-military arena. The only other agency receiving more than a smattering of mention on this question was AID. Some CDs also made a general distinction between foreign affairs agencies and those domestically oriented but having some international programs. These responses are listed in Table IV-2, and total more than thirty because multiple citations were solicited.

Methods of Problem Solving

Country directors had to solve problems in spite of such difficulties, and they employed a variety of techniques besides the interagency group in this effort. The most useful tool in these efforts probably was knowledge of other's problems and outlooks, gained over a period of time. The explanation given by one African CD was typical:

> I think the first element in effective interagency relationships is the constant contact between my desk officers and their counterparts in other agencies. . . . They should be seeing each other constantly. Then when a problem comes up, they know each other's viewpoint, up to a point at least. (CD #18)

Another provided more detail on the possibilities and limitations of this approach:

154

TABLE IV-2

AGENCIES OR DEPARTMENTS
MOST DIFFICULT TO DEAL WITH

Treasury	18
Agriculture	16
Defense	16
Agency for International Development	4
Domestic Agencies in general	4
Bureau of the Budget	3
United States Information Agency	2
Labor	1
Commerce	1
Justice	1
Interior	1
Federal Power Commission	1
Bureau of International Organization Affairs (State)	1

One of the prime things necessary for a country director to have success is to know the key people in other agencies on a close and flexible basis. . . . If you don't do this, you run the risk of being nitpicked bureaucratically. This close tie can only go so far, of course—on matters of fundamental difference, the greatest friendship in the world won't resolve them for you. Leadership and persuasion won't work, and the issue will have to be fought out at higher levels. (CD #27—paraphrase)

A related service which could prevent many problems from becoming unnecessarily difficult was to insure distribution of basic facts to all parties. Because so many agencies participate in some issues, this was not always easy:

You have to be sure that they see all of the communications and that we have received all of [the other agency's] communications. . . . In point of fact the problem I have right now largely originated because there was not complete across-the-board distribution of all the pertinent messages. (CD #9)

More generally,

> the technique of trying to assure a favorable channel for decisions you are going to want in the future is largely to fill an information role. You need to provide information relevant to the country in question, whether or not it is favorable to your own case. (CD #4—paraphrase)

One Asian CD, just returned from duty in the country for which he was responsible, saw his knowledge as his most important asset:

> It's just that I happen to know more about those programs than most people back here do, from having been intimately involved in [country X]. . . . Without that expertise, I suppose you could do it, but it would be much more difficult, because I know where skeletons are buried in many of these programs, and I know where corners have been cut. I know what we planned two and three years ago, and what the arguments were for and against. This is extremely useful. I've got longer continuity on this country and on these programs than [do] my colleagues in any other agency. (CD #39)

Another key to success was to avoid becoming a bureaucrat in the pejorative sense. There had to be a premium on finding how to get things done, and results counted and not one's own sensitivities and prerogatives. (CD #2) This required flexibility and a willingness to accommodate other agency positions. (CD #11) Ultimately, the hard problems had to be confronted.

> There's a certain amount of rug-merchant work that goes on; one is aware that another agency will have a special interest, and one sometimes plots one's tactics . . . very

carefully. But I don't think that you can ever achieve the kind of result you want to achieve if this is what's paramount in your mind. My own belief is that sooner or later . . . they've got to put their cards on the table [and] you've got to put your cards out on the table. . . . I like to talk the thing out, really find out what's on the other fellow's mind. If he's got a real problem, then it is a problem to be dealt with. (CD #24)

Similarly, another said:

The country director is not just representing the State Department. He's trying to understand what the other guy has in mind. He may have a very legitimate problem. There's no reason he hasn't got a right to his views, just as the State Department may have a right to its position. I think that 90 percent of the problems can be solved with this technique. (CD #1)

In the event that none of this background work resolved the problem, the CD still had other ways of forcing action:

Now, very often you get a bureaucratic hangup from a guy who's just sitting on something that he doesn't like and he doesn't know why he doesn't like it, so he just wants to nitpick the thing to death, or it just kind of gets buried. At that time, you get the stick of dynamite out, and you call his boss up and say, "What the hell's going on? Let's move. If you've got a problem, let's talk it out, let's not sit on this one," and therefore you don't have the problem. . . . And, of course, in the last resort you always have your boss calling up his boss, calling the assistant secretary or the deputy assistant secretary or somebody like that. [But] that you save. By and large, I think you very rarely have to resort to that. (CD #1)

While almost all CDs preferred to negotiate at their own level, knowing when a problem should move up was also important. The country director should

157

not wait too long, and [should] know when to call in the heavy artillery. In other words, don't gnaw away at these problems too long and get them too hard frozen in concrete. Know when to run up to the front office and ask them to call in at higher levels and break deadlocks. (CD #41)

There was wide agreement that the country director was inviting difficulty if he did not insure an issue was clearly focused as early as possible. Drafting a message or an instruction was the most effective way to accomplish this:

[A draft] concentrates attention very much on the issue, whereas long discussions may not. An actual instruction, in the form of a cable directing the ambassador to do something, focuses attention miraculously, because either they approve it, or disapprove it and do something [else], because it is going to go out. (CD #16)

Drafting a message or instruction also helped the CD gain acceptance for his proposals since the drafter of a telegram is often the prime controller of the process in bureaucracy. (CD #36) Far more coordination was carried out by reacting to drafts and then clearing them in person or by phone than by meetings. (CD #31) There was strong support by CDs and opposite numbers on the advantages of drafts over general discussions as a decision-forcing device.

More generally, decisions were reached by negotiating, persuading, and building support rather than by raw confrontation. One CD felt that ultimately, what was involved in resolving problems was

argumentation and the process of negotiation. I personally don't try to bulldoze things through, and cite the presidential order which gives certain authority to the State Department. [It's] better that we look at the law, look at the regulations, look at the established policy guidelines, and try to get something through on the basis of negotiation. (CD #16)

This did not mean, however, that means to "facilitate" a favorable outcome were not sought:

> Sometimes one enlists support through informal communications channels of the ambassador or the country team. Other times one plots one's course very carefully, escalating to the other fellow's superiors. That I do as little as possible. But there are some occasions when you have a pretty good idea that you're going to get full support from higher levels here. (CD #24)

At times alliances helped to bring a dispute with a third agency to a satisfactory conclusion:

> In [one] case, another agency was also interested in the same operation, and we've been fighting the battle with this other [official], and [it was] just one headache after another. And I just said, "Now, look, in this round, old boy, you carry the ball to this guy. I'm tired of beating myself to death." Well, you know, we finally got him to move, but it's plodding. You hit him and hit him, and it finally works. That agency had a greater interest than we did in the problem, and we finally got him to move. (CD #1)

As this example shows, persistence was also a necessary talent for the successful country director. As one said, "you really need a tough manipulator who can keep these people's feet to the fire until they make the right decision." (CD #39)

Country directors thus had a variety of techniques and approaches available for dealing with interagency problems. None, of course, provided automatic solutions, and the success of the individual country director ultimately depended on the intensity of conflict, his own persuasiveness and expertise, and the degree to which he was accepted as overall coordinator by his opposite numbers.

TWO EMBASSIES AND TWO FUNCTIONS: CONFLICT AND BALANCE

The country director's major remaining interactions were with American missions in his countries of responsibility, and with representatives of those countries accredited to the United States. In each case, the country director was the primary link between the mission and the U.S. government. It was his responsibility to insure that official policy was accurately transmitted to each mission, and to secure an adequate hearing for their points of view. An inherent tension existed between performance of these aspects of the CD's role and his responsibilities to place relations with his countries into the broader context of United States interests. The more sympathetic the CD to the requirements of positive bilateral relations, the more likely he would be considered too parochial by his opposite numbers in the Washington bureaucracy.

American Missions Abroad

It will be recalled that country directors were directed to be "single focal points in Washington to serve our ambassadors."[35] While the more junior desk officers and officers-in-charge had held similar responsibilities, they had often been hampered by the disparity in rank and experience between themselves and the ambassadors. They thus tended to be restricted to housekeeping details, while the ambassadors looked higher in State, to the assistant secretary in most cases, for guidance. Differences in rank between CDs and ambassadors were narrowed, so that in most cases the country director became the ambassador's primary Washington contact. Thirty-seven of the forty-six CDs interviewed said that ambassadors worked directly with them.

[35] Rusk, "Message to His Colleagues."

Ambassadors who chose to deal directly with the assistant secretary or even higher generally represented the United States in major countries, and apparently believed their problems or personal status required senior attention. This mode of operation was not necessarily in the ambassador's own best interest, because it slowed the reaction time of the government:

> In a place like [country X], where you almost always have a high-powered ambassador, they have a tendency to cable for the president or the secretary of state's eyes only, often using the first person and emphatic "I implore you . . ." form. This has little effect, because the senior officials will ask the country director what he wants to do about the problem, anyhow. (CD #34—paraphrase)

Of course, an ambassador who routinely corresponded with the CD could emphasize his concern by writing to a higher official. This could strengthen the CD's hand:

> Once in a while, when [the ambassador] has something that he thinks needs the attention of the assistant secretary, . . . he will write directly to him, but he will be sure to send a copy to me with a little note saying, "I wanted to show you how much weight I attach to this by writing directly to the assistant secretary. I know you would have brought this to his attention, but I thought it might help you in working. . . ." (CD #28)

If it was to the ambassador's advantage to use the CD as his primary contact, it was to the country director's benefit for him to do so:

> When it becomes apparent that an Ambassador and a Country Director work as a closely knit team with views and objectives almost always in harmony, some of the former's magic rubs off on the latter. "What is the use," asks the wise bureaucrat, "of fobbing off the Country Di-

rector today if there's likely to be a rocket in tomorrow from the Ambassador on the same subject?"[36]

This implies that the ambassador and the country director almost always agree. This was not always true, of course, but when across-the-board agreement exists between post and CD, its source needs exploration. If it occurs because interchanges of information and opinion lead to a mutual understanding of both bilateral relations effects and domestic demands, such parallelism may indicate a balanced perspective about global U.S. interests. But if it reflects a papering over of real differences and a slavish adherence to the ambassador's views by the country director, a danger exists that parochialism will dominate. An example of the latter possibility shows how it may arise:

> We don't really find ourselves in opposition to them. We try not to second-guess them on matters where they really are involved, where they're on the ground and judging what's happening. . . . Differences tend to be glossed over, rather than dealt with directly or bluntly. . . . One moves with care, if one is an FSO-2 or even an FSO-1, in challenging a Career Minister or a Career Ambassador with thirty-five years' experience behind him, who's the president's own man by appointment and who has access to the secretary. (CD #5)

This was perhaps an unusual case, since thirty-four of forty-six CDs said that there was a difference of perspective between themselves and the embassy staff which could lead to taking opposing sides on some issues. The delicate task for the country director was to decide when to side with and when to oppose the post, based on his own evaluations of proposed actions. One experienced CD explained the balancing act he had to go through:

> When you are in country X, your responsibility is that you're supposed to find all the information that bears on

[36] Spain, loc. cit.

an issue, and you are supposed to make recommendations. . . . And, of course, you are particularly interested in making sure that the U.S. government, a great and sometimes unwieldy organization, easily distracted, doesn't overlook the importance of your country, the importance of what the U.S. should try to be doing. So you try to make the best possible case for your country. . . .

Back here, starting at the office level, the country director level, you have a dual responsibility. You have that responsibility of getting the most appropriate and the best attention for the countries in your area, but the fact of it is that you now have several instead of one country. There may be competing interests among those several countries already, so you're no longer the advocate for the plaintiff or the defendant, you're sort of the trial court. Then you also know . . . from past experience that the assistant secretary has certain doubts; that AID has told you there just won't be any money for that purpose; that there are just too many other priorities. So you know a lot about the Washington scene; you know how difficult it will be, that certain things really will be impossible despite what the field recommends. And, of course, you have opinions of your own by the time you get back here. . . .

So: No man can serve two masters, but you have to try. . . . You know obviously that you just have to try to straighten this out for balance. That's supposed to be one of the traits of the business: to retain the confidence of the people [in the field], and to retain the confidence of the people in Washington. [Laughs] (CD #3)

It should be remembered that senior officers in the field and the CD usually had the same background, each having served many years in the Foreign Service, and each having experience with the country or at least the area concerned. Differences in perspective therefore cannot generally be attributed to differences in socialization. Rather, the primary cause was the different environment in which each side operated:

> When Ambassador [X] went out, because of a combination of circumstances he had an exceptionally long period of briefing. . . . For almost two months, I was seeing him day in and day out. I think the two of us were in complete accord on a whole range of things. We had a chance to discuss them, talk them out thoroughly, and reach a clear meeting of the minds. It's been very interesting [to see] . . . the way in which we proceeded to diverge, each taking our respective positions. . . . You're bound to take these positions, and I'm not all that concerned about it. I think there's a certain amount, if you will, of difficulty between the field and headquarters. (CD #41)

More succinctly, one CD said this phenomenon was "like looking through different ends of a telescope—you get an entirely different view." (CD #11)

This difference of perspective was generally observed. It was not related to the level of contact between the CD and the embassy. It was equally likely to occur whether the CD communicated with the ambassador or with the deputy chief of mission (DCM), as Table IV-3 clearly shows.

TABLE IV-3

LEVEL OF CD CONTACT WITH EMBASSY

Difference of Perspective	Ambassador		DCM		Other*		Total	
	N	%	N	%	N	%	N	%
Yes	28	75.7	6	75.0	1	100.0	35	76.1
No	9	24.3	2	25.0	–	–	11	23.9
Total	37	80.4	8	17.4	1	2.2	46	100.0

Notes: Cell percentages based on column sum; marginal percentage indicates proportion of total N in each category.

* Atypical case where CD had responsibility where there was no field post. Difference of perspective answer based on previous experience.

The country director's task was therefore to insure that embassy arguments and recommendations were receiving full consideration without accepting them in every case or compromising a broader viewpoint. There was some irony in his position, since he was likely to be seen by opposite numbers in Washington as suffering from "localitis" at the same time the embassy felt he was slighting the interests of bilateral relations.

Devices employed to keep disagreements within bounds were similar to those used to minimize agency differences in Washington. The central thread in each case was good communication. In the words of one CD, "We are all victims of our own environment. The role of the country director is to make each understand the other's environment." (CD #1) In addition to the formal telegrams, the primary means of remaining in close contact were visits back and forth, the telephone, and the "official-informal" letter. The latter was frequently employed, because it was a semi-private channel:

> The official-informal . . . [is] a way of giving the embassy some of the background thinking on a problem that you're unwilling to put in a message and have everybody else read. That's about what it comes down to. . . . If, for example, you have a complaint, a reprimand in effect of some sort vis-à-vis the embassy ("Why haven't you been doing this?" or "Why on earth did you come in with that nutty idea?"), then you would use the official-informal, and then you don't spread around the word. (CD #5)

Because these letters required no clearance, they were useful for exchanging half-formed ideas, asking for help in bringing pressure on a recalcitrant agency, or sounding out reactions to initiatives that the CD or the ambassador might be considering. In spite of recurring campaigns to suppress them because they deprived some interested parties of full information and were not always filed as were more formal communications, their use was virtually universal. When available, the telephone was also of great help, particularly during fast-developing episodes.

Most country directors thought, however, that nothing was as helpful as an occasional trip to the post. Unlike the letter, phone call, or telegram, trips made it possible to discuss a whole range of matters, large and small:

> Very often, you get a tendency for things to go on in a certain direction, which you'd like to stop, or at least change or divert. A trip to the field or a consultation back here is practically the only way you can do it, because you've got to be able to sit down and talk about the whole pattern which has been established. And a trip to the field is most important, because an ambassador is limited in his effectiveness by effectiveness in the embassy down the line. . . . The only way you can find out is going to the field. (CD #18)

A frequent complaint of CDs was that stringent budgetary limitations had been placed on such travel. Many CDs saw this as false economy given the benefits that could accrue:

> I've been out of [country X] three months and I've been on this job two, and already I find that I'm getting a little bit out of touch. I would think it essential to visit the post at least once a year, and I would hope that the department would have enough money to make this possible. I think it's pretty shortsighted if they don't. (CD #39)

It would be misleading, however, to assume that there was a constant strain between post and CD, even if there were occasional disagreements. These differences were "more in sorrow than in anger, for all concerned." (CD #16) Embassies relied on the country director, but recognized that differences were inevitable:

> They do depend on the country director or the old office director very much, to push their problems, to be their

eyes and ears at home, to be their advocates—it's partially a servicing function. But at the same time they realize that [the CD] may from time to time have to take a different viewpoint. . . . They don't always expect 100 percent agreement with every suggestion, and they wouldn't think much of the country director if they got it that way. (CD #23)

Because of the higher rank of the country director compared to his predecessors, there was a general consensus among CDs and ambassadors that the embassy's needs were being better cared for under the new system. Adjectives such as "good," "close," "close and constant," "intimate," and "excellent" were used much more frequently by CDs to describe these relationships than were their opposites. Ambassadors surveyed in 1970 corroborated these comments, and preferred the CD arrangement by better than three to one.[37] In short, the interaction between field posts and country directors was probably the most satisfactory for each participant of any discussed.

Foreign Missions in Washington

Great variations in relationships with diplomatic missions in Washington were reported by country directors. The CD had limited latitude in dealing with foreign diplomats, simply because they were representatives of sovereign nations accredited to the president. He could try to persuade them to work closely with him, but had little recourse if they chose not to do so. Major differences were found in level and frequency of contact, warmth of relationships and the extent to which approaches to other parts of the U.S. government were channeled through the CD. Factors accounting for these variations included the personality of the ambassador and his sense of status, the range of embassy activity and interests, the current state of relations between

[37] See Chapter VIII.

the United States and the country in question, and the diplomatic experience of the country and its representatives.

The modal pattern of CD-foreign representative contact saw the CD dealing directly with the ambassador on most but not all matters. Relations with the ambassador and his staff were frequent and contained a significant amount of informal interchange. By a much narrower margin, the country director was the primary U.S. government contact for these representatives.

Embassies were encouraged to work through CDs when the new system began, and most did so. Thirty country directors indicated that foreign ambassadors worked directly with them on most matters. When these ambassadors were instructed to make representations at a higher level, meetings were arranged through the CD, and he was frequently present when they took place. Seven said that they dealt with the minister or minister-counselor of the embassy (the second-ranking official) while the ambassador always dealt at higher levels; three found themselves working with a lower ranking embassy official; five had a mixed pattern with some ambassadors working with them and one or more operating at higher levels; and one had no representatives of his country in Washington. The primary reasons an ambassador worked at higher levels were the importance of his country's relations with the United States and his own personal preferences. Major allies and nations such as Japan and the Soviet Union, usually represented by very senior and prestigious ambassadors, were able to demand and obtain direct contact up to and including the president, and routinely with the secretary of state. Certain ambassadors were instructed always to deal only at the most senior levels of government, as one CD explained:

> The [representatives of country] have a style: they want to deal with the center of power; they want to deal through Washington rather than through our embassy in [X]; and they want to deal at as high a level as possible

168

in Washington. So [Mr. Y], in charge of defense in [X] wants to deal with Mr. Clifford, and this is the way that [their] whole operation is focused, so you get direct communication between [Mr. Y] and Clifford. (CD #12)

In other cases, the choice was personal and could interfere with the embassy's ability to present its case:

One very rank-conscious ambassador from a new and minor country tries to go to the assistant secretary or the deputy assistant secretary. This is unwise. He would do better by taking up problems in the first instance with the CD. (CD #27—paraphrase)

Sometimes a combination of personal pride and country importance presented a delicate problem:

Relations with the [representatives of country X] in Washington are not as close as I would hope, but this may be due to the fact that I am new here and have not had time to develop them, and because the previous ambassador from this country established a pattern, since he spoke only to President Kennedy, Secretary Rusk, and possibly God. (CD #36—paraphrase)

CDs tried to develop helpful relationships with foreign ambassadors, as one explained, so that they would be more inclined to work through them. (CD #29) Ultimately, however, this depended on what he was able to accomplish for the embassy:

One of the keys as to whether or not the ambassador will work directly with the country director is an understanding on his part about the lanes of power in State. If he understands them, and finds that the country director is in them, he will deal with him. If he finds that the country director is just a beefed-up desk officer, he will not take the time to deal with him and will make his personal approaches at a higher level. (CD #36—paraphrase)

When compared to the desk officer, the country director was generally held to be able to do more for the ambassador, because of his additional rank.

The closeness of relations between the embassy and the CD was determined in part by personality and operating style, and was also influenced by the state of relations between the two countries. If relations were tense, either side might limit interchanges with the other to what was required by diplomatic protocol:

> Our relations are really quite limited with the [country Z] embassy, but this is the way the [country Z] government wants it, and we recognize this and respect it. . . . [Country Z] is in an extreme state of xenophobia right now, very much pulled into their shell, and I think one way in which we've managed to keep in pretty good relations under this correct frame of reference is by respecting this. (CD #41)

Another CD noted that because of the August 1968 invasion of Czechoslovakia, social relations with participating countries had been curtailed to indicate U.S. government displeasure, and contacts limited to formal business. (CD #40)

The formality or informality of CD-foreign mission relations also depended upon personal and cultural preferences of the diplomatic personnel, as one CD explained:

> There are very few African diplomats here who have had a great deal of experience, and therefore we're advising them on things, or they're consulting with us on things that wouldn't be normal, traditional, diplomatic practice. To an African, by and large . . . the personal relationship is extremely important, and you won't get much other than formal cooperation unless you establish it. (CD #18)

There were advantages for the CD in close relations, as one from EA found:

I can now say things to them that if we had a more formal and distant relationship I would not be able to say, and they've begun to gain a certain confidence that I really have got their interests at heart—that I'm not just a watchdog, you know, with a fundamentally hostile attitude toward them. . . . And they're readily accessible to bounce an idea off, too. If you're wondering what the [country X] reaction to something is, it's very easy to take one out to lunch and find out what it is. Helpful—but not definitive. (CD #7)

Ultimately, however, the warmth and degree of formality in relationships was a choice of the foreign government and embassy staff.

The frequency of contact between the CD and the diplomatic mission, as contrasted to its warmth, depended on the nature of bilateral business and whether it was carried on predominately in Washington or the foreign capital; the amount of assistance the mission required; and the degree to which the CD was the primary Washington contact. The interviews showed that four CDs had primarily formal contacts with the embassies, limited to relatively infrequent diplomatic activities; thirty-three included their relationships in the primarily informal and frequent category; five said that their relations were informal but infrequent (reflecting little bilateral business conducted in Washington), and five found mixed patterns because of different operating styles among their countries of responsibility. There were none in the formal-frequent category, suggesting that frequent contact led to more informal relationships.

There were three basic reasons for infrequent contact, assuming there was no freeze in relations: Limited bilateral issues existed with the country; most bilateral discussions were conducted between the American embassy and the host country's government (rather than through the country's Washington embassy); or the local embassy bypassed the country director. In the first category, one CD noted

171

that his local ambassadors were basically inactive. They did no lobbying and had little reason to talk to other agencies since there were few American programs in their countries. (CD #2) In the second category, several country directors found their countries chose to deal with the American embassy in the field:

> I think it's true of most countries where we have programs, and probably true of most countries, period, that more of the really substantive work is done through our embassy in that country, than the other way around. . . . Their operation here is more one of keeping themselves informed, [of] trying to gather additional information on attitudes within the American government and American public, rather than of action. It's very unusual for them to come in and make a representation to us on an operational problem. (CD #7)

The third major reason for infrequent relations was an embassy's choice to deal with other parts of government directly, as in the following case:

> I don't have particularly close contact with their political counselor, and their ambassador doesn't see too many people, either. In part, they run a congressional lobby, but their heaviest emphasis is on public relations. The embassy staff tries to be friendly, but they avoid becoming involved in substantive matters with this country directorate. The economic minister is very active, and does a considerable amount of work with other parts of the government. In short, contacts with the [country A] embassy here are not an important part of our work. (CD #42—paraphrase)

Frequent interactions, however, did not necessarily indicate that the CD was the embassy's primary contact. There was almost always considerable interchange between embassies of larger countries and other parts of the government, along with frequent communication with the CD.

State has never required that all approaches to the U.S. government come through its geographic offices, and CDs were somewhat ambivalent about this. It would be impossible and possibly undesirable for them to handle or monitor all contacts of the more active missions:

> We've never tried to establish a flat fiat that nobody in our government can talk to a [country B] official without clearing with us. We'd be swamped with them if we ever tried. Secondly, I've never tried to tell the [country B] embassy here that they can't, if they want to, go to the Department of Commerce or whatever. Again, it would be too many. Moreover, I don't want [country B government] to clap a lid of that kind on our people in [their capital], either. (CD #6)

However, some country directors had difficulty following embassy activities, particularly if other U.S. agencies chose not to keep them informed. Most thought it best to encourage direct contacts, but also to insist they be kept informed of major substantive discussions. One CD described how this was managed:

> I know the [country C] representatives have a purchasing mission, and they deal a lot on technical problems of procurement, and financial arrangements, and shipping and insurance, agricultural commodities. Well, there's no sense in their coming through us on that sort of thing, but on basic questions of policy, such as whether or not we will have a PL 480 agreement this year, and if so what's the magnitude of it, and what sort of payment terms. . . . They know that if there are policy questions, the department wants to get involved, and they tend to submit their requests through us. (CD #28)

In other cases the CD was the primary contact, particularly for countries which did not have experienced representatives in Washington:

173

Since they may not have quite as wide-ranging contacts in this country . . . as some of the older, more established countries that have been here a long time, they might tend to look a little bit more to us for assistance in things that the older established countries do on their own, without bothering us at all. We try to help them in every way we can. On the other hand, we try not to let this interfere with carrying out our own policy, protecting our own interests. (CD #23)

In such situations, a strong CD's help could have a salutary influence on U.S. relations with that country.

It is understandable that patterns of relationship between CDs and embassies should be extremely varied, when one considers the great differences in countries and their interests. The CD's responsibility was to provide what assistance he could, to monitor the activities of the embassies, and to be the focal point for them in Washington, even if they did most of their work with other agencies. One can generalize, however, that those embassies whose ambassadors dealt directly with the country director were much more likely to use the CD and his staff as their primary U.S. government contact than were those embassies whose ambassadors dealt at higher levels of the government. Table IV-4 gives details of this relationship.

One remaining facet of the country director-foreign embassy relation deserves mention: whether there was a risk of the CD's becoming an advocate for the foreign government at the expense of United States interests. As detailed in Chapter III, slightly less than one-third (twelve of forty-one asked) said this was a potential problem, but none felt it was insurmountable. One of the majority who believed it need not cause difficulties explained why:

Relations are better, of course, if you can give them what they want, but the representatives of the countries I deal with are pretty civilized, cosmopolitan people, and can extract the personal regard from the professional duty.

TABLE IV-4

CountrY Director-ForeiGN EmbassY Relations

Highest Ranking Foreign Representative Dealing with CD	Is CD the Primary U.S. Government Contact for Embassy?							
	Yes		No		Mixed		Total	
	N	%	N	%	N	%	N	%
Ambassador	20	87.0	7	36.8	3	75.3	30	65.2
Minister/ Counselor	1	4.3	6	31.6	–	–	7	15.2
No. 3 Man or Lower	–	–	3	15.8	–	–	3	6.5
Mixed	1	4.3	3	15.8	1	25.0	5	10.9
Not Codable	1	4.3	–	–	–	–	1	2.2
Total	23	50.0	19	41.3	4	8.7	46	100.0

Notes: Cell percentages based on column sum. Marginal percentages based on proportion of total N in that category, either row or column. Mixed code means that CD in question had one embassy in each of two categories. To find total number with at least one embassy in a category, add the total in the mixed category to that category total.

So I feel no tension if I have to tell them something unpleasant. If anything, there may be a tendency to blame them too much if things don't work out pleasantly. (CD #15—paraphrase)

It will be recalled that some CD opposite numbers were not so sanguine about the CD's ability to retain objectivity. Several CDs took specific exception to this allegation of bias, arguing as one did that "It is our duty, or my duty, to be an advocate, not of the countries, but of our best interests with respect to [them], whatever the problem may be." (CD #19) Another said that those who felt that he and his staff were too favorably inclined toward the group of countries they dealt with were victims of fallacious reasoning, confusing awareness of realities about their area with advocacy. (CD #2)

In general, one can reasonably conclude that CD relationships with foreign embassy personnel were generally effective, although their nature was out of the CD's control for the most part. There were, moreover, indications that a sensitive CD could have a favorable impact on U.S. relations with his countries of responsibility, by helping them to carry out their own representational responsibilities.

CONCLUSION

The interactions of the country director as he attempted to control and monitor U.S. relations with his countries of responsibility were indeed complex. He was clearly the "man in the middle," attempting to remain on satisfactory working terms while asserting his right to be included in all major aspects of U.S. government activity for his countries. His task was complicated by the incompletely defined and only partially accepted role he filled. Success in such circumstances was primarily the result of his own persistence, abilities, and knowledge, since it was clear that he would have to earn his right, as an individual, to be an important figure in his particular segment of the foreign affairs community.

The central thread running through all the interactions discussed was contact and communication. In each element of the total pattern, the CD's ability to effectively carry out his responsibilities depended on his skill in making himself useful. His only chance of doing so was to be able to communicate useful information and analysis, and to gain trust and respect by the way in which he carried out his duties. Success was uneven, but the country director at least had become someone to be reckoned with, if not the dominating figure that his advance billings proclaimed him to be.

Chapter Five

The Country Director in the Policy
Process: Points of Impact

*The country directors, this group of totally unknown indi-
viduals, are really representative of a tremendous power,
and can and do influence major events. You can say fairly
that this is a very significant group in terms of action, because they put up the choices and make the recommendations.* DEPUTY ASSISTANT SECRETARY,
GEOGRAPHIC BUREAU, 1969

T HE emerging country director role and the nature of
the interaction patterns in which CDs participated
provide a basis for exploring the important question
of the influence they exerted in the policy process itself.
Role strength and impact on policy are substantially interdependent, since a strong, legitimized CD role helps make
considerable influence possible, while skill exhibited by individual CDs in the policy process aids in gaining acceptance for their role. This relationship requires more specific
attention to the way in which CDs might affect policy outcomes.

In Chapter I, it was argued that it is misleading to conceive of the policy process as being composed of discrete
steps following naturally in set sequences. As Gore has written, "decision making is not a smooth-flowing process dis-
pensing choices when and where they are required."[1] There
are, however, certain recurring features that can be separated for analysis, as long as the essential "seamlessness"
of the whole is not forgotten. The twisting interaction by
which policy emerges does have certain points supplying

[1] William J. Gore, *Administrative Decision-Making: A Heuristic
Model* (New York: John Wiley & Sons, 1964), p. 21. Cf. Joseph
Frankel, *Making of Foreign Policy*, for essentially the same argument
in a foreign policy context.

177

the impetus for the rest of the process. Any actor who can control or influence these points has a great potential for strongly affecting final outcomes. In this chapter, attention is turned to some of these aspects of the policy process as they are relevant to the country directors, in order to better gauge their importance in policy making and to illuminate some elements of the developing CD role not previously emphasized.

PROBLEM DISCOVERY AND FORMULATION

One very important such point is the situation[2] or occasion for decision[3] which is perceived by one or more actors as requiring some change in current thinking, policy, or operations. In short, a problem is seen to exist, leading to consideration of new action by some actors.[4] The problem, however, is not a given; it must be defined. One weakness of rational models is that they assume that the stimulus or problem is clear and is interpreted identically by all parties. In fact, actors "have to identify and formulate their problem."[5] Perception thus becomes of critical importance, for "we never respond to the actual event or situation but to our view of it."[6] If actors' views of a situation vary significantly from reality, or if limitations on possible action subconsciously restrict perceptions to what can be coped with under existing constraints, conceptual failure, "the failure to grasp the meaning of the situation," is likely.[7]

Because the problem must be developed, opportunities for influencing decisions exist at the very beginning. The

[2] Snyder, Bruck, and Sapin, pp. 80-82.

[3] Robinson and Snyder, pp. 440-442.

[4] Consideration of action is used, since discovery of a problem requires that it be given some attention, but not that something ultimately be done (if development of the problem leads to the conclusion that nothing can/should be done, or if the matter is not pressing and no agreement can be reached).

[5] Lindblom, *Policy Making Process*, p. 13.

[6] De Rivera, p. 31.   [7] Ibid., p. 66.

problem as formulated will be the starting point for all subsequent analysis and adjustment. It follows that how and by whom the problem is defined is important both for analysis and for outcomes. As Frankel argues, "In some situations [lower ranking officials] may exercise a decisive influence on further developments by determining the original formulation of the issue."[8] Similarly, Wilensky writes of

the many opportunities experts have to influence "policy" at times and in ways far removed from formal or informal policy deliberations: they can "crystallize" the policy when the policy is loose, sharpen the definition of the problem when specificity is low, fill the vacuum when the boss is busy or time is short, use official policy pronouncements as a lever.[9]

The CD was in fact able to "direct" some outcomes by the way he formulated problems. Frequently, of course, a problem was routine or administrative, and defined rather precisely by the time it came to his attention. Requests for information, logistic support for the embassies, arrangements for a visit of a foreign dignitary, or queries for information framed by others for embassy action are representative examples. In other instances, a complex problem might be structured by someone else. As Deutsch suggests, "some policy alternatives are implicitly stressed, and others perhaps already foreclosed by the way the United States Ambassador has worded his report from the foreign country where he is stationed."[10] The point is generalizable to actions of all other participants.

[8] Frankel, p. 7. As discussed previously, this is the reason that some CDs felt it was very important to arrange to be the individual who drafted an instruction.

[9] Wilensky, p. 31.

[10] Deutsch, p. 92. One recent example of this occurred during the Dominican intervention of 1965. See Jerome Slater, *Intervention and Negotiation: The United States and the Dominican Revolution* (New York: Harper and Row, 1970), and John Bartlow Martin, *Overtaken by Events* (New York: Doubleday, 1966).

But other situations presented opportunities for a CD to control problem formulation himself, and thus determine procedures to be followed. Sometimes, of course, "competitors" elsewhere attempted contradictory definitions reflecting their own concerns and perspectives. When this occurred, the nature of a problem as well as the response to it became the subject of partisan analysis and the bargaining and adjustment process. For example, one CD explained how an accepted definition of a problem was likely to influence the outcome:

> If it's a matter that others feel is essentially political, they'll tend to accept the argumentation that we put forward. If they regard it as something that ought to be decided on grounds outside the political sphere, they're likely to be more resistant. Occasionally, you'll run into a situation where another party will say, "Well, this is absurd on military grounds, or what have you, but if you want to present it as a compelling political necessity, then of course we'll accede." (CD #14)

Although the boundaries separating one class of decision situation from another were not always clear, it is possible to distinguish those not amenable to CD definitional influence. Primary, of course, was whether it was well understood by the time the CD became aware of it.[11] If it was, or if he accepted some other official's right to formulate it, his influence at this point was minor. If, however, the situation was ambiguous but seemed likely to have an impact on relations with his country, he was often able to impose his view of the problem. Thus, complex matters involving essentially bilateral questions usually presented a very important opportunity for major CD input.

In one such instance, what was initially seen as a military assistance problem, the major responsibility of Defense, as-

---

[11] Either because the situation was relatively obvious, or because an acceptable formulation had been developed elsewhere.

sumed larger proportions when it was shown that the agreement would cause a severe strain on the economy of the recipient country. Upkeep and maintenance of the equipment in question would eventually cost more than the equipment, and would be borne by that country. Formulation of the problem thus came to include economic development (since maintenance funds for the equipment would have to be diverted from development programs), and the viability of the regime (if reduced developmental efforts led to unrest and/or insurgency). At this point, many agencies had become involved, and the agreement for assistance was ultimately modified to lessen the effect on the domestic economy of the recipient country. (ISA #2, CD #41)

More generally, it seems fair to say that decision situations lacking clear precedents and/or standing in uncertain relationship to existing policy (in the sense of guiding principles or general plans) are those in which working-level officials such as CDs have the greatest possibility of defining a problem, and therefore of determining the thrust of the action eventually taken.

One CD argued that whether a policy existed was often more important for outcomes than the substance of a question, and that a critical element was

> marrying the problem with the policy. Sometimes this is not easy. Some problems don't seem to fall within the policy on something else, but do in some other way, and sometimes you have to marry it in two or three different ways. (CD #18)

This "marrying" of policy and and problem, of past and proposed future actions, presented both opportunities and a paradox. A CD was more likely to make a decision himself if it could be justified within existing policy: "Whether or not you make a decision yourself depends on the way it fits into the framework of existing policy. You are unlikely on your own to make a sharply divergent decision." (CD #36— paraphrase) If a CD or similar official felt strongly about

181

a particular action, he might be tempted to search for precedents showing it fit existing policy (AID #3) or that his interpretation of a regulation followed precedent and therefore should be controlling. (CD #16) To the extent, however, that a problem was formulated so that it could be subsumed under existing policy, freedom of action was constrained. If the CD's interpretation diverged from understood policy, and he asserted it did not, his credibility and perceptiveness would be called into question, probably damaging his efficacy.

The CD's potential influence for policy outcomes was most important when he desired change from existing practice, since only then would his participation offer the possibility of modification (if some actor does not advocate change, it is almost certain none will occur). But as we have mentioned, the greater the change advocated by the CD, the more likely enacting decisions will be made at higher levels. The paradox, then, is that the CD's influence for policy outcomes was likely to be greatest in precisely those instances when he was unable to make the decision on his own authority. That is to say, a working-level official is probably more likely to be able to make a decision at his level if it falls within existing policy; but he is likely to have more influence (in the sense of his input directly determining outcomes) in those cases when a sharply divergent decision appears to be called for.

Problem formulation has several important ramifications for the remainder of the process. It may determine the time available for solution. If deadlines exist, such as the opening of an international conference, a scheduled presentation to Congress, or the impending visit of a foreign representative, then some course of action must be decided upon before that time. Such deadlines may also be self-imposed, as setting a date for a major speech, or acceptance of the view that a matter is ripe for action and the occasion should not be allowed to slip away. In a crisis situation, a short time frame may be "imposed" on the actors, but all deadlines are not the result of crises. If a problem is formulated as requiring quick resolution, the process by which a solution is found may differ qualitatively from one without this constraint. A need for a rapid decision may limit the number of alternatives considered.[12] At the same time, more useful information is likely to be brought to bear, as Wilensky has written:

> Only the big (costly, risky, innovative) policy decisions that are also very urgent are likely to activate high-quality intelligence, because deliberation then moves out of channels toward men of generalized wisdom, executives and experts alike, communicating informally and effectively at the top.[13]

Similarly, one CD said that "the bigger the issue and the more urgent it is, the more reasonable people and agencies become to deal with." (CD #26) Compromise was more likely to result, thus changing the final decision, even if a CD or other participant felt he would prevail if more time were available:

> It seems that you're always under the pressure of time. . . . There are events that happen, or are going to happen, and you have to do something, or you're trying to get something resolved before a certain time. And unless it's extraordinarily important, you can't fight your way through the appeal mechanism. Therefore, you tend to settle for a compromise, because half a loaf is better than [none]. (CD #6)

Definition will also affect the way a complex problem is factored. The idea of factoring is developed by March and Simon, and it results from the complexity of situations that

[12] Robinson and Snyder, loc. cit. In some major episodes, however, this may not be the case. A wide range of possible reactions, for example, seem to have been considered in the 1962 Cuban missile crisis, before a shipping blockade was decided upon.

[13] Wilensky, p. 81.

do not permit all aspects of a problem to be considered in detail by single individuals or units. Specifically,

> a fundamental technique for simplifying the problem is to factor it into a number of nearly independent parts, so that each organizational unit handles one of these parts and can omit the others from its definition of the situation.[14]

In the case of foreign affairs problems, factoring is probably more prominent on technical matters or subsequent decisions than on general policy. For example, preparation of the Country Analysis and Strategy Paper (CASP)[15] for Latin American countries was undertaken by a factoring process, with subsections developed by each agency for its own programs. At the same time, ratification of the whole package was accomplished collectively. Factoring may be unsuccessful, if several participants try to define a problem as primarily their own, or at least to claim an expanded role for themselves. Relying on legal officers for interpretations of the law in a given situation is an effort at factoring, but it breaks down if they try to involve themselves in day-to-day problem solving. It also must be remembered that it was unlikely that a CD would be the only one to receive stimuli indicating that a problem existed, and thus allowing him to decide how the problem would be factored. Several actors were likely to recognize the existence of a problem at nearly the same time. Each was then likely to formulate the entire problem from his own perspective, including what other participants might be expected to do and what was within his own domain. If so, factoring itself would become subject to the process of decision unless all agreed.

It should be clear that problem formulation can further preferred outcomes and/or enhance the bureaucratic position of the official who prevails. It may allow one actor to gain control of the action, or at least to increase his own

---

[14] March and Simon, p. 151.   [15] Described in Chapter IV.

potential influence. A CD often had an opportunity to do this because of his central position and his knowledge of the country and United States' intentions toward it, subject to certain constraints. If his interpretation was greatly at odds with those of other actors, or if he excluded those with legitimate interests, the result was likely to be reformulation on the basis of different interpretations, weakening his input. Furthermore, he might find himself excluded in the future by those slighted currently. His problem was to gain acceptance of his formulation by demonstrating his fairness and perceptivity, rather than by imposing it through bureaucratic subterfuge or withholding information.

Selection of Participants

Intimately related to problem formulation is the question of who participates in problem resolution. It is possible that a well-defined problem will still present an opportunity for selection of those to be involved, but definition clearly influences participation.

If formulation answers the question what is to be decided, and factoring how the job is to be done, selection of participants of course reflects who is to decide. The country director often made this sort of evaluation, which involved not only the level of decision ratification, but also which offices, departments, bureaus, and even individuals were to have an input. Who participates may be critical if change is a possibility, because the support or opposition of a major actor may be the deciding factor. There may be more latitude than one might expect to significantly alter participation. Not all levels within State or another department are likely to be involved in a given problem, and it may be presented in such a way that those favorable to a particular outcome are included or excluded, depending on the preference of whoever "had the action." Similarly, particular units or individuals in other offices and departments may

185

be excluded,[16] or included for clearance purposes only after a solution has been essentially developed by the drafter in consultation with others.[17] One example illustrates these considerations. A country director, in concert with an NSC official, decided that a foreign nation's request for support of its experimental space program was in U.S. interests. Knowing that the functional office concerned with space matters in State was unsympathetic and that success was more likely elsewhere, emphasis was placed on the military aspects of the program, action was channeled to the department's Politico-Military Group, and the resulting policy developed along the lines desired by the NSC staffer and the CD.[18] The same sorts of differences were often present in the interaction between CDs and functional specialists as to whether an issue was a matter of bilateral relations or of global application of a functional policy. It is also important to note that representatives of various units may not be gathered to work out a decision, but rather to backstop or legitimize one already made by a smaller group of actors.

A related phenomenon is the tendency of an official to define a problem as logically belonging to his own unit, whose abilities and talents are well known, rather than to another, which is more of an unknown quantity:

> He is likely to feel that his organization is much more qualified to make the "proper" recommendation if they [have] available the required data.[19]

[16] Unless, of course, they discover through informal channels that they are being bypassed and make a demand to be included. See William Jones, pp. 3-7, 14.

[17] As indicated earlier, most CDs felt that a failure to clear was unintentional most of the time, whether on their own part or when others left them out, and several noted that a complaint usually brought an end to the problem. Pruitt, however, found this was more of a difficulty for the XYZ office in his study. See Pruitt, pp. 25-26.

[18] This example based on description provided by one of the participants.

[19] William Jones, p. 15.

In one such instance, a CD explained how his office had gained additional responsibilities:

> I regard the protection of our citizens in these countries as a political matter, and will take charge of handling them immediately, rather than leaving them to the people in the protection and representation section of the Bureau of Security and Counsular Affairs, where they would normally be handled. I feel they get better, quicker action as a result in these unfriendly countries than they do elsewhere, even where relations are less difficult. (CD #40—paraphrase)

The choice of level to which a problem must be carried before resolution is possible depends on what those at each level can do on their own, and what must be done indirectly through referral to others.[20] This distinction is more meaningful than one between an official acting alone and acting in concert with others, since in a collective process it would be an extremely rare and trivial instance when no one else was involved.

Contrary to what one might expect using a hierarchical model of organizational activity, the CD usually decided whether he could deal with a problem. He thus influenced even decisions which he could not make alone:

> It's the role of the country director . . . to know at what point and to what extent he can commit State, without appealing to superior authorities, and what things he

[20] Blankenship and Miles make a similar classification, describing a manager's decision-making behavior in terms of frequencies of initiation (when he calls problems to the attention of others or refers them to superiors); consultation with and by peers, superiors, or subordinates (not listed separately above, but of course a part of the collective process); and making or approving the final choice (similar to what the CD does on his own). See L. Vaughn Blankenship and Raymond E. Miles, "Organization Structure and Managerial Decision Behavior," *Administrative Science Quarterly* 13 (June 1968): 108.

would have to or should appeal to higher authorities. (CD #19)

Information on this point was solicited by asking, "What types of decisions do you make? What determines when a decision has to be made at a higher level?" Bureaucracies are usually said to operate by formal rules, but only twelve of forty-three CDs asked this question said even "rules of thumb" existed which could be applied to specific situations. Thirty-one said this determination was made as a result of experience, instinct, a feel for the way the bureau operated, or some variation on these points. Furthermore, examination revealed that there was little if any difference between the rules of thumb cited and the more informal criteria mentioned by CDs who said there were no such rules.

Decision situations were likely to be seen as requiring higher level attention if artifacts of the organizational structure of State or the government limited the CD's ability to find a solution at his level. Twenty-four CDs cited disagreement at their level as a major cause of escalation to mutual superiors; fifteen mentioned problems crossing jurisdictional boundaries and therefore requiring coordination by a common superior; and seven said problems sometimes "entered" the system at a higher level; for example, as the result of a call from a senior official in another agency to a CD's superior. Unless the problem was trivial, it was usual to refer a proposed solution back to the official who was first appraised of the problem, even when the details had been worked out elsewhere. Finally, three CDs noted that legal requirements made it mandatory that certain decisions, sometimes quite routine in nature, be ratified by a specific official.

Other matters were taken to superiors for idiosyncratic or personality reasons. Foremost were those of particular interest to a higher official, mentioned by twenty-five CDs. This should not be confused with matters taken to higher levels because of their importance. Rather, these citations referred to known interests of specific superiors in certain countries or in functional areas where they had assumed responsibility and indicated their interest (e.g., refugee problems). The operating style of superiors was also involved according to seven CDs, since some preferred to follow day-to-day operations, while others relied on CDs to bring to them only matters which required their attention. Four CDs therefore generalized that a new CD would be more likely to take a higher percentage of matters to the DAS or assistant secretary, until he had determined what sorts of things they wished to see.

None of these reasons is inherently connected with the weight of the problem. But in other instances, the decision to refer a matter upward was intimately tied to its perceived importance, as twenty-five CDs suggested. Realization that higher level attention was required was dependent upon the experience and working relationships of the CD, since this category is less explicit than others previously mentioned. Some such situations were clear, such as developing crises, or those involving one of the "five or six countries which are treated differently because of their importance to us." (CD #12) In other instances, only a subtle understanding of the country involved, the American domestic political context, or the longer range implications of a proposed action might suggest higher level attention was needed. These included major policy issues (defined as those involving a change in major U.S. goals in relations with a country), cited by eleven CDs; those involving new departures in programs or activities, mentioned by twenty-four; or those which had a potentially high level of U.S. domestic political interest, and on which public/congressional/White House attention was likely to be directed toward State, as noted by twelve.

Given this discretion, the CDs' proclivity for solving problems assumed importance. It often determined whether they would ask a superior to make or to ratify a decision, or merely inform him afterward of what had been done. Twenty-six of forty-three CDs with whom this topic was discussed volunteered that they attempted to do as much as possible themselves, rather than taking borderline matters higher up. Most others implied agreement and might have responded affirmatively to a direct question. The reasons given were basically two: to relieve superiors of as much as possible, and to have those with expertise and intimate knowledge of a problem (i.e., the CD and his opposite numbers) work out a solution, rather than more generally oriented senior officials. However, there are reasons to suspect that few CDs took the risk of being called to task for errors of commission. Only rarely did a CD say he had been questioned by a superior who wondered why he had not been consulted. There may be reluctance to admit that one had been overruled or reprimanded for exceeding his authority, but these statements gain credence because some assistant secretaries and DASs felt that the problem was more likely to be one of referring too much upward, rather than too little. The inferential conclusion is that most CDs were not particularly aggressive in assuming responsibility for borderline decisions. However, it should be remembered that a CD who wished a major change in policy or program might take a matter to his superiors not because he was reluctant to accept responsibility, but to increase support for the modification and therefore the probability that it would be accepted.

CONTROL OF INFORMATION

The presence or absence of information could also have a major impact on policy outcomes. First, some information must be received by some actor from some source suggesting a problem may exist. It may come from intelligence or diplomatic sources, from the media, from within the organization, or from analysis of past events by the actor himself; but something must occur or be discovered that leads to dissatisfaction with what is currently being done. After the resolution process begins, information will be marshaled by all participants to buttress their own interpretations or to help find some common position on which all can agree or at least "live with." Finally, information on the effects of a particular action may indicate that no further action is necessary, or may start another episode. Because of the importance attached to relevant information, anyone who could determine what information was circulated to whom assumed a position of some strength and influence.

In general, the CD was well placed to obtain necessary information and to enhance his own position by overseeing the access of others to it. He received sole possession of very little that concerned his country, but he was privy to a wider range of information than anyone else, with the possible exception of the American ambassador, including much that pertained primarily or entirely to other units of government. As one 1973 CD who had also served in another agency argued, "we know everything," compared to superiors or others with more limited functional concerns. Most agencies and bureaus of State sent their telegrams to the field only after clearance with him, and most CDs tried to insure they were not bypassed. Similarly, the CD received copies of incoming telegrams, letters, and documents from almost all those attached to the embassy.

Even those with their own communications channels to Washington superiors, such as the CIA and the military, often sent CDs information copies of messages. Furthermore, many CDs attempted to gain access to communications not marked for them by developing close working relationships with opposite numbers who were addressees. Because those elsewhere in government frequently received only communications dealing with their own agency's activities, differing understandings of a situation were common. It was for this reason that a majority of CDs and almost all of the opposite numbers interviewed found there was some advantage to the interagency meeting on country problems

191

that allowed the more important information to receive a wider airing.

Information requirements were not limited to current situations. The country director who had recently served in the host country had an extra edge, since opposite numbers were unlikely to have had such experience. If the CD could blend expertise gained in the field with comprehensive knowledge of current conditions, other agencies would be hard pressed to challenge his interpretations, and more obliquely, his recommended course of action.

This did not prevent challenges resulting from conflicting goals, but did give the CD a strong position on what was desirable with respect to his country. When the CD lacked knowledge about other agency programs, however, some of his advantage dissipated, particularly since his opposite numbers had often been dealing with agency programs for long periods as opposed to his one or two years as a CD.

It seems fair to conclude that CDs were influential because of their partial control of needed information, but that this was primarily a function of past experience, individual initiative, and expertise, rather than of the strength of the CD role.

There was also variation in influence resulting from control of information according to the information levels and expertise of opposite numbers. When actors in other parts of government had as much or more background with respect to the country, the CD's relative control was less and his influence over policy was likely to come from other factors.

SEARCH FOR ALTERNATIVES

Identification of alternative means and evaluation of the consequences of each is a cornerstone of rational models of decision making, with the alternative promising optimal consequences being selected after utilities have been calculated. Simon argued that this is unrealistic; that most human decisions tend to be made on the basis of satisfactory outcomes rather than optimal ones; and that consideration of alternatives would end when one satisfactory one was discovered.[21] This important modification confronted the problems of limited rationality and uncertainty, and was the source of the idea of search for alternatives. March and Simon posit an inverse relationship between the amount of satisfaction in a given situation and the amount of search that takes place for possible alternatives to it.[22]

A later formulation by March and Cyert is even more to the point here. They suggest that "problemistic search" is stimulated by and directed to finding a solution to a particular problem, and is "simpleminded" because it reflects simple concepts of causality. It is based on two rules compatible with an incremental model of the policy process: First, search takes place in the neighborhood of the problem symptom; and second, it takes place in the neighborhood of the current alternative. Only if application of these two rules do not present a "satisficing" solution does a third apply; search takes place in organizationally vulnerable areas (where slack exists, or power is weak).[23]

In many instances such search does occur if problem formulation does not predetermine a solution. It may be employed by an individual, such as a CD, in reaching a position he can support, or may be a feature of the collective process where search seeks a solution acceptable to all participants.

At the same time, search, even for a "satisficing" alterna-

[21] March and Simon, pp. 140-141, provides one discussion, and similar arguments are found in much of Simon's other work. But cf. Louis G. Gawthrop, *Bureaucratic Behavior*, pp. 89-95, for the suggestion that as the degree of risk associated with uncertainty increases, officials will shift from attempts to "satisfice" to attempts to find the one best alternative. This of course would increase the amount of search in such situations.

[22] March and Simon, pp. 173-174, provides one example.

[23] Richard M. Cyert and James G. March, *A Behavioral Theory of the Firm* (Englewood Cliffs, N.J.: Prentice-Hall, 1963), pp. 120-122.

tive, is not automatic. The basic tenet of the concept is that search results from dissatisfaction with the current situation or already viable alternatives to it. Wilensky, writing to the March and Simon and the Cyert and March conceptualizations, cautions that

> organizational theory often assumes that where an existing policy satisfies organizational goals there is little search for alternatives but that when policy fails search is intensified. This assumption underestimates man's capacity for clinging to prophecies already proven wrong. The failure of a prediction lays waste actions taken in preparation for its fulfilment. Thus, men use a variety of ingenious defenses to protect cherished convictions under the onslaught of devastating attack.[24]

Providing some supporting evidence, Thomson argues that the Vietnam involvement developed because a variety of misconceptions and situational factors prevented recognition of failure, and allowed hopes that policies being followed would ultimately succeed to prevail.[25] De Rivera suggests that emotional bias in favor of one alternative may cause a reluctance to search for others, and that "freezing" of perception and meaning attached to a situation at the time an initial decision is made may prevent a different perception of the situation or its meaning.[26] Deutsch believes that because of costs attached to it,

> search for the supposedly "best" strategy is apt to stop as soon as any *acceptable* strategy is found at tolerable

[24] Wilensky, p. 78. This is not the same argument made in this study, that dissatisfaction is the source of suggestions for change. Wilensky's point is that the failure of current procedures may not be perceived, and so no dissatisfaction will arise. The argument here, which is not inconsistent, is that when and if such failures are perceived, dissatisfaction will arise and may result in suggestions for change.

[25] James C. Thomson, Jr., "How Could Vietnam Happen? An Autopsy," *Atlantic Monthly* (April 1968), 47-53.

[26] De Rivera, pp. 119, 123.

costs in terms of search and computation, provided that no alternative and equally attractive strategy has emerged.[27]

Finally, dissatisfaction with current efforts may not develop early enough to prevent disaster or at least unfortunate results. Developing consequences of a chosen solution may require considerable time, causal relationships between decision and consequence may be erroneously posited, and no utility calculus may be available. All this suggests that search may not occur, or if it does, may not develop usable alternatives.

Evidence from country director interviews supports this interpretation. The CD was submerged in a sea of problems small and large. There was a premium on getting things done, by whatever method (and however intuitively). (CD #2) The need for quick solutions deterred search for better ones. Another CD explained that you could actually "know too much":

> Very often there is a tendency to try to get everything: all the facts, all the information, every last bit of information together before you make a decision. If you do that in the United States government, you'll never make it. . . . You've got to have some time to move, or you'll never do it. . . . You have to go off not fully cocked, occasionally! (CD #14)

Another said one had to be forceful and persistent, or other actors would be likely to draw the process out unacceptably long. (CD #21)[28]

Informational factors also inhibited search. While the strong reliance on precedent and a desire for knowledge about past episodes often led CDs to consult the Bureau of

[27] Deutsch, p. 124. Emphasis in original.

[28] This might be considered a corollary to Parkinson's law. Instead of "work expanding to fill time available," it might be phrased, "agreement on a particular alternative will be delayed as long as it is possible to do so."

Intelligence and Research (CD #33), what was turned up there was often of little use in suggesting current alternatives. One CD believed that what is "most deficient of all is the sort of retrospective intelligence [about] what really did happen at an earlier period." (CD #7)

Another search limiter was reluctance of lower level officials to disagree with superiors. Yet, "middle-level managers, and even lower level employees, sometimes have a near monopoly of insight into feasible alternatives,"[29] because they alone may have sufficiently detailed knowledge. Such alternatives may be submerged as a working-level official arrives at a recommendation he presents to his superior. This was one reason that William Gaud, when AID administrator, disliked the merged offices in ARA-LA, since through them AID and State points of view were reconciled and presented to higher levels without adequate (from Gaud's point of view) consideration of possible alternatives. Some CDs countered by contending that alternatives had been adequately developed, but agreed a danger of insufficient search did exist. (CD #35)

Another pitfall was that what appeared to be search efforts might actually be intended to provide support (or "backstopping") for decisions already made.[30] One CD, when discussing the possible use of a program budgeting system, saw its primary utility as being "to justify a course of action which has been less salable to other agencies." (CD #30) To be fair, this might support a "correct" policy rather than put over a personal preference, but the possibility clearly exists for using devices and techniques designed to improve the alternatives under consideration to support previously determined positions.

[29] Wilensky, p. 29.

[30] See Roger Hilsman, *Strategic Intelligence and National Decisions* (Glencoe, Ill.: Free Press, 1956), p. 43, for a discussion of backstopping, which he defines as "either a chronological history of events leading up to a problem or a mechanical search for facts tending to support a policy decision that has already been made." The term has the latter connotation in the text.

Finally, the essentially reactive nature of much of foreign relations (and of the duties of the CD) tended to limit search to particular responses to perceived stimuli. The decision to follow the Truman Doctrine in support of Greece and Turkey was made in the space of five days and the fundamental positions developed within thirty-two hours after the British government informed the State Department that it would no longer be able to support those governments.[31] However wise and prescient that decision, it was hardly the result of intensive search, for at no time was any alternative other than picking up where the British were leaving off actively supported or considered.

To conclude, it may be erroneous to assume that foreign policy or problem solutions emerge only after intensive examination of many possible courses of action. Neither the rational model of the decision process implying consideration of all possible alternatives, nor the limited rationality model of Simon may give sufficient indication of how problems in foreign policy are resolved. In summary, the amount of search for alternative courses of action will be reduced when: inadequate perception prevents recognition that current performance is unsatisfactory; an emotional bias exists in favor of a current alternative; the costs of search are great in terms of time or other resources; a quick solution is needed; or when a current alternative or policy is strongly favored by a superior.

ADJUSTMENT AND ANALYSIS

Without repeating what has been said before, it is useful at this point to relate adjustment techniques to resolution of foreign affairs problems. As suggested earlier, there is interplay between social adjustment and intellectual analysis, with the latter becoming an important tool of the former

[31] John H. Stutesman, Jr., "The Architecture of a Decision: How the Truman Doctrine Evolved," *Foreign Service Journal*, 43 (July 1966), 19-20. See also Joseph Marion Jones, *The Fifteen Weeks*.

and thereby changed in its characteristics. Personal relationships clearly affect the weight given to analysis, as one CD indicated:

> I have worked with some people . . . whom I don't respect much in general, and I very often [have] caught myself turning down things, or reacting negatively to things, which I shouldn't have reacted negatively to. . . . Respect is important: if you can gain respect, you can get a hearing. On the other hand, if you're dealing with somebody you don't respect, somehow you've got to close that part of your mind, and try to take what he's saying for what it is, and analyze it outside of your own feelings about the man, and see if it is a good idea. (CD #18)

This reflects the obvious point that disputes of policy are not played out in the abstract—a man wins or loses as well as a particular alternative policy approach or course of action.

For difficult problems, CDs and opposite numbers were both interdependent (since actions of each participant contributed to or interfered with others' goal achievement) and partisan (in that they did not assume that shared criteria existed sufficient to govern adjustment acceptable to themselves and all other relevant actors).[32] Analysis was therefore used to persuade others that a proposed solution would serve *their* values, rather than overarching ones shared by all. Lindblom refers to this as "partisan analysis" and argues that others will listen to such persuasion because they operate in a world of uncertainty and can never be completely sure their own suggested solution will ultimately serve their own values, and because their reputations depend on the success of their policies.[33] This give and take helps a policy maker to clarify his own goals. Partisan analysis is not frustrated by lack of agreement on policy goals as a rational means-ends analysis may be, and need

[32] Lindblom, *Intelligence*, pp. 21-22, 28-29.
[33] Lindblom, *Policy Making Process*, p. 33.

not demonstrate one best policy (since it need only persuade a partisan with respect to the current situation he faces).[34] These characteristics suggest that consensus and appeasement are the bases of successful policy development when several actors or organizational units participate. This acts to make policy choices less innovative than the objective situation may require.

Partisan analysis is only one form of partisan mutual adjustment,[35] but Lindblom's emphasis on it parallels the great importance ascribed to persuasive techniques by country directors. One argued that persuasion was likely to be the most productive way of insuring the predominance of one's viewpoint:

An effective policy is one which everybody [agrees] on and is enthusiastically carrying out. So we are much better off in persuading other agencies to see things our way; and if they see them differently, they are much better off to persuade us to see things their way than trying to pull an end run, and go around or above us. (CD #19)

Another explained his techniques in terms almost identical to Lindblom's:

You try to clarify the thing, try to get something pinpointed, get down to the guts of the problems between agencies—what is it that is bothering the other guy—and then you try to look for a solution. . . . You're using essentially persuasive techniques, and analytical persuasive techniques. (CD #1)

[34] Ibid., pp. 33-34.

[35] It is essentially the same as "partisan discussion" in Lindblom's description in *Intelligence of Democracy*, which is defined as a form of negotiation "in which X and Y induce responses from each other by effecting a reappraisal of each other's assessment of the objective consequences of various courses of action (where bargaining alters the consequences, partisan discussion exchanges information about unaltered consequences)," p. 331. See also his *Policy Making Process*, p. 71.

Others argued that persuasion was a necessity, in the absence of authority to enforce their own views:

> I don't think that a country director, whatever you put in the directive, is going to be able to order the other agencies around. . . . It's more a question of persuasion than ordering. (CD #16)

In part, this was because

> institutional structures are essentially not built by directive. They are built by interests, and as long as the Department of Defense [and] the Central Intelligence Agency remain enormous, powerful, financially totally independent, and in comparison with State, enormously larger institutions, their independence and their judgment is going to be reflected in an unwillingness to subordinate themselves, except at the very highest levels if necessary. Or, unless by cooperation and consultation— and I think that this is the only thing that is going to do it. (CD #5)

As previously discussed, facts and expertise provided by CDs were among the most powerful tools in their repertoires. A reputation of knowledgeability helped build acceptance for them, and furthered the possibility of persuading others to go along. (CD #29) In another's words, the CD "has to establish, within the bureaucracy in Washington, that he does have expertise in depth on that country." (CD #24)

At times, of course, the CDs employed other adjustment techniques. Most of these could be classified, using Lindblom's scheme, as that form of manipulated partisan mutual adjustment[36] called negotiation, in which "X and Y, in a certain variety of ways, induce responses from each other."[37]

---

[36] In manipulated PMA, X as a condition of making his decision induces a response from Y, while in adaptive PMA, X seeks no response from Y. Lindblom, *Intelligence*, p. 330.

[37] Ibid., p. 331. Thus, as with some of the others to be discussed,

Bargaining (inducing responses by conditional threats and promises) was common, although limited by the usual inability of the CD to threaten sanctions sufficiently disliked to evoke desired responses. Nevertheless, in some instances the threat of carrying a problem to higher levels was successfuly used, particularly when the CD's relationship with his superiors was such that he could move more quickly than his opposite numbers.[38] Similarly, there was some additional leverage since a decision taken against the CD's will might never be implemented in the field, providing the ambassador were agreed and it could be ignored without consequence. (CDs #19, 34)

Compensation (X induces a response by a conditional promise of benefit) was used less frequently, since the CD's limited resources and imperfectly defined role meant credible promises of benefit were seldom possible. At times, however, reciprocity (calling in an existing obligation or acknowledging a new one by either or both X and Y) was employed, since given the frequent interaction of country directors and some opposite numbers, future support might depend on current acquiescence. (CD #18) Indirect manipulation (X uses any of the other forms of manipulation to induce a third decision maker to induce Y to make a desired response) was also used, most usually when a CD and one opposite number supported the same proposed solution, and when the opposite number was in a better position to bring a recalcitrant third party around.

Two final types of manipulation which are not forms of negotiation were infrequently employed. Authoritative pre-

---

partisan discussion is a special case of the general category of negotiation. In the following paragraphs, definitions in parentheses, unless otherwise noted, are taken from ibid.

[38] At times, this technique resembled Lindblom's "prior decision" form of negotiating, wherein "X takes a prior decision to induce Y to respond rather than forego the advantages of coordination with X." Ibid. CDs #7, 9, 15, 36, and 37 made explicit mention of the advantages that "speed of escalation" could have for a CD.

scription (X prescribes a response to Y, who concedes X's authority) occurred only when the problem was defined as being predominantly the CD's responsibility, since one major departure from formal prescriptions about his role was his inability to make authoritative recommendations about many problems concerning his countries. Unconditional manipulation (X induces a response from Y by unconditionally altering the advantages or disadvantages to Y of various responses) was very seldom used, simply because the CD was not in a position to carry it out.[39]

Lindblom also posits three types of adaptive PMA: parametric (X adapts to Y's decisions without regard for consequences for Y); deferential (X seeks to avoid adverse consequences for Y); and calculated (X does not wholly avoid adverse consequences for Y, but still adjusts his decisions out of consideration for such adverse effects). While admittedly impressionistic, it seems likely that parametric PMA was most practiced by country directors, since they often reacted to strong positions and previous decisions of others; for example, when they altered proposals in light of Treasury's strong opposition to foreign expenditures that would adversely affect the balance of payments. More generally, successful CD operations called for "continual exercise of initiative, within the limits of respecting the sensitivities and the authority that other parts of government have." (CD #6) Deferential and calculated PMA were of course possible, if country director actions could have adverse effects for other actors.

This brief survey is not intended to argue definitively that Lindblom's scheme provides a precise fit with the realities facing the country director, but rather to suggest that a major portion of CD problem-solving and policy-making be-

[39] The most common form of unconditional manipulation is the granting or withholding of funds for an agency's operations. Ibid., p. 78. As has been seen, one of the complaints of CDs was the inability to alter other agency fund usage, much less to grant or withhold such funds.

havior was conditioned by the presence of other actors with different views, and by a subsequent need for mutual accommodation.

It may be helpful here to summarize the ways country directors participated in the process of problem solving. When a problem was perceived by a CD, he made a preliminary analysis of the situation, drawing upon experience and information to arrive at his own position and attempting to be as rational as possible given uncertainty about means-ends relationships and outcome preferences. He interacted with concerned opposite numbers using partisan analysis and other techniques in an attempt to find an acceptable, agreed solution. Problem reformulation, search for other alternatives, and shifting positions might result. If resolution was not possible at the CD level, the matter either was carried upward until solved by someone with agreed authority, or dropped if no immediate solution was required.

Certain accepted rules, conventions, and procedures largely controlled this process.[40] Chances of success were enhanced by knowing when short cuts could be taken and when one had to "play by the book." (CD #12) Such rules prevented hostility from building up, and helped regulate conflict. For example, all participants acted as partisans in support of their own perceived personal and agency interests, but were unlikely to try to muzzle any one participant once he had been conceded a legitimate interest. As one CD noted, it was necessary to allow each actor to make his "pitch" even if it was clearly unacceptable, so that he could tell his superiors that he made "the old college try" and future cooperation would not be jeopardized. (CD #31) Similarly, since participants at each level had a vested interest in resolving problems themselves, pressures existed

---

[40] The prominence of rules, along with the previously mentioned cooperation of experts and subordination of analysis to the play of power, are the underlying mechanisms of the policy process listed by Lindblom. See his *Policy Making Process*, p. 30.

for making the system work. It was held to be just as well to "cave in" after the battle had been fought and lost, unless there was a compelling reason for attempting to gain reversal. (CD #29) Conversely, some account was taken of the intensity as well as the content of the views of the various actors, and of the centrality of an agency interest. Those with less intense opinions and less organizational involvement tended to defer to those with more.[41] The adjustment system thus tended to flag major controversies, since problems were most likely to be escalated for resolution when two or more opinions were intensely held or when conflicting assertions of agency primacy existed.

Several final points ought to be mentioned concerning adjustment and analysis techniques. First, although proper timing is not itself an adjustment technique, a sense of the atmospherics, preoccupations of other actors, and their interests sometimes suggests which technique should be employed in order to maximize payoffs.

Second, some actors, such as CDs, can be partisans of a different order than the others. Their interests may be to find any solution others will accept, rather than support of one substantive proposal against others. A CD whose primary concern is maintenance of warm and productive relations with given countries may have no substantive preference in a dispute between say, the Department of Agriculture and a foreign government over conditions under which that country's exports will be admitted to the United States. (CD #37) Any solution will be acceptable to him, as long as relations with that country are not appreciably harmed. A CD thus may be an expediter (or coordinator) in some instances, and a partisan participant in others. (CD #17)

Third, the need for accurate information may provide opportunities for an energetic partisan. A higher official in

[41] This is one reason definition of the problem as being of central importance to one's own agency was important for success in pushing a particular course of action.

one agency explained that in order to obtain information, he had instructed his secretary to put all calls through rather than screening them. As a result, in one instance an aggressive CD exploited the contact to influence and persuade him, with the result that the decision reflected the latter's preferences.

Finally, the fact that the adjustment process provided solutions did not mean that it did so easily. Another reason for an incremental style of policy making and problem solving was the delicacy of a mechanism easily thrown out of equilibrium. One CD argued that this constituted a bias against change:

> There's a great tendency to say, "I'm here, and this is the policy I'm defending, and that is essentially my job." It's very easy to get into that rut. It's so easy to find reasons for not doing things, because doing things always ruffles all kinds of feathers and rocks all kinds of boats and complicates your life incredibly, and forces you into an enormous amount of new work and new argumentation and persuasion and negotiation, and is more likely than not to create trouble. (CD #5)

CLOSURE

Although foreign policy problems are never solved in a finite sense, nevertheless at some point a particular episode ends. This act of closure may result from agreement on a course of action/inaction, from referral to a central coordinator, or from an understanding that puts the problem in suspended animation for a period of time.

Actors desiring resolution of problems need to obtain such closure, since decisions do not emerge full blown, but rather grow[42] or evolve.[43] When quick agreement is possible, or when limited time is available, closure may not be difficult, although the alternatives may present excruciating

---

[42] Gore, p. 67.   [43] De Rivera, p. 134.

choices. But when disagreement is sharp and action can be deferred, an episode may continue interminably unless a way can be found to end it. This was a prime reason for the emphasis given by country directors to "getting things done," (CD #2) knowing how to "push a problem through the maze," (CD #33) and being able to "get the ball rolling," (CD #23) or to "cut red tape." (CD #31) Knowledge and experience were seen as the primary guides to expediting closure by applying such techniques as drafting a cable (CDs #42, 16, 27, and others), escalating to a higher level (CDs #7, 37, 4, and others), and persistence. (CD #21) Style was considered to be extremely important in accomplishing this, (CD #18) and human relationships contributed mightily to the ease of obtaining an outcome, if not necessarily to its content.

One often hears that the primary characteristics of the policy process are conflict and dispute. In some instances, however, an actor's initial task may be forcing others to consider a problem he perceives, rather than winning acceptance for his own proposed solution. Mobilizing other agencies to deal with a problem was perhaps as difficult as anything a CD had to do, (CD #39) and some effort was usually needed to accomplish it:

> There are opportunities that call to be exercised, [but one must find a way] of getting representatives in other agencies moving on something that needs to be done. This is what I was trying to do yesterday in a meeting, when I was bringing up a general policy area that bothers me, and [where] I'd like to see some action. Now, I don't know what will happen—this was only an initial go. (CD#43)

Given many simultaneous developments, such persistence by one actor may be the only way of avoiding a failure to deal with a problem while favorable outcomes are still possible. One redeeming grace of a multiplicity of decision makers, if each is attuned to a slightly different set of signals, is that less opportunity exists for such failures (assuming, of course, that it is ultimately possible to convince others that a problem does exist). At the same time, perception by one actor will be to no avail if he is not able to bring an episode to conclusion.

CRISIS AND NONCRISIS SITUATIONS

If the country director had difficulty in attracting attention to some perceived problems, in other cases there might be entirely too much interest from his point of view. These were the "flaps" or crises, when high-level consideration was prompt and continuing. One CD described how the organizational responsibility for a recent crisis evolved:

> It started out, the first week or so, before it was apparent that we were going to be in a full-fledged warlike situation, that I was chairman of the task force. And this was an interagency task force, not just [the bureau] or just the Department of State. And then it grew and the deputy assistant secretary was put in charge and I was made his deputy; and then it grew further and the assistant secretary was put in charge and the deputy assistant secretary became his deputy, and I was put in charge of what was called the operating staff of the task force—the troops who had to carry out the orders, and prepare the policy studies and staff the special watch we kept up in the operations center on a twenty-four hour basis. (CD #28)

The decision to create a task force, a very common occurrence in crises, was made at the top, partially for symbolic reasons:

> We simply got instructions from the secretariat that we were to establish a [name of area] task force. . . . We felt that we could deal with the crisis without doing that, at least in its early stages, just by our own traditional ties

with other agencies and our own internal operating procedures. But there was great pressure to have some more unique and dramatic mechanism to show that the crisis was being coped with. . . . I don't know that we really came up with a better policy as a result, but I suppose that it did keep an awful lot of people in other agencies in the picture that would have felt left out if it hadn't been done this way. I don't have any brief either for or against having it done that way. It's sort of traditional that if you get a crisis, you establish a task force on it. (CD #28)

The concept of crisis has connotations of urgency as well as importance. Ideally, the term would be reserved for the latter meaning, that is for situations where important values or policies are under severe challenge, whether the time frame is long or short.[44] In government the urgent often takes precedence over the critical, because something must be done immediately or at least expeditiously. Vital has explained how the "men on top" become prisoners of the time available:

When a particular problem begins to loom large on their political, and therefore mental, horizon and requires closer attention, other matters will have to be pushed aside. . . . It therefore follows that the major criterion determining which matters will take precedence cannot be that of intrinsic importance, but rather their urgency—which is another way of saying that energy and thought

[44] In terms of importance for the nation, both the Cuban missile crisis, played out in a few days, and the continuing balance of payments crisis from the mid-sixties on could be considered critical with respect to possible outcomes, although the time frames differed drastically. Recent studies of the unique nature of crisis situations include Charles F. Hermann, *Crises in Foreign Policy: A Simulation* (Indianapolis: Bobbs-Merrill, 1969); and Thomas Halper, *Foreign Policy Crises: Appearance and Reality in Decision-Making* (Columbus, Ohio: Charles E. Merrill, 1971).

tend to be concentrated on the immediate, rather than the fundamental.[45]

For present purposes, what is essential is that certain situations, characterized by urgency and by some (although not necessarily fundamental) importance tend to be handled somewhat differently from those that are more routine. Some consequences of problems being formulated as requiring immediate attention have already been cited, including consideration of fewer alternatives, better intelligence usage, more reasonableness in the adjustment process, and possibly a more compromised solution.

Another feature of crisis situations is the tendency referred to above for senior officials to take over. Although working level officials may be resentful and may feel that critical decisions are being made by individuals with inferior knowledge, there is little alternative, as Cleveland has written:

> The highest officials of our Government spend their time on crisis management because there is no other way for responsible men to take responsibility for crucial decisions.[46]

Another CD had perhaps a more realistic view of his role in crisis situations than the one cited previously, recalling that when a *coup d'état* occurred in his country of responsibility, he was first on the scene in the department's Operations Center, joined shortly thereafter by the DAS and assistant secretary. The end result was a "three-way" view given to Rusk and Katzenbach the next morning. In other words, "the matter wasn't taken out of the hands of the country director—there was just more input to the decision." (CD #31)

[45] Vital, pp. 95-96.
[46] Harlan Cleveland, "Crisis Diplomacy," *Foreign Affairs*, 41 (July 1961), 638.

In such situations, there is a tendency to ignore formal channels and to draw upon whatever expertise is available. One CD, speaking of Secretary Rusk, differentiated routine and crisis situations:

> I think there may be confusion between two types of situations. One, the ordinary day-to-day running of the department, where the secretary will go through organizational channels; secondly, a crisis situation, in which he might want to walk down the hall . . . and get sort of a direct link between himself and the guy who's running the problem at the working level. (CD #12)

Because of this desire to insure inclusion of necessary expertise, the task force has come into increasing use. While it may be true in general that "relevant actors in any policy issue cannot be identified in advance,"[47] the task force is in part an attempt to specify most of them, and to put them in close and continuous contact, so that the time required to define actors by the adjustment process and assertion of interest can be cut short. Similarly, such group decisions may reduce the time required to build support for what is ultimately decided. The country director was almost certainly at the heart of such task forces, and his overall knowledge, if respected, might be the link which allowed them to function effectively.

If organizational constraints are lessened during a crisis, others may be even more compelling. If time is available, it may be possible to develop resources or organizational programs necessary to carry out a preferred course of action even if they do not exist when a solution is chosen. In a crisis, only what is immediately available can be employed. Uncertainty is likely to be intensified, resulting in greater uneasiness than usual about what is possible or likely to be efficacious. Perceptual limitations in problem formulation or in conceptual ordering of the situation may be even more difficult to overcome, because of frantic search

[47] Bauer, p. 15.

for any certainties that can serve as point of departure. This can result in development of false analogies with past events, or in reliance upon false or dubious mental pictures of the world, simply because there is no time for corrective evolution or for input of other perceptions.

In a crisis situation, then, organizational constraints are likely to become less important, while those related to resources, uncertainty, perception of the situation, and time available may be even more difficult to surmount.

Constraints

Throughout this study mention has been made of several factors that must be considered by policy actors, including limited resources, the need for quick decisions, precedent, external circumstances, and previous commitments. Taken together, these constraints restrict what government can do, and limit the options available to actors attempting to deal with current problems. As Gore notes,

> Perhaps even the bargaining models are limited to the extent that they depict organization as an agent essentially free from societal constraints, from its own traditions, and from the expectations (often backed by counter-sanctions) of groups interested in what an agency does.[48]

Even unanimous agreement may not lead to action if resources are unavailable. Resource problems are at the crux of many policy disagreements. As March and Simon observe, "There is no particular problem associated with dividing an unlimited pie."[49] Material resources are the "fundamental common denominator for all government business,"[50] and the lifeblood that keeps a problem solution

---

[48] Gore, p. 156. By bargaining models, he means those such as Lindblom's. In an immediately preceding passage, he has criticized the rational models even more harshly as being naive, in that they ignore the emotional side of man's nature.

[49] March and Simon, p. 123.   [50] Vital, p. 57.

or policy alive. Without them, the best analysis and most perceptive problem formulation will not result in satisfactory responses. If resource lacks are perceived as constraints, the only alternatives seriously considered will be those that can be carried out with available resources; if such deficiencies exist but are not taken into account, any course of action decided upon is unlikely to be implemented. One CD explained how such constraints can wreak havoc with the best laid plans:

> There's no doubt that what you might want to achieve, what you think the policy should be, is bound to be affected, and maybe substantially affected, by external pressures. You may decide that it is in the best interests of the U.S. to try to achieve a certain position on [an] area, and suddenly a Middle Eastern war comes along, over which we had no control, and sends a shock wave throughout [these countries] that can knock your well-laid plans into a cocked hat. Or, if for overriding reasons —let's say a cut in the congressional appropriations for AID—word comes down that every program is going to have to take its cut, that goes for your countries too. All of your arguments about how important it might be to increase our aid to country X are out the window. (CD #3)

It follows that previous commitments making heavy drains on available resources are likely to deter action requiring additional resource allocations, however desirable it may seem.

Other constraints also take their toll. Analysis may be weakened by the unavailability of people necessary to do it properly:

> In the State Department, you are not free to go out and hire people to meet specific job requirements the way you would do your hiring in an automobile factory. You

212

get a limited number of people to choose from, and you have a peculiar, complicated set of jobs. (CD #12)

This may limit the development, creation, or discovery of alternative plans of action. Precedent and the momentum of present policy also limit alternatives, since a major decision often acts to force subsequent problem solutions to conform to stated principles or guiding rules. Pressure from agency constituencies may have the same result if they inhibit flexibility in meeting objections of others involved. (CD #16) One CD summarized many of the constraints:

> You are much more conscious [in Washington] of the constraints that are put on your policy-making functions by the need for congressional support, the need for funds, for public opinion in this country, for the positions and parochial views of other government agencies, other bureaus, and offices in this bureau. . . . You have to work out a policy, not necessarily in the ideal way, but within what is possible against competing needs and other pressures. (CD #19)

Even a general mood may inhibit solutions which at other times might be accepted, as for example during a change of national administration. (CD #22) Similarly, options that go against a superior's known views are not normally likely to be given serious consideration. One must have a

> day-to-day knowledge of what [his] immediate superiors are concerned about—where they feel pressures, where there may be matters that impinge on other countries or might set a precedent for other countries. (CD #9)

Perhaps the most compelling constraint of all is uncertainty about the situation, about what would be efficacious in dealing with it, or about what one's goals ought to be.[51]

[51] See Thompson, pp. 159-163, for a discussion of some of the major sources of uncertainty.

The greater the uncertainty, the more desirable it may seem to do nothing. Acceptance of the viewpoint that most problems ultimately take care of themselves may foreclose actions which should have been seriously considered.

Finally, future avenues of action may be severely restricted by outworn adherence to slogans and other simplifying devices originally applied to make it possible to work with complex situations. Wilensky argues, for instance, that "self-righteous Cold War rhetoric, rooted in the facts of past conflicts, served to perpetuate policies long outmoded."[52] Similarly, distorted perception may prevent operationally possible options from being considered, thereby acting as a cognitive constraint.

In short, many limitations exist which together narrow what is or seems possible. This is yet another reason that action agreed upon is likely to differ only marginally from what has gone before, since solutions similar to existing policy are likely to seem more certain in their possible results than unknowns, and are more likely to successfully navigate the currents and eddies of the adjustment process.

SUMMARY

This chapter has attempted to place the country director in the larger context of policy making in the U.S. government. It should be emphasized again that there is some danger in treating this process as one of sequential stages since some steps which are separated analytically may be absent, may occur out of order, or may be repeated. Even the initial formulation of the problem may be modified if later perceptions cause abandonment of the original definition. Search for alternative solutions may not take place in a particular episode, and problem formulation and search may themselves be a part of the adjustment process. Constraints limiting potential courses of action will be much more re-

[52] Wilensky, p. 20.

strictive in some cases than in others. In most episodes these constraints may make it likely that agreed means to attack a problem will differ only marginally from previous policy and solutions, but in some where they can be circumvented, highly original alternatives may be possible, even if not selected. Just as the adjustment process may be easy or extremely difficult, so in some instances closure will be obtained with little effort, while in others it may never be achieved and the problem left in limbo. Even with respect to the differences between crisis and noncrisis situations there may be no clear distinction, with some arguing that a crisis exists while others prefer to handle the problem in a more normal fashion.

In any event, the CD was so located in the foreign affairs community as to have considerable potential impact in all of these aspects of the policy process. The strength and nature of his actual influence in a given episode started from what came to be accepted as the CD's proper role, as considered in Chapters III and IV, and varied from one episode to another according to the structure of the particular situation, as discussed in this chapter. But the full part CDs came to play in the policy process cannot be fully understood without consideration of the role of incumbents as individuals, for much depended upon how each viewed his role and the situations he encountered, and the talents and abilities he was able to draw upon in carrying out his responsibilities. It is to these individual factors we now turn.

Chapter Six

Individuals and the System

The basic and rapid changes in the nature of the world and in the role of the United States have clearly called into being a new and enlarged concept of foreign affairs, and this in turn entails a different conception of the role and kinds of personnel engaged in it. THE HERTER COMMITTEE

SINCE the CD role was in many respects poorly defined, idiosyncratic factors became very important determinants of CD behavior. The individual CD's personal preferences and abilities influenced the style and content of his performance to a necessarily large degree. The wide possibilities were indicated in the description by one of them of what had happened in his bureau:

> I have noticed that about 40 percent of the country directors through time have been in what I call group A, who set out to be active and not take decisions upstairs, and to take on the functions of the ambassador to a small and necessarily modest degree. Another 40 percent are in group B, and they are good staff men, treating their job like desk officers with more experience and higher rank. The other 20 percent swings from one side to the other. Nobody in State has told group A to "cut it out, slow down," nor come to group B and said, "You've got the responsibility—use it." (CD #15—paraphrase)

Given the numerous contenders for policy influence, a CD carried maximum weight when he combined knowledge and expertise with an aggressive interpersonal style, building prerogatives for his position and accustoming others to rely on him and to include him in their deliberations. While this did not mean that he would prosper by being antagonistic, the seven or eight generally mentioned as being the strongest and most effective were all outgoing

216

and aggressive in approach.[1] The passive CD was less of a problem for other agencies, but also less likely to prevail when disputes arose. The individual CD was more likely to be influential when he could provide services and expertise for other participants in the policy process. To the extent that Secretary Rusk was correct in asserting that the primary problem in government was not bureaucratic warfare but avoidance of responsibility,[2] the CD who chose actively to take charge and to assist others with their duties would increase his influence. There is no necessary inconsistency between other agencies defending their prerogatives and at the same time avoiding responsibility and welcoming someone who would provide leadership, as long as their legitimate interests were given consideration.

In such circumstances, it becomes important to know something about the proclivities and attitudes of individuals filling the CD positions, both to help gauge how likely they were to assert themselves, and because the way they conducted themselves had a critical impact on the development of norms and expectations about what CD behavior should be. In the sections that follow, attention is turned first to FSOs generally, since almost all CDs were selected from this group, and then to the perspectives and experiences of CDs themselves.

The FSO as Country Director

George H. Mead has drawn attention to the importance of the relationship between role and self (the sense of personal identity or "the set of all standards, descriptions, and concepts held by an actor for himself").[3] Building on

[1] Opposite numbers were asked which country directors they believed to be most effective in carrying out the intentions of the concept, whether or not they agreed with it.

[2] Rusk, testimony of December 11, 1963, reprinted in Jackson Subcommittee, *Administration of National Security*, p. 403.

[3] Biddle and Thomas, *Role Theory*, p. 10.

217

Mead's work, Sarbin advanced the hypothesis that "the effectiveness or validity of role enactment is related to the degree of congruence of self and role."[4] When self and role characteristics are in conflict, "enactment is likely to be invalid and unconvincing."[5] Moreover, the behavioral styles of initial incumbents of positions help set the role tone for subsequent ones. As Turner argues, "to the extent to which roles are incorporated into an organizational setting, their persistence is intensified through traditions and formalization."[6] Therefore the self-images of FSOs chosen as country directors were bound to have a double impact: They not only conditioned their own behavior, but also helped define the CD role, thus affecting the behavior of their successors in these positions.

Much attention has recently been given to many aspects of socialization, self-conception, and morale of FSOs. A brief overview of these studies suggests there may be cause for concern about the ability of many of them to accept the new responsibilities implied by formal requirements of the CD system. These findings are not conclusive, but since many of the negative opinions arise from within the service itself, they should not be taken lightly. One of the earlier investigations was conducted by Regis Walther in conjunction with the work of the Herter Committee staff. He concluded, after a comparison of a sample of eighty-seven young FSOs with a like number in other government service categories, that

> compared with a number of other occupational groups the Foreign Service officer tends to score high on the Self-confidence, Academic Data, Problem Analysis, Resourceful Accomplishment, Empirical-Intuitive, Persuasive Leadership and Autonomous scales. These results suggest that he likes work that combines interpreting data and influencing other people. His style for analyzing information tends to be impressionistic and intuitive rather than

[4] Sarbin, p. 550.   [5] Ibid.   [6] Turner, p. 555.

formal, methodical, and statistical; his preferred style for working with a formal organization is to do the work himself rather than to work through a hierarchy. He greatly values personal intellectual achievement and places a moderate value on formal status, social service, and the approval of others.[7]

These conclusions are compatible with part of the argument contained in a widely circulated letter written by six mid-career officers, arguing for changes in style. Among other things, managerial and team elements were held to suffer when compared with individual activities:

> The task of coordination and direction suffers principally from inattention: Foreign Service officers come late and unprepared to executive responsibilities. The habits of diplomacy, characterized by individual brilliance, organizational caution and a continuing effort to widen areas of agreement are not the habits of the good executive or manager.[8]

Chris Argyris, in his controversial study of the "living system" of the department, makes a related argument, contending that the norms of the Foreign Service, which he considers particularly helpful in predicting behavior under stress, act to induce a low risk-taking posture. Such norms include withdrawal from interpersonal difficulties and conflict; minimum interpersonal openness, leveling, and trust;

[7] Regis Walther, *Orientations and Behavioral Styles of Foreign Service Officers*, Foreign Affairs Personnel Study, 5 (New York: Carnegie Endowment for International Peace, 1965), 16. The scales mentioned in the passage refer to the Job Analysis and Interest Measurement (JAIM), a comprehensive battery of tests devised by Walther. See also the Report of Task Force VII, "Stimulation of Creativity," pp. 291-339.

[8] Charles W. Bray III, Peter D. Constable, Morris Draper, Robert T. Hennemeyer, Frank S. Wile, and David E. Zweifel, "1966: Are We Obsolete?" letter to John M. Steeves, director general of the Foreign Service, reprinted in *Foreign Service Journal*, 43 (November 1966), 27.

219

mistrust of others' aggressiveness and fighting; and withdrawal from such aggressiveness and fighting.[9] Low risk-taking proclivity is an inherently *status quo* orientation; and a lack of aggressiveness/assertiveness was unlikely to lead to a strong CD role.

Rufus Burr Smith, a senior Foreign Service inspector, considered the problem of developing management talent such as that required by the CD more directly, and his conclusions were somewhat pessimistic. He argued that experience, advancement, and individual career preferences "produce an intellectual emphasis on narrow political analysis rather than broad thinking on the overall problems of foreign relations."[10] On the management side, Smith asserted that "Foreign Service experience in the middle grades gives little training in the management of personnel, the allocation of resources, or other functions of executive management."[11] He contended, however, that a graver malady was the attitude of FSOs themselves: "Even more fundamental is the continuing failure of many senior officers to recognize that they are in fact executives."[12]

If an organization is not geared to new responsibilities, the individual who does try to operate in new ways may run afoul of tradition, precedent, and current norms to the detriment of his own future.[13] Much attention has been focused on this problem, emphasizing organizational patterns, management, and personnel systems (selection, training, assignments, evaluation of performance). The 1968 report of a committee of the American Foreign Service Association advocated a completely revised personnel system, incorporating all foreign affairs personnel in a way de-

[9] Argyris, pp. 3-9.

[10] Rufus Burr Smith, "Problems of the Foreign Service," *Foreign Service Journal*, 46 (June 1969), 29.

[11] Ibid., p. 30.   [12] Ibid.

[13] For a recent commentary on this problem in State, see Andrew M. Scott, "Environmental Change and Organizational Adaptation," *International Studies Quarterly*, 14 (March 1970), 85-94.

signed to broaden their perspective and experience.[14] The 1970 reform effort spearheaded by Deputy Under Secretary for Management William Macomber, Jr., had much the same emphasis, with a particular focus on what could be done to enhance openness and creativity in the Foreign Service and in State generally.[15]

The organizational milieu may in fact be the key to the problem. The most comprehensive study of individuals in the Foreign Service suggests that they may be more receptive to a managerial approach than often believed. If true, system changes may translate such attitudes into more effective role behavior. This study, John Harr's *The Professional Diplomat*, is based primarily on survey of a 20 percent random sample of the entire Foreign Service conducted in 1966 using a comprehensive self-administered questionnaire. When asked to evaluate a series of recent changes, the sample was highly favorable toward placing operational responsibility for all overseas programs in State, toward a managerial role for the ambassador, and toward the emergence and development of the "country team" concept.[16] One must question whether there is a parallel willingness to accept the increased responsibility that such changes would imply, but these responses are somewhat encouraging to those advocating new approaches to foreign relations management. Another question indicated the same tendency. The sample was asked to rank order eleven diplomatic functions in order of descending importance (the point of reference being the extent to

[14] Committee on Career Principles of the American Foreign Service Association, *Toward A Modern Diplomacy* (Washington, D.C.: American Foreign Service Association, 1968), passim.

[15] See Chapter VIII.

[16] Harr, p. 236. Responses were weighted from 1 (Bad) through 5 (Very Much Needed). All three of the changes cited showed an average score of between 4 and 5, and in the case of the first, overall responsibility for State, 75 percent of the sample chose a maximum (5-point) answer.

which each was/should be at the core of the diplomatic profession). Harr weighted the results by assigning eleven points to first choice, ten to second, and so on. The first four choices were as follows:

RANK ORDERING OF DIPLOMATIC FUNCTIONS[17]

Function	Total Weighted Score	Number 1st Choices	Number 2nd Choices
1. Managing and coordinating a variety of programs designed to advance U.S. interests in the host country	5,477	260	96
2. Conducting negotiations with representatives of foreign governments	5,328	164	142
3. Reporting on significant events and trends in the host country	5,057	61	155
4. Influencing citizens of the host country to understand and support U.S. policies	4,321	41	69

It is somewhat surprising that the managerial aspect was ranked slightly higher than the traditional functions of negotiating, reporting, and influencing. Some of Harr's other data suggest an inconsistency between this finding and the job attitudes of the FSO, but the FSO may be more willing to accept new sorts of responsibilities than he is usually given credit for, assuming the organizational setting ever begins to encourage such behavior.

COUNTRY DIRECTOR PERSPECTIVES

Additional insight into the preparation of FSOs for carrying out new aspects of the CD role can be gleaned by in-

[17] Ibid., p. 243, Table 41.

vestigating the attitudes and opinions of those who actually filled these jobs, or who observed and worked with them at firsthand. One way of exploring whether dimensions previously identified as necessary to an expanded role were seen as legitimate by CDs themselves is to examine the attributes, qualities, and experiences they felt necessary for effective performance. This is an indirect measure, but does shed light on their ability to perform a new role effectively. CD opinions on this topic were sought by asking, "What qualities, styles, and experiences are needed for a country director to be able to perform effectively?" Numbers of responses in each category are undoubtedly smaller than if the question form had required agreement or disagreement with a set list of attributes and experiences.

Most mentioned was experience in the area or country of responsibility. Thirty-eight of the forty-three CDs asked cited this point, in terms ranging from "useful" to "absolutely vital." This did not appear to be a function of whether a CD had experience in his area, for the positive references were almost equally high in either case (see Table VI-1).

TABLE VI-1

SERVICE IN AREA OF RESPONSIBILITY

Importance of Area Experience to CD	Previous Service in Area?[*]					
	Yes		No		Total	
	N	%	N	%	N	%
Important	23	85.2	15	78.9	38	82.6
Not Mentioned	1	3.7	4	21.1	5	10.9
Not Asked	3	11.1	–	–	3	6.5
Totals	27	58.7	19	41.3	46	100.0

Notes: Cell percentages based on column sums. Marginal percentages based on proportion of total N in that category.

[*] Service in Area defined as service in country of responsibility for country directorate covering only one country; Service in Area defined as service in one of countries for country directorate covering two or more countries.

As noted previously, there was general agreement among the opposite numbers that few CDs could be faulted on their substantive area knowledge. Comments such as the following were typical:

> All of the ones I've dealt with are good in terms of experience and knowledge of the area. (USIA deputy assistant director)
>
> The ones I deal with in Latin America are first rate on this score. (DOD/ISA deputy director)
>
> Of the Country Directors I've had direct contact with, I have fairly good confidence in their ability and knowledge of their countries. (political appointee, Department of Agriculture)

The area knowledge of the CDs was clearly an asset in developing sensitivity for problems and expertise necessary for leadership. Nineteen of the country directors interviewed had not served directly in the area assigned to them, but most had wide experience in the same region and were thought to be able to master relevant area details quickly.

The breadth of view of country directors and their competence in nonpolitical matters was rated less highly. Many opposite numbers thought CDs were not as knowledgeable as they should have been about nonpolitical issues. The following comment of an AID regional deputy assistant administrator is representative:

> They do get in deep on the political side, but some of them do not read "the economist's language." This is due both to experience and to their main concern with political matters, which causes them to place short-term political considerations above economic and social considerations in their area of responsibility. (AID #1— paraphrase)

Some opposite numbers were concerned that CDs were primarily political specialists. This was not *prima facie* evidence of lack of knowledge of, and concern for, other activities, but it was likely that such officers would be less sensitized to nonpolitical issues. This possibility was corroborated to a degree by CD responses. Only twelve mentioned the desirability of senior foreign affairs experience, which was usually defined as having served in several areas of the world and in a variety of positions calling for increasing responsibility and for some experience outside the political realm (e.g., economic reporting, politico-military affairs, administration).

Two other attributes related to the leadership and breadth of concern dimensions were also mentioned by a number of country directors. One, cited by sixteen CDs, was having relatively senior-level Washington experience, so that one was able to use the bureaucracy to accomplish his objectives. As one said,

it's difficult to put a guy in a country director job who hasn't had previous Washington experience [and isn't] knowledgeable in the techniques of a bureaucracy. It's a strange town. It's got its own mores. You can learn the mores, but I've seen guys come in without that background, and it takes them six months to a year to find [their] way around and know what levers to pull. When to be tough, when to be soft, and so forth. How to play agencies. We don't have authority in the sense of command authority, but you do have a great deal of authority, if you know how to use it. (CD #1)

The other attribute was managerial experience, mentioned by eighteen CDs. One explanation of the value of such experience was given by a Latin American CD:

[The country director] has to have, I think, a certain amount of experience in program direction, either in the department or in the field. . . . In other words, some skill at leadership and at execution, some executive authority [in] a capacity that he has already performed in, whether he's been a DCM, or senior counselor at a mission, or

225

something of that kind. At least the head of a very large section, so that he's been dealing with people that he supervises. (CD #23)

In this context, several emphasized the importance of being able to delegate and not becoming enmeshed in small details, because "so much happens that if you can't delegate, you get lost very quickly." (CD #13) Another reason that managerial talent was necessary was that the range of topics covered was vast ("everything from mushrooms to F-4s"), and the CD had to be able to keep everything moving and make good use of his staff. (CD #42)

With respect to managerial competence, opposite numbers were again less impressed than with CD area knowledge. Because State was not an agency with large programs, there were relatively few jobs below the DCM-CD level where an officer could gain executive experience, and FSOs were at a disadvantage, at least initially, in positions requiring management of people and resources. One assistant secretary noted that new country directors were frequently too timid in asserting themselves, and that he had to keep emphasizing that they had to take charge, to manage, and to be "self-starters." He continued that he noticed a very definite "learning curve" in their performance, as they became more accustomed to aggressive leadership and learned their way around Washington. (STATE #13)

It is more difficult to relate past experience to the activity dimension, in that the extent to which a CD became a planner or initiator rather than just an operator/reactor was circumscribed by the demands placed on him. Similarly, his status was determined only indirectly by his background. If he were an acknowledged expert on his area, he personally would have higher status than if he were not. For the most part, however, status appeared to be a function of the support (see Chapter VII), authority, and latitude given CDs as a group, and the breadth and leadership they exhibited.

Certain other attributes and talents were also mentioned. Thirteen CDs cited the importance of being able to make decisions rapidly and to act quickly and decisively. Interpersonal skills also received a good deal of attention. Most mentioned was the ability to deal with others effectively using tact and diplomacy (10), while others looked to the same point when they suggested a flair for leadership (4), political skills (3), articulateness (3), and persuasiveness (2). Also listed were several traits helpful in coping with substantive problems. These included judgment (6), a sense of proportion and balance about priorities (3), an analytic mind (3), flexibility and responsiveness to new ideas (3), the ability to anticipate problems (2), a sense of when to act and when to wait (2), and patience (2). Since none of these were presented in response to yes-no choices, many CDs who did not mention them specifically undoubtedly subsumed them under more general categories. Table VI-2 summarizes these responses.

The Department of State *has* selected superior officers as country directors, as measured by traditional indicators. By September 1973, 153 individuals had been or were CDs. A bachelor's degree was held by 97.4 percent (149)—better than the 86 percent of all FSOs who had that level of education reported by Harr in 1962.[18] Moreover, 84 had advanced degrees, including 15 Ph.D.'s. Most had already had successful careers, since they were FSO-1s when they became CDs, or were promoted to that rank during or immediately after their CD tours. On another widely used indicator of those who are "making it"—average age in

[18] John E. Harr, *The Anatomy of the Foreign Service: A Statistical Profile*, Foreign Affairs Personnel Study, 4 (New York: Carnegie Endowment for International Peace), 14. The overall percentage has been rising, however, as older officers without degrees retire, since the new recruits do have at least B.A.'s, virtually without exception. Nonetheless, the high CD percentage is impressive when compared with the education levels of those of roughly the same age, the proper level of comparison, as Harr's study cited here (completed in 1962, published in 1965) reflects.

TABLE VI-2

"What Qualities, Styles, and Experience Are Needed
for a Country Director to Be Able
to Perform Effectively?"*

Quality	Responses
Experience in the area/country of responsibility	38
Managerial ability and experience	18
Previous experience in the Washington bureaucracy	16
Decisiveness, ability to act and make decisions quickly	13
Senior Foreign Affairs experience	12
Interpersonal skills	
Ability to deal with others with tact, diplomacy	10
General leadership talents and skills	4
Political skills	3
Articulateness	3
Persuasiveness	2
Problem solving and mental skills	
Judgment	6
Sense of proportion and balance about priorities	3
Analytic mind	3
Flexibility and responsiveness to new ideas	3
Ability to anticipate problems	2
Sense of when to act and when to wait	2
Patience	2

* Number of responses greater than 43 because multiple responses
were solicited.

grade—CDs also showed up very well. As a group, their
average age when promoted to their current rank, whether
FSO-1, -2, or -3, was substantially younger than the average
age at promotion of all FSOs in each of the same three
ranks. CDs came to their jobs with a wide range of area experience, 108 of 153 having served in one of their countries
of responsibility, and 26 more in a related or neighboring
country. Finally, most moved on to other important jobs,
such as ambassador, DCM, counselor at a large post, important staff positions, or senior training.[19]

[19] Appendix A contains more detail on this and other characteristics
of the individuals who hold or have held country director positions.

But it is disquieting that excellent FSOs have not been able to have more impact as CDs. This may be a sign that there are too many problems for them to overcome without more help, but it is also possible that the outstanding FSO by traditional measures may not have the mix of talents and experience required for the peculiar responsibilities of the country director. Some impressionistic evidence bears this out. Almost everyone interviewed was asked to name incumbent CDs who were carrying out assigned responsibilities particularly well. The replies must be evaluated with care, since certain CDs were much better known to respondents than others, and some excellent ones were no doubt slighted. Even so, the same CDs tended to be cited by a whole range of sources. Almost 80 percent of incumbent CDs at the time of the study (38 of 48) had "standard" careers, having come into the Foreign Service by the examination method. Only ten had entered in other ways (as Wristonees, later lateral entrants, or returnees to the service from outside government). Yet the eight CDs most cited as outstanding were split equally between the two categories and the two most mentioned both entered laterally. There are two possible reasons, assuming some validity in these responses, for this imbalance. It is conceivable that those who enter the Foreign Service in atypical ways are particularly well qualified, since they have to overcome a certain negative bias. But it is also possible that their experience outside the Foreign Service has better prepared them to be CDs than the experience an FSO normally gains within it.

Some confirmation for the latter view comes from comparison of the specializations of all incumbent CDs at the time of the primary interviews with those cited as being particularly effective. The whole group was heavily weighted toward the political cone, the traditional glamor specialty of the Foreign Service (25 political; 11 political/economic; 6 political/military; 3 development; 2 economic; 1 political/consular; 1 political/international organizations).

Yet only two of the eight "strong" CDs were solely political specialists, while the other six were divided between political/economic (3), political/military (2), and development (1).[20] This finding is at least suggestive that officers whose career specialties bring them in closer contact with the programs and activities of other agencies, and/or force them to deal with several types of issues may be better attuned to a broad view of their responsibilities when they become CDs than is the case of those who lack such breadth of experience. In short, more diverse career patterns may serve as an "inside" equivalent to the apparent advantage of "outside" preparatory experience cited above.

The opinions of opposite numbers, the career patterns of CDs, and their own comments all suggest that most CDs were more likely to exercise an expanded leadership role by virtue of their area expertise than by their breadth of concern and wide experience in areas other than political affairs. They were not in general prepared to cope with the new elements of the CD role. There were, of course, notable exceptions, but the conclusion must be that on balance the experience of the CDs was not such as materially to enhance the possibility that the new elements of the CD concept would be successfully incorporated into their operating styles.

PERSONAL SATISFACTION

It was obvious that country directors were sometimes frustrated by their inability to assume strong leadership. Yet almost all those interviewed found compensations and indicated a reasonably high level of personal satisfaction.

Opinions were solicited by asking first, whether job content was satisfying for the current stage in one's career, and second, whether being a CD had utility for gaining further

[20] Derived from information provided by the Special Assignments Division, Office of Personnel, Department of State, in early 1969.

advancement. In each instance strongly positive responses were obtained.

Only three of forty-three CDs found their jobs not particularly satisfying, and one qualified this by saying that there was little it was possible to do with respect to his country, but that he would have enjoyed being a CD for other countries very much. Of the other two, one was a very senior Class-One Officer nearing retirement who implied he was dissatisfied primarily because he had hoped to have a higher position; and the other said that while the CD job was good for a man's career, he soon found himself bored with it. The enthusiasm of the other forty varied considerably, but all said they basically enjoyed their work. Comments ranged from "good," and "interesting," to "one of the choice jobs in the department," "there are no others in Washington of comparable interest at this level," and "demanding, but unparalleled in terms of straight interest." Although differing degrees of verbal flamboyance on the part of CDs interviewed make any conclusion somewhat impressionistic, the forty with a positive opinion of their jobs appeared to divide into two groups of twenty. The first could be classified as very satisfied, and the second as reasonably so. One reason for these positive evaluations was that the CDs were overwhelmingly political specialists, for whom a position of responsibility in a geographic bureau was a key post. One would expect to find those who succeeded in obtaining positions in their specialty to be basically contented, all things being equal.[21]

With respect to the utility of the CD position for one's career, there was wide agreement that these jobs were useful, subject of course to good performance. Two CDs said

[21] Throughout its history, and particularly recently, the Foreign Service has encouraged officers to take up specialties other than the political one, but has found it difficult to convince FSOs, who thought that political specialists not only had more interesting jobs but also better chances of advancement and of ultimately gaining ambassadorial posts.

that the CD job was not as important or helpful as being an OD under the former system; five said that it depended upon when in his career a man held the job; and three said they were not sure of its effect. The other thirty-three with whom this topic was broached all felt that it was helpful to be a CD. It was not, however, held to be a *sine qua non* for further advancement: "It is useful for education if nothing else"; and "having responsibility is what is useful." Others regarded it as one of the jobs where a man could demonstrate he had the talents needed for positions of greater importance and sensitivity: "It is useful if you can show you can pick up responsibility." In short, despite the many difficulties CDs faced, almost all were pleased with their assignments as country directors.

This finding, somewhat surprising in view of the ambiguous and somewhat difficult positions in which CDs often found themselves, provides grounds for supposing that the somewhat restricted CD role which ultimately developed was reasonably congruent with their expectations and with their self-images of what a CD should be.[22] In part this no doubt reflected skepticism about the likelihood of their being accepted as government-wide foci for country-level activities and policy. But along with the emphasis they gave to area as opposed to programmatic, managerial, or leadership experience as preparation for being country directors, it provides grounds for believing that CDs themselves tended to be more attuned to the residual elements of their role than to those parts which required new orientations and patterns of enactment. What can be called the "political officer mentality," a product of their past experience and socialization in the Foreign Service, seems to provide one more additional reason for the limited development of new role elements. If they themselves did not expect to lead and did not assert their right to do so, others were unlikely to follow.

[22] See notes 3 through 6 of this chapter.

Chapter Seven

The Country Director Experiment: Some Perspectives on Attempted Organizational Change

. . . proposals for significant change are likely to founder unless they have: (1) the support of the leadership corps of the Service itself, as in the case of the Foreign Service Act of 1946, or (2) aggressive, even ruthless, follow-through by the very top political officers in the State Department, as in the case of the Wriston recommendations, or (3) both.

FREDERICK C. MOSHER

ALTHOUGH the Department of State is frequently characterized as the most tradition-laden and Byzantine of Washington's bureaucracies, many of its officials cannot fairly be accused of a reluctance to attempt alterations in its organizational patterns in order to improve performance and contend with changing circumstances. It is equally clear that changes have not always come easily and have almost always been resisted. Many that might have improved foreign affairs management have failed through lack of support. Moreover, those that have become permanent and accepted have generally become woven into the fabric of tradition and orthodoxy and are themselves zealously defended against subsequent alteration. The record of the country director system provides an opportunity to learn more about the phenomena associated with organizational change in government, and shares significant features with efforts to innovate in other organizational settings.

State, of course, is not the only organization where reform has been an issue. A premium has come to be placed on change and adaptation, whether by individuals, corporations, associations and private groups, or government institutions. Finding new ways of adjusting structures and procedures to meet new needs or to deal with old ones more effectively sometimes seems to be the major function of complex organizations today.

Our preoccupation with change, however, does not mean that we understand its complex dynamics, or that a planned organizational change will have its intended result. Indeed, as Bennis has written, "no viable theory of social change has been established."[1] The two predominant models of organizational analysis maintain directly contrary positions about change and why it occurs. The Weberian "rational" model treats the organization as an instrument designed to meet expressly announced goals, regards "changes in organizational patterns . . . as planned devices to improve the level of efficiency," and tends to assume that departures from rationality "derive from random mistakes, due to ignorance or error in calculation."[2] By contrast, the "natural-system" models, which can be traced from Comte through Michels to Selznick and Parsons, tend to

> . . . regard the organization as a whole as organically "growing," with a "natural history" of its own which is planfully modifiable only at great peril, if at all. Long-range organizational development is thus regarded as an evolution, conforming to "natural laws" rather than to the planner's designs.[3]

Both models contain much that is true, but neither suffices by itself. Any viable interpretation of organizational change must be attentive to both planned elements and unintended consequences.

Techniques of inducing change in organizations are extremely varied, but all are obviously based on an assump-

---

[1] Warren G. Bennis, "Theory and Method in Applying Behavioral Science to Planning Organizational Change," *Journal of Applied Behavioral Science*, 7 (October-December 1965), 339.

[2] Gouldner, pp. 404-405.   [3] Ibid., p. 406.

tion that programmed or planned change is practical, whether one relies on structural, technological, or humanistic approaches.[4] There is a certain developing optimism among practitioners of this art, summarized in Bennis's assertion that "the proportion of contemporary change that is planned or that issues from deliberate innovation is much higher than in former times."[5]

Yet it is incontestable that changes do not always work out as planned and, equally important, that the change which "issues from deliberate innovation" is frequently an unanticipated consequence rather than a reflection of the planner's design. Certainly, the country director reorganization produced results only partially reflecting what its designers apparently desired.

In the pages that follow, the CD system is examined from the perspective of the organizational modification it represented, in contrast to its previously discussed operational characteristics. The two are of course related, and much that has been presented earlier on such topics as the developing country director role is as important for understanding how organizational change occurs as for evaluating the place of country directors in the foreign policy community. But here, the intention is to look behind what happened when the CD system began to operate, to how and why it developed as it did. Conclusions from the empirical investigation of the country director change which appear to have wider relevance are presented in the form of summary propositions in the course of the discussion.

[4] See Harold J. Leavitt, "Applied Organizational Change in Industry: Structural, Technological and Humanistic Approaches," in March, ed., *Handbook of Organizations*, pp. 1144-1170, for a summary of such techniques. Leavitt's *Managerial Psychology*, 2nd ed. (Chicago: University of Chicago Press, 1964), develops the same themes, and Chris Argyris, "Effectiveness and Plannning of Change," *International Encyclopedia of the Social Sciences*, XI, 311-319, provides another useful summary of approaches to modifying organizations.

[5] Bennis, p. 337.

How Change Begins

A key tenet of recent work on organizations is the not un-reasonable notion that efforts to change them reflect dis-satisfaction with their performance. March and Simon's general search model states that "the lower the *satisfaction* of the organism, the more *search* for alternative programs it will take."[6] Feldman and Kanter strengthen this statement by contending that "the *major* variable affecting the initia-tion of search is dissatisfaction."[7] Downs extends it by sug-gesting that dissatisfaction with current programs or pro-cedures may result not only from poor performance but also when "normal search reveals some opportunity to sig-nificantly improve that performance."[8]

Mere recognition of inadequate performance levels or of new circumstances does not mean changes will be forth-coming, or if they are, that they will meet the perceived need. There will always be some impetus for innovation, but the response to it is not predetermined, and the form it takes is dependent upon factors other than the perceived need. Specifically, the argument here is that:

Proposition A: Although attempts to change organiza-tional structure, procedure, personnel or policy can result from either *internal* or *external* dissatisfaction with or-ganizational efforts because of poor performance or changed circumstances, successful corrective action de-pends upon *internal* factors and interactions with closely associated organizations.

In the current example, new circumstances and a need for better and different kinds of performance at the work-ing level were obvious to many long before it was begun in

[6] March and Simon, p. 48. Emphasis in original.

[7] Julian Feldman and Herschel E. Kanter, "Organizational Decision Making," in March, ed., *Handbook of Organizations*, p. 622. Emphasis added.

[8] Downs, p. 272.

1966. State's declining position in the foreign affairs community, the frustrations of several presidents with its performance,[9] the many previous efforts to reform and modernize the department,[10] and the several antecedents of the country director system discussed in Chapter II are all indicative of the presence of both internal and external dissatisfaction with the existing state of affairs.

In this situation, further attempts at organizational adaptation were to be expected, for little in the way of significant progress had been made toward solving many of the basic problems which were the source of earlier calls for reform. But without the involvement of certain individuals and a particular set of circumstances, the country director system would not have emerged in the form or at the time it did.

[9] See Chapter I.

[10] Among the many recent proposals suggested by individuals are those presented by John Franklin Campbell, *The Foreign Affairs Fudge Factory* (New York: Basic Books, 1971); I. M. Destler, *Presidents, Bureaucrats, and Foreign Policy*; and Lannon Walker, "Our Foreign Affairs Machinery: Time for an Overhaul," *Foreign Affairs*, 47 (January 1969), 309-320. Official and quasi-official studies have been prepared by the Bureau of the Budget (1945); the first Hoover Commission (1949); the Rowe (1951) and Wriston (1954) committees, both composed of outsiders appointed by the secretary of state; internal groups within State such as the Chapin-Foster study (1945) and a whole variety of programs under the auspices of Deputy Under Secretary for Administration William Crockett (1961-1967); outsiders sponsored by private foundations (Herter Committee, 1962); presidential ad hoc groups (the Du Flon study of 1955 and the Heineman task-force report of 1967); outside organizations under congressional committee contracts such as The Brookings Institution (1951 and 1959) and Syracuse University (1959); "think tanks" with foundation support (Institute for Defense Analyses, 1968); a professional association (the American Foreign Service Association, 1968); and several others. More complete listings and citations for the studies which have been published can be found in Destler, op. cit., p. 297, n. 3; Arthur G. Jones, *The Evolution of Personnel Systems for U.S. Foreign Affairs: A History of Reform Efforts* (New York: Carnegie Endowment for International Peace, 1964); and Frederick C. Mosher, "Some Observations About Foreign Service Reform: 'Famous First Words'," *Public Administration Review*, 29 (November/December 1969), 600-610.

Developing the format of change, building support for it, and neutralizing opposition were all required. They are examples of internal factors alluded to in Proposition A which determine whether change will be begun, and if so, whether it will be successful. It is always difficult to causally link a series of actions leading to a given outcome in organizations, particularly in those as large as the federal government, but certain conditions must be met for organizational change to be initiated:

> *Proposition B*: Suggested changes will be successfully initiated when
> 1. Resources and support needed to make the change are available within the organization or to those who can impose the change on it; and
> 2. Those with such control of resources and support are convinced that the change is needed and act to advance it; and
> 3. Powerful opposition to the change either does not exist or can be neutralized.

This proposition refers only to the initiation of a change, not to whether it is successfully implemented in the sense of meeting the original expectations of its designers. Changes such as the CD system should be seen as being dependent upon two sets of factors: those which are necessary for them to gain acceptance as part of the formal program of the organization, and those which influence whether the actions taken to reach the goals of the reform are effective and lead to fulfillment of the purposes of the change. This distinction can have considerable importance, for the resources, support, and reduction or elimination of opposition which occur before a change is formally made may not carry over or be available to insure that what the advocates of change had in mind actually comes to pass. In short, ordering a change or course of action is not the same as placing the order into effect.

The country director experiment provides substantiation for this line of argument.[11] The prime movers of the change, U. Alexis Johnson and William Crockett, were able to cite the additional demands for leadership which would presumably be levied upon State under the NSAM 341 system to justify reorganization of the working level in the geographic bureaus. Although Crockett in particular had long favored a general flattening of State's hierarchy, they based their case on the need to provide the additional support and staff capabilities for the assistant secretaries who were to head the Interdepartmental Regional Groups under the new procedures, and on the advantages of forcing more decision making on bilateral problems to the working level. Both purposes were to be served by upgrading the individuals in charge of relations with individual countries.

In spite of considerable doubts on the part of the assistant secretaries (who might have been expected to favor the change because it would in theory assist them), Johnson and Crockett were able to convince Secretary of State Rusk that this step was desirable, and to gain what appeared to be his strong support. More generally, they were so situated in the department (the former being the department's liaison to General Taylor in developing the NSAM 341 system from which the CD system followed, and the latter in charge of its organizational, management, and administrative areas) as to be able to control information about what was going to occur while at the same time overseeing planning for it. The result was to limit the possibility of opposition being manifested to the degree that it presented a real challenge to introduction of the CD arrangement. Additionally, Crockett was able to prevail in the negotiations about the number of country directorates to be established in each bureau, overcoming the considerable recalcitrance of many officials in them.

[11] For an extended discussion of the origins of the CD system, see Chapter II.

Thus, it was rather easy to meet the conditions presented in Proposition B which seem necessary to successfully initiate organizational change. Yet there were some potential problems which were to make implementing the CD change more difficult. This could have been anticipated, for some were carryovers from the period before NSAM 341 began to be discussed, when something like the CD system had been proposed but had failed to generate enough support to receive serious attention.[12]

The Implementation of Change

The country director case strongly suggests that over and above a perceived need for change and the means to initiate reform, several factors play an important part in determining whether a design for change will come to fruition. They include the organizational climate, the attributes of initial position incumbents who fill new positions created by the change, the perceived utility of their role, whether that role challenges the prerogatives of others or the self-conceptions of the position incumbents themselves, the presence or absence of role inconsistencies, and the degree of operational support for the change generally and for those filling new roles in particular. In the following sections, each of these will be taken up in turn, except for the attributes of initial position incumbents, which have been discussed in detail in the preceding chapter.

As preliminary points, it should be noted that some of these factors are interrelated (e.g., strong support for a new role is likely to make the organizational climate more favorable to that new role), but all need not be present for successful implementation to occur. Each point listed is itself a summary, and any one of them may display countertendencies. For example, some aspects of the organizational climate favored the CD change while others opposed it.

[12] Chapter II.

Success or failure should not be viewed as a dichotomous variable. It is likely that a major change which has enough support to be promulgated will have *some* effect, even if it does not fully meet original expectations.

Organizational Climate: The Environment of Change

Two elements determine whether the organizational milieu is conducive to a given change: attitudes about change generally, and the reception accorded the specific proposal. While these are related, it is possible that a given change will be accepted even where the general orientation does not encourage change, or conversely that a particular idea may be rejected on merit even where change is welcomed.

Within State, distrust of organizational change, always latent, had become manifest by 1966, due to the activities of Deputy Under Secretary for Administration Crockett.[13] Many officers, particularly in the more senior ranks, were dubious about applying management theory to the department, and ambivalent about the nation's expanded foreign operations. Other agencies, having successfully asserted their independence from State in the 1950s and early 1960s, were skeptical at best about reforms that might even partially deprive them of policy control over their own activities.

At the same time, some individuals were deeply concerned about the sprawl of the foreign affairs bureaucracy, and wanted to make it more responsive to the policy goals of the administration. This feeling motivated those who developed the NSAM 341 change, and clearly lay behind the White House request for General Taylor to undertake his study. In State, the first stirrings of opinion in favor of moving the United States "Toward a Modern Diplomacy" were noticed, which coalesced shortly after the NSAM 341 and country director changes into the successful efforts of the "Young Turks" of the Foreign Service Association to take

---

[13] Discussed more fully in Chapter II.

241

over the leadership of that professional organization of diplomats.[14] These officers, drawn primarily but not exclusively from the younger members of the Foreign Service and related groups, were strongly receptive to innovation and after 1966 supported the country director concept with considerable force.[15] These interwoven tendencies provided some base of support for change, but from the first, several specific problems clouded development of the country director system.

The first was the murky relationship between the country director and the NSAM 341 system announced simultaneously. While State sources confirmed the essential unity of the SIG, IRGs, and CD levels, others questioned this interpretation, particularly whether the CD shared the assistant secretary's executive-chairman authority. Since the SIG/IRG components were introduced by presidential announcement while the CD appeared only in supporting State Department documents, this viewpoint was widespread.[16] It produced a tendency to take the CDs less seriously and, at worst, a belief that State was trying to use NSAM 341 unfairly to further its own interests.

A second difficulty, especially within State, was a proclivity to see the change as purely administrative in thrust, and of little importance for the conduct of foreign relations. For some, it was merely a way of creating senior jobs for the then current excess of Class-One and -Two Foreign

[14] The quoted phrase is the title of the previously cited report of the American Foreign Service Association. It contains a comprehensive program of organizational change for State and the foreign affairs government, and is a good summary of the ideas of the "Young Turks."

[15] Activities of the reformers in State are described in Leacacos, pp. 456-467; and referred to in almost every issue of the *Foreign Service Journal* in the late sixties. Some of the Nixon administration reform efforts (see Chapter VIII) were directly attributable to this group of officers, called collectively "The Movement," and represented in their successful bid to take over the Association by a self-styled "Group of Eighteen."

[16] This argument was made by a range of interviewees in other parts of government.

Service officers. Credence for this interpretation was given by U. Alexis Johnson, who wrote that "the working out of this concept will of course require more rather than fewer qualified senior officers and thus presents additional opportunities for the Foreign Service."[17] Moreover, the CD change was often identified with others made under the aegis of William Crockett, a view held by Crockett himself: "The Country Director concept, which followed some months after my program of M.O.P. [Management by Objectives and Programs], was exactly analogous in objective and thrust."[18] Thus there was a certain "guilt by association" in the minds of those unsympathetic toward Crockett and his restructuring activities. These "administrative" rationales for the CD change obscured its intended leadership and coordination aspects.

A third problem was the limited attention the change received. The announcement of NSAM 341 generated considerable press coverage, but the country director was ignored. Much of the comment focused on individuals rather than the system. There was speculation that McGeorge Bundy's resignation as White House national security advisor was a major reason for creating the system, since it would absorb some of the responsibilities he had held,[19] and some surprise that Under Secretary George Ball was chosen to run the Senior Interdepartmental Group in view of his opposition to the administration's Vietnam policy.[20] There was also skepticism because there was, for some, "a question of whether enough of the right men are in enough of the right spots for the new arrangement to work in

[17] Johnson, p. 6.   [18] Crockett, letter to W.I.B.

[19] Murrey Marder, "LBJ Gives the State Department New Power," *Washington Post*, March 5, 1966. In his press conference at the time of the announcement, General Taylor denied any connection and said he had been working on the new system long before he knew of Bundy's impending departure.

[20] James Reston, "Washington: The Johnson System," *New York Times*, IV, March 6, 1966, p. 10.

practice."[21] Even this coverage quickly evaporated, for on March 7, three days after NSAM 341 was announced, the Abba Schwartz resignation story broke, and the press was occupied with it to the exclusion of other comments on State for the better part of March.[22] The changes thus received little continuing public emphasis at the time discussion would have been most useful in setting the boundaries of the SIG/IRGs/CD field of activity.

Fourth, since the system was not operating when announced (discussed in Chapter II), few results were apparent until months later and momentum was lost. It was deprived of the impetus associated with initial publicity, and the opposition circumvented by the initial secrecy and imposition of the change from the top surfaced with considerable vigor. One school of organizational and management theorists would dispute this argument on the grounds that the only way to insure effective change is to have the participation of those who will be affected in the planning stages.[23] This may be true in some contexts, particularly in small organizations, but it may be difficult if not impossible to have effective rank-and-file participation in determining specific details of changes in one as large as State.[24]

[21] Joseph Kraft, "State's New Role," *Washington Post*, March 9, 1966.

[22] Full details are contained in Abba P. Schwartz, *The Open Society* (New York: William Morrow, 1968).

[23] This of course refers to the "human relations" school of organizational theorists. Formulations would generally resemble the following: "Decisions imposed by the leader are not likely to be lasting or effective." Leavitt, p. 264. There is a diversity of views in this school, but for a brief discussion, see Edmund P. Learned and Audrey T. Sproat, *Organization Theory and Policy* (Homewood, Ill.: Richard D. Irwin, 1966), pp. 3-7, passim. A recent critique of the human relations school and its emphasis on participatory management may be found in Nicos P. Mouzelis, *Organization and Bureaucracy: An Analysis of Modern Theories* (Chicago: Aldine, 1968), pp. 112-118.

[24] It should be noted, however, that one of the goals of Deputy Under Secretary for Administration William B. Macomber, Jr., in the reform program of 1970 was to have proposals developed within State

A related series of developments also affected the climate the CD system encountered. While State was fleshing out the CD structure, efforts were also being made to activate the SIG and the IRGs. On March 10 Harry Schwartz, a career FSO who had aided General Taylor in preparing NSAM 341, was appointed SIG staff director.[25] The staff started small and remained that way, since Under Secretary Ball wanted to proceed cautiously. (STATE #1) Also, Schwartz felt at first that he did not have time to brief new people, and in any event did not want to add staff members before there were jobs for them. (NSAM #1)

A critical point for the SIG was Ball's attitude, as the man designated to run this new instrument which was not of his own design. By one report he was enthusiastic (STATE #14); by another, from someone perhaps closer to him, he was waiting to be convinced of its usefulness (STATE #1); while a third believed that Ball was more of an individual operator than a team player, and that he was less attuned to resource problems in underdeveloped areas for which the SIG was designed than to the more structured problems of NATO and Europe. (STATE #15) The question soon became academic, for a transition was in the offing which effectively stopped SIG development for nearly a year. It was reported as early as May 1966 that Ball intended to resign,[26] and he eventually left State in late September. He reportedly did not want to start anything during his last few months he could not finish, and the SIG became relatively unimportant to him. (STATE #1) With Ball's impending departure, the SIG entered what has been called

---

by those who would be affected by possible changes. Nevertheless, the final decisions were made by the senior officials of the department, and the recommendations of the various task forces Macomber established were advisory only. See Chapter VIII for discussion of the Macomber program and its relationship to the Country Director system.

[25] *Washington Post*, March 10, 1966.
[26] *New York Times*, May 12, 1966.

its "dormancy" in July 1966, and in the next year only three meetings were held, primarily because Nicholas Katzenbach, the new under secretary, consciously opted not to use it.[27]

Thus, by the time the CDs were appointed, the SIG had lapsed into slumber. While some IRGs did come to operate effectively, the system had lost its balance wheel and driving force, and the aspects of the country director role related to the NSAM 341 system failed to develop. This heightened the tendency to consider the country director simply as an office director with a reduced area of responsibility, or as an officer-in-charge with a new title.

In summary, the organizational climate which greeted the CD change was not auspicious. The incompletely specified relationship of the CD to the NSAM 341 system, the assertion that the change was made primarily for administrative convenience, the lack of initial attention the system received, the delay in activating the country directorates, and the early impotence of the SIG all acted to weaken the country director concept and to cloud its role in the foreign policy process.

Utility

If a new role is positively valued by other participants who interact with role incumbents and shows utility for the work of the organization, it will probably be seen as legitimate.[28] One way this can come about is for role incumbents to provide services that assist other actors in performing their own functions.[29]

[27] Information on SIG meetings taken from an unpublished SIG staff study of November, 1968, from which the phrase in quotations was taken. Additional details on the SIG may be found in Chapter IV.

[28] This usage derived from Turner. See Chapter III.

[29] Conversely, if the new role either is not useful, or if it challenges the prerogatives of incumbents of existing roles, it will be negatively valued, will tend to be seen as illegitimate, and sanctions, if available, are likely to be applied.

A new role may be useful for others either by emphasizing what is residual or what is new. If residual role elements are primarily valued, then the change may not "take" even though the role as performed is legitimate. This appears to have been true with respect to country directors. There was evidence that both American embassies in the field and foreign embassies in Washington were pleased with the service they received from country directors, and that the CDs were more useful to them than the CDs' predecessors because of increased rank.[30] Yet providing such service was a traditional function of geographic officers, and only peripherally reflected new elements of the CD role. In the department, there was some success in bringing country expertise closer to the assistant secretary, but the new element—direct contact—was lessened by deputy assistant secretaries acting as a partial layer between CDs and the policy level.[31] The secretary of state did not normally deal directly with country directors, except in rare cases, and the change did not appreciably alter the operations of senior officials. (STATE #16) In the interagency arena, the country director role came to be positively valued primarily because of satisfactory performance of residual elements. The CD was seen as a source of country expertise and as a central repository of information. He was adjudged to be a legitimate participant in discussions on most problems, with the primary function of bringing a State Department, bilateral-relations, and international-political perspective. He was useful as an initial point of contact with State, and in some cases as an expediter who could facilitate agreement.

There was less evidence that new aspects of the CD role were valued, or even much of an issue. While CDs felt they were gradually coming to be accepted as overall coordinators,[32] it was clear that other agencies saw their mandate as

[30] See "Summary of Views from Chiefs of Missions," Appendix III to the TF VIII, pp. 368-371. See also Chapter VIII.

[31] See also Chapter IV and Chapter IX.

[32] See Chapter III for discussion of the data upon which this statement is based.

being to coordinate, not to direct or to manage. Moreover, agreement about the coordinating aspect of the role weakened in specific policy disputes. Even if, as some CDs and others in State contended, the CD could force many decisions to be made at lower levels than previously, this was frustrated to a degree by failure of other agencies to delegate to CD opposite numbers at the same level, and by a tendency to escalate a problem if a more favorable decision might result. Since the CD was unable to act either as overall planner or as a prime initiator of ideas and programs, new role elements associated with these activities had little utility for others.[33]

On balance the CD role had considerable utility for other participants in the foreign affairs community, but the benefit derived primarily from competent performance of residual elements. While the CD role was useful enough to warrant its retention, the intent of the change to provide aggressive new leadership at the country level as well as services, had largely been frustrated.

Role Conflict

As previously introduced, role conflict refers to inconsistent norms and expectations about a given role held by multiple actors or internalized by an individual. If conflict develops about what constitutes legitimate activity for incumbents of new positions, sanctions are likely to be applied and cooperation withheld when possible, at least with respect to contested role elements. Conflict in the current instance was somewhat minimized since some new elements of the CD role failed to develop. It was hardly realistic, for example, to assume that a CD would attempt to take full responsibility for all U.S. activities in his country, or that he would be

[33] See Chapter III. The possible exception to this generalization was in the merged AID and State Bureau for Latin America, where the CASP system made it possible for the CD to plan, to initiate, and to exercise a strong coordinating role, even if final decisions were ratified at a higher level.

able to do so if he tried, in the absence of fundamental changes in the structure, mores, and operating styles of the federal government. The CD's concern with bilateral relations was seen as legitimate and necessary to avoid a narrow focus on functional or technical problems or on a global policy that might be inappropriate in individual instances. This did not keep policy disputes from arising and certainly did not mean others agreed the political/foreign relations perspective should be controlling. Conflict occurred when others considered guidance provided by the CD to be excessive. Legal requirements, established operating patterns, and allocation of budgets to individual agencies made a CD role stronger than persuasion and coordination an unrealistic goal. At times he could prevent proposed actions, but only for strong and compelling reasons.

Little conflict existed over more traditional role elements. The CD was used more than his predecessors as the basic point of contact for foreign and U.S. embassies, and there was no disagreement about the appropriateness of this pattern. He was welcomed as a central source of country information both in other agencies and in State, and he was in a position to influence policy considerably, if his expertise and competence warranted it.

In some respects, role conflict is the obverse of utility. When an actor such as a CD is useful to others, there will be little question about the legitimacy of helpful role elements. Conflict was not so great that the CD was impeded in his functions as a State Department official. Efforts to gain government-wide dominance were opposed, that is, when a CD attempted to live up to the letter of his formal responsibilities.

Cross-Pressures

If some role elements are mutually inconsistent, the role occupant must either emphasize some and ignore others, or attempt to balance contradictory sets of prescriptions. This can lead to immobility and unconvincing role performance.

The situation is analogous to that which exists when self and role characteristics are incongruent, except that there is no evidence of such incongruence when elements of the role are themselves in opposition.[34]

There were two related cross-pressures lessening CD effectiveness. First, as both direct subordinates of the secretary of state and primary Washington contacts for American ambassadors, they faced a potential conflict between the requirements of global policy and harmonious relations with their country or countries. A CD concentrating on advocacy of the case of the ambassador in the field was unlikely to be able to take a broad view of wider U.S. interests. Perhaps more importantly, he was unlikely to convince others of his objectivity even if he managed to square both considerations in his own mind.

Second, formal prescriptions implied that the CD should use his wisdom and experience, together with a "presidential viewpoint," to blend many diverse considerations. But if the CD came to the policy-making forum as essentially an advocate of one conflictive viewpoint (e.g., State Department official urging primacy of political considerations, or special pleader for good relations with his countries), other participants would remain unconvinced of his neutrality.

In short, there were built-in conflicts between role elements which made it virtually impossible for the CD to carry out all of his intended functions, forcing him to engage in a continuous balancing act.

Support

Just as resources and assistance in neutralizing opposition are necessary for organizational reform to be begun, so continued support from those able to apply sanctions to opponents is essential. As Mosher suggests in the passage introducing this chapter, the right kinds of continuing support may be the *sine qua non* for successful implementation

[34] See Chapter III.

of plans for organizational change. Without it, the impact will be dampened, for many actors will choose current certainties over future uncertainties, even if their own situation may improve as a result of changes in procedures or organization.[35]

Several indications of lack of support for the CD change were manifest. Some resulted from the CDs' close ties with groups and other actors who themselves did not have strong roles, while others were due to failure to strengthen the country director himself.

Those in the first category may be grouped under the rubric of role linkage, which refers simply to the notion that the nature of interaction between the CD and his opposite numbers was partially dependent upon relationships between the CD and his hierarchical superiors. The most critical linkages were those between the CD and the assistant secretary, and between the CD and the secretary of state. Their importance was recognized implicitly or explicitly by most supporters of the CD change. For example, one official involved in the reform efforts of the Foreign Service Association "Young Turks" believed that the CD was properly not included in NSAM 341 because he was a subordinate of the secretary of state, and a personal mandate for him was therefore unnecessary. He argued that if the CD were strongly supported by his assistant secretary (acting as executive chairman of the IRG), appeals from the country director's decisions were unlikely to succeed. (STATE #17) Since the SIG and IRGs did not become effective interagency mechanisms, however, the CD was deprived of this source of support. Only one of the forty-six CDs interviewed for this study believed that he had more clout due to linkage to the assistant secretary as executive chairman of the IRG. (CD #37)

On the other hand, the linkage between the CD and the assistant secretary *qua* assistant secretary could sometimes

[35] See Crozier, p. 226, passim.

251

be very helpful to the former. If the CD's actions supported the interests of the assistant secretary, then appeals to the latter would show the CD reflected State's position accurately, and the CD would be challenged less frequently. A forceful CD, given wide latitude and consistent support, could be a formidable opponent for another agency, as one indicated:

> *Question*: Do you find people in other agencies bypassing you and going directly to the assistant secretary?
>
> *Response*: They're welcome to do it—the last guy that did it got his head chopped off. You know, I'm perfectly aware of this, when somebody might think he's going to try it. I'll get the assistant secretary alerted. By and large this is a problem of where your assistant secretary is going to back you. (CD #1)

While some CDs did find this sort of close relationship with their assistant secretaries, it was by no means universal. Moreover, even those assistant secretaries who later indicated they had come to prefer the CD system over the office director bureau format did not appear to *use* the new arrangement in an aggressive way or attempt to force it to work up to its full potential. They did not demand that other actors channel everything relating to specific countries through the CDs, and they were in large measure responsible for proliferating the number of deputy assistant secretaries, blunting the possibility of close and continuing working relationships between themselves and CDs. Their approach to the CD system can perhaps best be viewed as a passive one. An outgoing and assertive CD such as the one cited immediately above more often than not would find himself supported by his assistant secretary, and in general the CDs interviewed believed they were given sufficient latitude, although this did vary from bureau to bureau. But the burden of making the system effective in its interagency and interbureau aspects rested squarely on the individual

CD. The "aggressive, even ruthless, follow-through"[36] Mosher cites as being essential was certainly not forthcoming from the assistant secretaries.

There is admittedly a problem of delegation and internal authority in State. One prime mover of the NSAM 341 system feels that the CD could have been given a very strong role; that it would have been accepted in other agencies if the secretary of state had given strong indication that he wanted it that way; and that there was no prohibition on such delegation just because the CD was not included in NSAM 341. (NSAM #1) On the other hand, we have seen that the secretary of state believed that he could not deal with the country directors individually, and that he could not risk undercutting his assistant secretaries by building them up.[37] CDs received little explicit support from Rusk, and certainly much less than would have been the case under a more organizationally minded secretary who was committed to making the system work.

This is not to say that the secretary did not influence the CD role. In fact, it may have been more dependent on the secretary's standing in the Washington community than on how the secretary dealt with individual CDs. If State and the secretary in particular were the major force in foreign policy, country directors would be in a strong position as long as it was clear they were acting with the support and approval of their superiors. If, however, the secretary was bypassed in important foreign policy deliberations, then the status of country directors suffered along with his own.

Most CDs would have liked more support, but they differed considerably over whether it was possible to enhance CD status by a grant of additional formal authority, or whether the means chosen would have to be primarily informal. There was substantial sentiment for several modifi-

[36] Mosher, "Some Observations About Foreign Service Reform," p. 602.
[37] Rusk, interview August 14, 1969.

cations in the latter category. These suggestions derived from a common hope that they would clearly indicate the CD was responsible for relations with his countries, and that all problems involving those countries should be taken to him. First, some CDs argued that more explicit delegation and obvious support by top officials would be helpful. A greater effort to include the CD in ceremonial functions such as State dinners for visiting dignitaries and top level working luncheons at State was also favored by some, on the grounds that this would indicate the continuing support of the president and the secretary of state for the CD concept.[38] At times, exclusion of CDs from such events was an embarrassment and could snag working relationships:

> To be included would help somewhat, especially with foreign heads of state, particularly if you know and have worked with them. If you're not at the White House with them, they wonder why you're not there, and begin to think, "maybe he's not as important as I thought." (CD #15—paraphrase)

Similarly, another CD commented that local embassies and other agencies took these exclusions as an indication of the unimportance of the CD and therefore tried to conduct their business at higher levels. (CD #27)

Another who made the same argument extended it to a variety of other steps that could be taken:

> There are a variety of degrees of limitations of access to documents, incoming messages and so on—some are

[38] A check of guest lists for more than twenty State dinners during the Johnson and Nixon administrations showed that in no case was the country director included. The junior State Department official present was usually the appropriate geographic assistant secretary. The management staff of State on several occasions attempted to convince the chief of protocol and the White House social secretary that it would help to have the CDs included if they were really expected to live up to their formal role, but no success came from these efforts. (STATE #4)

more restricted than others. The country director is one of the first that gets chopped off—I think he ought to be last. Not that I don't get to see them eventually, but I have to fight my way, and steal my assistant secretary's—not steal, literally—copy of something. Well, it's twenty-four hours too late then. . . . I think, as a flat rule, that whenever the country ambassador, resident in Washington, sees somebody on the seventh floor, the country director ought to be present. Whenever he goes to the White House, I think the country director ought to be there. (CD #6)

One CD summarized this whole relationship between formal and informal ways of improving the CD's status succinctly: "One call from the secretary of state to the country director, bypassing all the other channels, would be worth ten pages of instructions." (CD #1)

It is of course possible that given the realities of current government norms and procedures, even significantly stronger continuing support for the CD concept would not have been decisive. It is clear, however, that far greater efforts would have been necessary for the CD to assume the role originally specified for him. One can fairly conclude that the CD concept was either oversold at the beginning and that a strong emphasis on government-wide leadership was not desired by the president and the secretary of state, or that as the CD system began to operate, it was substantially undersupported.

The difference between the support needed to initiate a change and that required to make it work is clear in the country director case. The advocates of the system in the beginning, with the exception of Secretary Rusk whose commitment was not deep, were not in a position to have much influence on how it actually worked when placed into effect. Crockett and his managerial planners could engineer a formal change, but since they were not involved in the substantive operations of the geographic bureaus or in the working relationships between CDs and those elsewhere in government, they could do little except urge that the CD concept be given a fair chance. Those most involved in the new system, particularly assistant secretaries and other officials in the geographic bureaus and less directly the seventh floor officials and staffs, were in practice the individuals whose support or lack of it would count most. But since they were frequently skeptical and had no personal commitment to the system, and in some cases had seen it imposed upon them against their will, it is not surprising that they did not expend a great deal of effort in attempting to buttress the newer and more controversial elements of the CD role. Without this support, the emphasis was almost inevitably placed by most relevant actors upon the more traditional role elements inherited from previous types of geographic bureau officers such as officers-incharge and office directors. Only occasionally was a particularly strong and well-situated CD able to function in ways more nearly approaching what advocates of the system had hoped for when they promoted the change.

CHANGE IN ORGANIZATIONS

The conditions and factors which affected the ultimate success of the country director system in State appear to have wider applicability since questions of organizational climate, role utility, conflict among actors, role uncertainty, and support seem to be inherent problems associated with organizational life. These important factors are summarized in Proposition C:

Proposition C: The degree to which a suggested change, creating a new position in an organization, is successfully implemented (as opposed to initiated) is primarily the result of the informal norms and expectations that become associated with the newly created position. Successful implementation is most likely when:

1. Organization climate is favorable to change and innovation.
2. Initial position incumbents are qualified by socialization, background, operating style, and predisposition to emphasize intended performance goals of the change.
3. New roles associated with new positions show signs of having high utility for the operations of the organization and related or associated organizations.
4. New role components do not challenge prerogatives of other existing roles or self-conceptions of position incumbents, thus lessening the possibility of role conflict.
5. Role elements are consistent with each other, reducing the possibility of immobility due to cross-pressuring.
6. Continued and genuine (as opposed to pro forma) support for new role elements and for position incumbents is forthcoming from those most directly concerned with the new position and/or in a position to apply sanctions to opponents inside and outside the organization.

The record of the country director experiment in State does not directly relate to other forms of organizational change not involving the creation of new positions and the development of roles associated with them, but it does seem plausible that many of the same factors and conditions are relevant in other contexts as well. Certainly support for such changes from those in positions where they must be reckoned with must be forthcoming, and a favorable organizational climate supportive of change will enhance the possibilities of success. Utility of suggested changes for the organization will lessen opposition, and consistency of the change both internally and with existing prerogatives of others should have the same effect. Thus the basic argument presented in this chapter and summarized below may be of value in conceptualizing problems associated with many forms of organizational change.

The starting point for any organization change, unless one assumes it springs entirely from whim, must be dissatisfaction with the current state of affairs. This need not be universally felt, nor for that matter sensed within the organization at all if it is sufficiently strong outside it. Such dissatisfaction may surface because of poor performance, but may also occur if it seems possible to improve upon what was previously considered satisfactory achievement. There is nothing startling about all of this. What may be less obvious is the contention that successful implementation of corrective change depends upon factors internal to the organization and upon interactions between its members and other actors in closely associated organizations. Change requires action, and action requires authority to prescribe new procedures, structures, personnel, or policy that will be accepted by organizational members. It also requires control of resources essential for the change, and the ability to thwart opposition by persuasion or sanction. Both legitimate authority and control of resources usually rest with the top or second levels of the organization itself, or in the case of a federation of related organizations such as the U.S. government, sometimes with the overall leadership. These might be called formal factors necessary for successful change.

Essential informal factors are even more dependent upon internal conditions in the organization, since they include receptiveness to change, the preparation and predisposition of personnel who fill newly created positions, the utility of the new position for the activities of the organization and those associated with it, the amount of support provided by those who "count," and whether there are conflicts between the intended change and what already exists. It is these informal factors which primarily, although not exclusively, determine whether a change that has been initiated (begun formally) will be successfully implemented (carried out so that its objectives are substantially met). Once a change is formally begun, the interplay of organizational life determines the ultimate effect.

A new position created by change will be accompanied by a role consisting of norms and expectations about why incumbents should contribute to the functioning of the organization. These roles result from formal instructions about the change, from residual patterns that carry over to the new position, and from new norms and expectations developing as the new-position incumbents begin to carry out what they interpret to be their responsibilities.

A change such as creation of the country director positions suggests the potential impact of change on decision-making patterns; if it and the accompanying innovations of NSAM 341 had been substantially implemented, the policy-making process would have come to function in a considerably different fashion. Power at the working level would have been much more centralized in the Department of State than previously. A strong role for the CD, the product of the formal and informal internal factors discussed in the study, would have led to substantial influence in the continuing and collective policy-making process. Legitimation, strength, and prestige of superiors and close CD relationships with them, continued support, delegated authority, strong and productive working relationships with opposite numbers, and the absence of dissonance about what the CD should do would have contributed to such a role. There are other factors that make a strong impact in the policy process possible. These include the ability to control problem definition, formulation, and participation in individual episodes; access to and control of information; and effective operating styles and high levels of performance. All are in some way interdependent with the strength of the CD role.

It has not been possible to make this argument for the interrelationship of organizational change (and new roles deriving therefrom) and decision making in as strong terms as would have been desirable. Since the CD change was only partially implemented, its effects were considerably dampened, and the result on decision making and problem solving was modest, albeit perceptible.

Yet the system had as many supporters as critics, and the perceived advantages and disadvantages of the system made further change, either toward scrapping the system or in the direction of strengthening the CD concept, an active possibility. The nature of these evaluations, the proposals for further change, and the prospects of further modifications taking place are the next subjects of discussion.

Chapter Eight

The Country Director's Future:
Survival, Modification, or Extinction?

To determine the best course to follow in the future, it is almost always useful to understand where we have been. Santayana's observation, that those who will not learn from history are condemned to repeat it, is as applicable to the narrow problems of bureaucratic form and organization as it is to the broader context to which Santayana applied it.

COMMITTEE ON CAREER PRINCIPLES,
AMERICAN FOREIGN SERVICE ASSOCIATION

A PARADOX of the country director system is that although it did not approach its intended purpose of gathering all the multifarious strands of U.S. policy and programs in individual countries under the strong control of one individual, it nevertheless became generally accepted and approved in its modified and less encompassing operating version. Of the many suggested changes in the system put forth almost from its inception, virtually all have been directed toward strengthening the role the country director could play. Again there is a paradox, for most of the actions actually taken which affected the system tended to vitiate the possibility of such a role developing. The diversity and track record of recommendations about the CD arrangement, when compared with what has actually transpired, shed additional light on how the system operated in practice, and allow further understanding of the difficulties encountered in implementing organizational change. They also provide clues about what the future is likely to bring with regard to the organization of State's regional bureaus.

EVALUATION: HOW GOOD IS THE SYSTEM?

By 1970 there was general agreement that the country director system was effective, and "preferable to any alterna-

261

tive form of organization. . . ."[1] Assistant secretaries gave it general, if mild, approval as noted earlier. United States ambassadors abroad, responding to a survey about the system, preferred it by more than three to one to the office director arrangement it had replaced.[2] Moreover, in spite of the severe limitations on their developing role, CDs interviewed also favored the new system to the old by the same proportion. Twenty-eight favored the CD system, six had no preference, nine favored the previous system and three were unable to compare the two. Most preferences, however, were mild in intensity,[3] perhaps reflecting the system's limited impact. Responses by bureaus are shown in Table VIII-1.

The greatest divergence of opinion was in the Bureau of European Affairs, and there were CDs in every bureau except East Asian and Pacific Affairs who preferred the previous system. In the Bureau of African Affairs opinion was as divided as in EUR, although preferences were less intensely held, possibly because the CD in AF was not truly a "country director" in the sense of having responsibilities for a single country. However, in EA, where the original geographic area conceptions were more closely adhered to, CDs preferred the new system unanimously.[4]

---

[1] TF VIII, "The Role of the Country Director," p. 342.

[2] TF VIII, "Summary of Views of Chiefs of Missions," p. 370. Not asked to compare the two systems directly, 27 of 35 who nevertheless made the comparison preferred the CD system, and the other 8 were served by arrangements which were new in name only, since the areas of responsibility of the former office directors had not changed when their titles were changed to country directors.

[3] Since these opinions were solicited by relatively unstructured questions and interpreted by the author, the system preference indicated is probably more valid than the intensity. Nevertheless, it was clear that the CD system was preferred by a very large majority of the CDs interviewed.

[4] See Appendix B for a listing of the countries assigned to individual country directors. Ultimately, the Bureau of European Affairs reverted part way to the older patterns of organization, featured by fewer office directors, each with more countries of responsibility. See following sections.

TABLE VIII-1
SYSTEM PREFERENCE

Bureau	Prefer CD Strong	Mild	No Preference	Prefer OD Mild	Strong	CDs Responding	Total CDs in Bureau
AF	–	3	1	3	–	7	9
ARA	3	4	1	2	–	10	10
EA	1	8	1	–	–	10	11
EUR	2	–	3	–	1	6	9
NEA	–	7	–	2	1	10	10
Sub-Total	6	22		7	2		
Totals	28		6		9	43	49

Note: Total CDs = 49; Not interviewed = 3 (2 EUR, 1 AF); Unable to make choice = 3 (1 EUR, 1 EA, 1 AF).

These preferences reflected perceived advantages and disadvantages of the new system, as well as the effect of the change on the respondents personally. Usually CDs found both good and bad in the new system. Most mentioned as an advantage was upgrading the individual responsible for bilateral relations. Sixteen CDs saw this favorably, but it led to a corresponding difficulty noted by five CDs: the downgrading of the desk officer (now called country officer), since the CD had a much narrower span of responsibility than the OD.

A related advantage, cited by fourteen CDs (including many of the sixteen above), was the elimination of some layering in the department. Only one said it had not diminished, while another argued that the same layers existed but that increased rank made them easier to deal with. Also related was the CD's ability to sign off cables and send them on his own authority, which was very useful in expediting more routine matters, and which the officer-in-charge had been unable to do. This was mentioned by nine CDs. To this extent, Secretary Rusk's hope that decisions could be forced downward was partially met. At the same time, it showed that high status for the CD had not materialized, for these CDs were clearly comparing themselves to the previous more junior officers-in-charge, not to office directors of equivalent rank.

A fourth advantage, cited only by CDs in ARA-LA, but important because it was mentioned by seven of ten interviewed there, was the ability of the CD to integrate significant elements of policy relating to his countries. This was primarily a function of the joint State and AID responsibilities held by CDs in that bureau.

Several other advantages were also noted. Four said that the CD system gave the working level geographic officer a more direct channel to the assistant secretary, but others indicated this had not been a major problem previously. Embassy relations were held to have been improved both with respect to U.S. missions in the field and foreign embassies in Washington, with five citing the former and four the latter, although one CD said that because of the change foreign embassy representatives actually attempted to deal higher in State than previously. Judging from the other responses, this apparently was an isolated case. Finally, two CDs said that State was able to react to developing situations more rapidly with the streamlined access to the assistant secretary, and many others might have agreed if asked directly. It is indicative of the limited impact of the system that only two asserted the CD was in a unique position to isolate country problems early as a result of his overall viewpoint.

The major disadvantages listed fell into four broad categories: those related to the nature of the smaller country directorates as opposed to the former offices; those which were manifestations of having fewer subordinates; those which were due to the need for more coordination at higher levels; and finally, those relating to asymmetry.

In the first group, six CDs said that since the CD had a

smaller geographic area than the OD, it was difficult not to have a narrower view, and three (including one of these six) argued that the smaller area did not give a senior man sufficient responsibility.[5] Five also said that the CD became too involved with details, interfering with the desk officers and making it difficult to convince superior FSOs of fairly senior rank to take subordinate jobs in the country directorates.

The second group of disadvantages cited were more the result of smaller offices, that is, offices with fewer officers assigned. There was a loss of flexibility, particularly when officers were on leave, traveling, ill, or detailed to task forces. An office was more easily able to cope with the absence of one or two of ten than one or two of five. Six CDs said that although in theory they were not allowed to have a deputy who could serve as an alter ego, there was a need for an officer who could act for the country directorate when necessary. Often the most senior desk officer was a de facto deputy, but since he also had primary responsibility for a part of the area, he had to sacrifice one part of the job or the other. The six CDs who made this argument said that while a full-time deputy was likely to be underemployed, the CD was often too tied to his office to function effectively. They concluded the solution was to have larger geographic units (i.e., like the old offices) with deputies rather than smaller units without them.

Another difficulty was that the CD could not deal with certain problems formerly within the purview of the office director. It was argued by seven CDs that more high-level coordination was needed, because some problems now involving more than one CD could have been dealt with previously by a single OD. One made the contrary point

---

[5] These responses clearly reflected a traditional view of life in State, for the measure of a man's success through the years has been how much of the world he was responsible for. These CDs did not feel that the added functional responsibilities made up for a reduced area, and therefore were not attuned toward such responsibilities.

since he believed that ODs had dealt bilaterally with each country on most issues, and that their large number of assigned countries meant only that they were less knowledgeable about each. Related to this, one CD said that more problems than previously went to the Regional Affairs offices. Finally, three CDs felt that CDs were not drawn upon as the ODs had been, as one put it, "as an inner committee for running the bureau." (CD #26) This was seen as both a function of the increased number of CDs and of their more limited geographic spans of responsibility.

A final disadvantage related to interagency matters, listed by three CDs, was that "by increasing the rank and the status of the [geographic officer] in State you leave him without effective opposite numbers." (CD #15) Since State was organized more deeply geographically than any other agency or department, upgrading the man in State placed him on a rank level held by those with much wider geographic areas in other parts of government. This structural asymmetry left him with no one of equal authority and detailed knowledge to work with.

With few exceptions, the advantages and disadvantages cited referred to changes within the Department of State. Furthermore, none are related to the SIG/IRGs arrangement, to which the CD system was initially linked. They indicate, as Spain has argued, that the CD change had the least impact in the field of interagency coordination.[6] One possible reason was cited by one of the more experienced CDs:

> On the face of it, I think I would prefer the old arrangement, because the reorganization only affected the State Department, it didn't affect any other agencies. And I think that's the key to the organizational effectiveness of the country director system. (CD #18)

It is hard to know whether to list differences between the CD and the OD system regarding interagency relations as

[6] Spain, pp. 35-36.

advantages or disadvantages, for directly contradictory answers were received when CDs were asked whether they fared better in this arena than their linear predecessors. Eight specifically commented that the CD had more interagency authority, while nine said he had less. On the negative side, comments ranged from "maybe even less" to "no difference whatsoever" to "interagency coordination has become more cumbersome." The affirmative responses were mild, indicating that any improvement was unspectacular, and were couched in terms such as "on balance, somewhat better," and "marginally improved." Thus, whichever side the CD took on this question, he would agree that the anticipated increase in authority had failed to materialize.

The advantages and disadvantages cited by the CDs interviewed in 1968-1969 paralleled those developed in the course of the Nixon administration management review of State, conducted during 1970. This program was announced on January 14, 1970, by William B. Macomber, Jr., deputy under secretary for administration, in a speech delivered to employees of State, AID, USIA, and the Arms Control and Disarmament Agency in which he addressed himself directly to State's weakened position in the foreign affairs community. After discussing some trends of the postwar era in terms similar to those employed in Chapter II, he asserted that "the key fact is that as an institution, despite many brilliant performances along the way, we have not met the challenge of foreign affairs leadership as successfully as we might have."[7] Macomber continued by emphasizing the Nixon administration's desire to attack these problems, and announced that task forces would be appointed to examine such areas as career management, performance appraisal, personnel requirements, training, recruitment, creativity, management evaluation, and manage-

[7] William B. Macomber, Jr., "Management Strategy: A Program for the '70's," speech delivered January 14, 1970; reprinted in *Department of State News Letter*, No. 105 (January 1970), 2-5. Cited passage from p. 3. Also reprinted in *Diplomacy for the 70's*, pp. 587-605.

ment tools. On January 28 thirteen task forces were appointed, including one—Task Force VIII—which was assigned to explore "The Role of the Country Director."[8]

Task Force VIII was chaired by former CD James Spain, whose earlier comments have been previously cited. Its members included six incumbent CDs, country officers, the director of the new Planning and Coordination Staff, a Regional Affairs office director and a DAS from a geographic bureau, and opposite numbers from USIA, AID, ISA, and the Bureau of Economic Affairs. After almost four months' work, it presented a report in June 1970 containing many recommendations and a detailed analysis of the strengths and weaknesses of the CD system, both as originally envisaged and as operating at that time. This comparison, prepared by a working group of the Task Force and published as an appendix to its final report, illuminates the differences between intent and practice.[9]

It is worth noting that several of the perceived weaknesses of the original CD system were held by the working group to have been attacked in part by the way the modified CD system operated (see Weaknesses 1, 2, 3 of I versus Strengths 3, 4, 5 of II in Table VIII-2). At the same time, some supposed strengths of the modified system—those relating to the intermediary role assigned to deputy assistant secretaries—were seen as drawbacks by the CD interview

[8] *New York Times*, January 29, 1970. The exact titles of the task forces and their chairmen are listed in *Department of State News Letter*, No. 106 (February 1970), 6. Full membership lists accompany each report as presented in *Diplomacy for the 70's*. See my "Diplomacy for the 70's: An Afterview and Appraisal," *American Political Science Review*, 68 (June 1974) for a more complete review of this program.

[9] Appendix II to TF VIII, pp. 360-367. The summary in Table VIII-2 is summarized from this report, which in addition to comparing the CD system as conceived and as modified, also lists strengths and weaknesses of other possible arrangements, including the former office director system, a formalized deputy assistant secretary system, an ambassadorial system, and some others which would involve a major restructuring of the foreign affairs community.

TABLE VIII-2

STRENGTHS AND WEAKNESSES OF ORIGINAL AND MODIFIED COUNTRY DIRECTOR SYSTEMS

I. Original Concept	II. Modified (Operational) Concept
Strengths	
1. Single, high-ranking responsible country level focal point with concentrated knowledge and significant delegated action authority.	1. Single, high-ranking responsible country level focal point with concentrated knowledge and significant delegated action authority.
2. CD able to devote time and attention to one, or at least a very few, U.S. and foreign embassies and ambassadors.	2. CD able to devote time and attention to one, or at least a very few, U.S. and foreign embassies and ambassadors.
3. Increased access to higher levels for action officers, with minimum number of intermediate layers.	3. Subregional deputy assistant secretaries help in supervision, easing workload of assistant secretary.
4. Encourages development of managerial ability.	4. Informal focal point, at the DAS level, for coordination of subregional policies and relationships.
	5. DASs provide assistance to CDs in dealing with other agencies.
Weaknesses	
1. Large numbers of CDs, creating difficulties of supervision by assistant secretaries, and infrequent contact for policy guidance.	1. CDs removed from frequent contact with and continuous guidance by assistants due to numbers and duties of DASs used as intermediaries.
2. Small country level staffs make shifting of personnel difficult, as in crisis situations.	2. Small country level staffs make shifting of personnel difficult, as in crisis situations.
3. Ambiguous authority and lines of contact for the CD with respect to other departments; no natural opposite number contacts.	3. Ambiguous authority and lines of contact for the CD with respect to other departments; no natural opposite number contacts.
4. No institutional focal point for coordination of subregional policies and relationships.	

Note: Information summarized from Appendix II to Report of Task Force VIII, reprinted in *Diplomacy for the 70's*, pp. 381-382.

sample. Neither system dealt with the major problems of ambiguous authority and lack of appropriate opposite numbers, each of which limited the CDs' potential for strong interagency leadership. As we shall see, the recommendations of the large majority of the whole Task Force tended to side more with the CD panel with respect to the deputy assistant secretary and improving authority. That is, in each case the thrust of the suggestions, if enacted, was to move closer to the original CD concept.[10]

PRESCRIPTION: SOME POSSIBLE MODIFICATIONS

Country directors and others who felt the current system had disadvantages were quick to suggest modifications. Similarly, Task Force VIII, set in motion by a general dissatisfaction with management of foreign affairs, made numerous recommendations for strengthening the country director system.

The major source of contention among CDs was whether it would be desirable or useful to give the CD more formal authority.[11] Fifteen said that it would be helpful and possible while seventeen said that mere legal authority was not enough, and that informal means were necessary. Specifically, nine CDs believed additional high level support was necessary, in order to indicate to others that the CD was valued by his own superiors. It was suggested that various means of building up the CDs' prestige could be used, including having them present at all sessions between ambassadors from their countries and any senior U.S. official, and

[10] Somewhat paradoxically, in practice the concept tended to be vitiated, for reasons to be discussed later.

[11] It should be recalled that NSAM 341, issued by the National Security Council and therefore government-wide in its inception, referred only to the SIG and the IRCs and to the responsibilities of the secretary of state, while the CD system designed to accompany these changes was promulgated in FAMC 385 by State, which had no legal applicability to other agencies.

invitations for them to attend appropriate State dinners and working lunches. Six CDs, including four of the nine above, made this argument. A related point, advanced by eight CDs, was the need for more guidance from the top specifying what the CD was expected to do. While this would not necessarily increase his range of authority, it would prescribe it more explicitly.

With respect to interagency problems, five argued for some formal budget control or review of other agency programs, as a means of insuring a formal input into relevant policy development of other agencies. Except in ARA-LA, at the time of the interviews no such review system existed. However, review procedures were developed informally in some individual cases, and some officials, including Bureau of the Budget representatives, advocated their adoption. (BOB #1)

Finally, several CDs asserted that the biggest favor that could be done for the geographic bureaus would be to cease and desist from making further changes, concentrating instead on making the current system work to its full capacity. This viewpoint reflected both a skepticism about the efficacy of organizational changes in improving performance, and a dislike of the inevitable confusion accompanying any major restructuring while new routines and operating patterns became established.

Once again, opinions of CDs and of Task Force VIII were essentially parallel. What is striking is the extent to which each resembled the previously cited comments by Secretary Rusk before the Jackson Subcommittee, efforts of William Crockett, and original CD concept. Since the primary finding of Task Force VIII, already cited, was that the CD system was the best likely to be found, its recommendations were directed to increasing the effectiveness and removing defects of the existing system, under the assumption that the structure of the foreign affairs community would remain essentially unchanged. It was noted, however, that

271

almost every aspect of our study of the director's role points toward the desirability of a more unified and integrated foreign affairs structure. If the director is to lead and manage, the more knowledge and control he has of economic and military budgets and programs, the more effective he is going to be. If his view is to be truly government-wide and not primarily political or diplomatic, he would be best situated in a unified foreign affairs structure.[12]

Organizationally, little change was recommended in the current assignment of countries to country directorates, but more rational guidelines were provided, replacing personal whims of assistant secretaries or short-run political exigencies as the determining factor. It was also suggested that periodic reviews of CD staff composition be undertaken and that a better effort be made to draw junior officers into the process by assigning more of them to country officer positions and by avoiding hierarchical patterns in country directorate operations.

With respect to relations within geographic bureaus, greater contact between assistant secretaries and CDs was urged, and it was strongly recommended that DASs be prevented from becoming a layer between CD and assistant secretary, by employing only one alter ego DAS and assigning others to functional responsibilities. Review of the division of labor between regional offices and CDs was encouraged, the objective being to assign all bilateral matters to the CDs. Finally, it was held that the CD should be given authority to sign all telegrams of whatever classification which dealt with bilateral matters.

Relations with the seventh floor and the White House needed considerable improvement, according to the report. Proposals included arranging for CD attendance at all meetings or social functions dealing with bilateral matters, as also suggested by the country director sample.

[12] TF VIII, p. 342.

The Task Force also argued that interagency powers of the CDs could be improved by a more explicit formal delegation of powers, perhaps in the form of a government-wide document issued by the White House or National Security Council. It was also asserted that more formal means were needed to insure that CDs received information copies of all messages sent to missions abroad.

Resources needed to enable the CD better to carry out his functions were also cited. These included sufficient travel funds for post visits by all officers on country directorate staffs; an adequate range of expertise on each CD's staff; and selection of personnel who were action oriented, possessed country and area expertise, skilled in program management and/or in working in the Washington bureaucracy, and who demonstrated broad understanding of problems and programs of other agencies. It was also suggested that the best available officers be assigned, regardless of their professional specialty, and that normal tour rotation be ignored in order to obtain the right officer at the right time. Training procedures and other means of insuring that officers had the background necessary to carry out managerial functions were also recommended.

Finally, it was recommended that periodic evaluation of country directorate performance, as the case with field posts, be carried out by the inspection corps.

PROSPECTS: THE CLOUDED FUTURE

To the reader who has had the patience to explore the CD system this far, these recommendations will not seem new.[13] It was reasonably obvious to anyone familiar with the system that certain modifications would increase the likelihood

[13] It is only fair to inform the reader that there was contact between Task Force VIII and the author during the time that both the initial version of this study and the task force report were being prepared. The latter had access to preliminary drafts and findings of this study, and the author benefited from conversations with members of the Task Force and participated in one meeting of the entire group.

that the original CD concept would be more nearly approached.

At the same time, even formal approbation of all these recommendations would not insure success, in the absence of norms and expectations by all participants that the new CD role was legitimate and these recommendations would enable it to be carried out. If the past has shown anything, it is that formal attempts at change are not enough. Willingness to carry out a new role by position incumbents, and acceptance of that role by opposite numbers and others affected is vital.

It must also be remembered that from some points of view, including some in State itself, a stronger role for the CD posed serious questions. It challenged existing roles and raised problems of a philosophical nature, such as whether a career official, neither selected by an incumbent administration nor confirmed by the Senate, should be delegated such power over bilateral relations. As one dissenter to the Task Force report argued,

> In my opinion, the country director neither can nor should play the major policy role contemplated by the Task Force, and could not play it even if all the Task Force's recommendations were implemented.
>
> He cannot play this role because the foreign policy function is a political one. . . . Though the foreign policy responsibilities of the president and the secretary of state are often delegated downward in the hierarchy, the country director is too far removed from the source of political power to evaluate, reconcile, and arbitrate the U.S. interests involved in any important issue and many unimportant ones as well.[14]

It is not clear, in short, that attempts to increase the CD's formal authority would be accepted, would work or, for

[14] Dissenting view of Arthur Allen to the TF VIII report, reprinted in Appendix I to that report, pp. 357-358. Quoted passage from p. 357.

that matter, would be in the best interests of State. Recommendations that seventh-floor principals deal directly with CDs, for example, with the latter keeping the sixth floor of their own bureaus informed, run the risk of weakening the critical assistant secretary level, and in any event do not square with the "chain of policy" or hierarchical operating pattern favored by Secretaries Rusk, Rogers, and Kissinger and probably their successors. A formal grant by an FAMC or NSC directive suggesting that the secretary and/or president wished CDs to have responsibility and authority throughout government would likely have the same effect as NSAM 341 attempting the same thing at higher levels in 1966—which is to say, not much. It too would probably become a dead letter.

It seems more plausible to expect improvement in foreign affairs at the senior working level as a result of the efforts of individual country directors. Outstanding ones may be able to develop expectations that CDs in general are valuable assets to be used at every opportunity. If so, then reform efforts should be directed to implementing those recommendations aimed at providing the most qualified individuals (those adapted to fulfilling initial role expectations) for those positions, at helping them develop needed skills and expertise at earlier stages of their careers, and at giving them necessary resources.

Progress toward making the CD system work better, if it comes at all, is likely to be piecemeal. One clear indication of the difficulties faced in improving the CDs' position is the limited impact of the Task Force VIII report. Few of its recommendations were followed by the time the "Diplomacy for the 70's" program ended with the departure of Macomber to become ambassador to Turkey; and given the unsettled question of how management functions were to be carried out in the future,[15] any future action springing

[15] Curtis W. Tarr was designated as acting deputy under secretary for management when Macomber left in April 1973, while retaining his position as under secretary for security assistance. By September,

from the program seemed unlikely. Moreover, those recommendations of Task Force VIII which had become effective were relatively minor, such as using "country director" as a generic name rather than title, with CDs being officially designated as "Director of _____ Affairs" (e.g., German, South African), and periodic inspection of country directorates as well as field posts by the new office of the inspector general.[16] Verbal support, at least, was being given efforts to broaden the pool of potential country directors and to emphasize activism and management skills as well as country expertise as essential criteria for selection to these jobs, but here few results had yet become obvious.

Certain other recommended actions were being undertaken, but for reasons directly contrary to those that had motivated Task Force VIII to suggest them. The Task Force had urged, for example, that the composition of country directorate staffs be periodically reviewed to insure adequate balance in terms of grade and opportunities for junior officers to serve in them, and sufficient functional expertise to make them more effective. During late 1971 and early 1972 such reviews were in fact conducted, but the thrust was clearly toward eliminating slots rather than possible expansion to meet the needs detailed by the task force report.

Some of the most important suggestions, such as a broader grant of formal authority to CDs by a secretarial or presidential instruction (FAMC or NSDM) not only had not been acted upon, but seemed very unlikely to be so since

Macomber's position still had not been permanently filled, and Secretary Kissinger's ultimate intentions in the management area were not yet known.

[16] Details in this paragraph are taken from Management Reform Bulletins issued by Macomber's staff which gave notice of recommendations of the program which were being placed into effect, from interviews conducted in January 1972 with two officers directly involved in the Management Reform program, and from subsequent discussions with CDs and others during the summer and fall of 1972.

they ran counter to certain trends and realities in policy making in the Nixon administration.[17] Similarly, with the possible exception of the Bureau of African Affairs, little had been done about deputy assistant secretaries acting as a layer between CD and assistant secretary by virtue of being assigned geographic responsibilities as well as functional ones.[18] Taken altogether, the limited results of Task Force VIII's efforts were not such as to provide encouragement for supporters of the country director concept.

This development stood in some contrast to indications given at the beginning of the Nixon administration that the CD's role might become even more prominent than previously, even though his superiors were clearly at a disadvantage in asserting themselves against White House dominance.[19] Secretary Rogers, in his initial message to State upon taking office, stated that

Country Directors, under the guidance of their Assistant Secretaries, will exercise leadership in the Washington community in policy and program matters relating to the countries under their jurisdiction and in support of our missions abroad.[20]

This formal statement, like those before it, was not effectively followed up. CDs were initially employed to develop

[17] Ibid.

[18] As of mid-1973. Several interview sources, as well as *Management Reform Bulletin No. 11* (March 24, 1971), which reports modifications made in the Bureau of African Affairs.

[19] There are many sources, particularly in the popular press, of the dominance of the White House, and particularly of Henry Kissinger over William Rogers, until Kissinger replaced Rogers as Secretary in September, 1973. See in particular John P. Leacacos, "Kissinger's Apparat," *Foreign Policy*, 5 (Winter 1971-72), 3-27; and I. M. Destler, "Can One Man Do?" Ibid., pp. 28-40.

[20] William P. Rogers, "Message on the Department of State's Responsibilities," February 7, 1969, reprinted in Jackson Subcommittee (National Security and International Operations), *The National Security Council: New Role and Structure* (Washington, D.C.: GPO, 1969), pp. 2-4.

information and answers in response to the blizzard of detailed questions prepared by the NSC staff, as part of their early 1969 efforts to conduct an initial review of a wide range of programs and to provide Nixon and Kissinger with preliminary status reports.[21] Several CDs in the Bureau of European Affairs were called upon prior to the February 1969 presidential visit to Europe. (STATE #4) The source of this information, a senior seventh-floor official, also said that President Nixon supported the CD idea; that the consensus was that the CD was generally establishing himself and moving toward what was sought originally; and that no major changes were planned. He also asserted that under the new system the CD had an important new responsibility as the key figure in preparing country papers for the NSC. The CD did continue this latter role, both by providing inputs for government-wide National Security Study Memoranda (NSSMs) touching on their countries, and by being a central focus, particularly in the early stages of preparation, for the supplementary country-based PARA (Policy Analysis and Resource Allocation) documents which began to be developed in 1971. These documents were geared to the budget cycle and were intended, after their adoption by the relevant NSC-Interdepartmental Group, to guide decision making by the sixth- and seventh-floor officials as well as by other agencies.[22]

[21] This paragraph based on CD interviews in early 1969 and from conversations with two former NSC staff members during the early fall of 1969.

[22] Interview January 1972. The PARA documents, like the CASP previously described, were basically programming documents, supplementary to NSSMs. The CASP system continued to exist, now called CASP II to reflect refinements in procedures. According to some sources, the CASP III documents were too elaborate, while the PARA presentations were too simplistic, and the ultimate goal was to merge the two procedures into one. It should be noted that no bureau or area of the world was covered by both CASP II and PARA. Rather, as programming efforts were extended to areas not previously involved, PARA was introduced, but those already using CASP II continued to

In some individual policy episodes, CDs were quite influential, for example during the Spanish base negotiations and to a lesser extent in the Middle East, where State and particularly Assistant Secretary Joseph Sisco had managed to counter the flow of decisions to the White House and CDs benefited.[23] The director for Asian Communist Affairs (later called the director for People's Republic of China and Mongolia Affairs) was active in preparation for the presidential China visit, was a member of the official party, and ultimately was assigned as one of two deputies when the Peking mission was established under Ambassador David Bruce.[24] In other instances, however, CDs were bypassed along with the rest of State.[25] This varying impact of CDs from case to case was similar to what had transpired during the Johnson administration.

Certain other developments cast substantial doubt on the Nixon administration's commitment to a major CD role. In July 1969 the assistant secretary for African Affairs, Joseph Palmer II, a strong supporter of the CD concept, exchanged assignments with ambassador to Libya, David D. Newsom, who had always preferred the earlier office director arrangement.[26] Shortly after taking office, Newsom reduced the number of country directorates from nine to six, yielding a pattern similar to that existing prior to 1966.[27] In the

---

do so. *Management Reform Bulletin No. 11* also gives some sketchy detail about the PARA operation in the Bureau of African Affairs.

[23] Interviews with CDs and others involved, January 1972.

[24] *New York Times*, February 13, 1972, March 21, 1973.

[25] For example, during the development of the new China policy and the economic measures announced in August, 1971, and generally during the tragic developments in South Asia during 1971.

[26] From an interview with an officer who had served with Newsom.

[27] This was announced on August 26, 1969. Prior to the CD change of 1966 there had been offices for Eastern and Southern Africa, Northern Africa, West Africa, and Central Africa, plus a regional affairs office. See Appendix B for areas covered by the nine country directorates between 1966 and 1969. The units after Newson's change were again called offices, and there was one each for Central, North, South,

spring of 1972 a somewhat similar change reduced the number of country directorates in the Bureau of European Affairs from ten to seven.[28] While there was nothing sacred about the original number of country directorates, it is interesting that assistant secretaries could, with little if any opposition, reverse the thrust of the 1966 change. There were no major alterations in the other three bureaus.[29] On two occasions country directorates were merged, once in ARA-LA and once in EA, but in the former this amalgamation was ultimately reversed and the original pattern restored.

By mid- and late 1971, however, two somewhat uneven but related trends could be discerned which seemed to pose the possibility of additional, although perhaps temporary, movement away from the original CD concept and the modifications suggested by the CDs and Task Force VIII. These were attempts to increase centralization of policy-making power on the seventh floor, at the expense of the geographic bureaus, including country directors; and continuing efforts to reduce personnel as part of the administration's larger drive to cut federal spending and the size

---

East, and West Africa, a regional affairs office, and a special staff for Nigeria.

[28] Prior to 1966, the Bureau of European Affairs had had five geographic offices: British Commonwealth and Northern European Affairs, East European Affairs, Soviet Affairs, German Affairs, and West European Affairs. Between 1966 and 1971 there had been nine country directorates, and for a period in 1971 and early 1972, ten, as a result of splitting the directorate for Eastern Europe into components of Czechoslovakia-Hungary-Poland and Bulgaria-Rumania-Yugoslavia. Appendix B lists the other 1966-72 areas of responsibility, and the offices in existence, after the 1972 reorganization.

[29] The changes that took place were as follows: the country directorates for Ecuador-Peru and Bolivia-Chile were merged in 1970, and again separated in 1971. The directorate for Eastern Europe was split into one for Czechoslovakia-Hungary-Poland and one for Bulgaria-Rumania-Yugoslavia in 1971, but merged again in 1972. The country directorates for Indonesia and for Malaysia-Singapore were merged in the same year.

of the bureaucracy. Taken together, it seemed that the country director's already limited freedom of action might be further restricted. Some positions in country directorates were eliminated, making it very difficult to provide CDs with additional in-house functional expertise, and reducing the possibility of making more junior positions available on CD staffs. At one period, in late 1971 and early 1972, some thought was being given to saving even more positions by combining some country directorates; one estimate was that the then existing forty-six units might be consolidated into as few as thirty. A year and a half later, however, the only further amalgamation that had taken place was the previously mentioned reorganization in EUR and the merger of the Nigeria directorate into the one for West Africa in AF which left the total number of units at forty-two. Several sources indicated that with one or two possible exceptions, no further changes were contemplated, unless additional unanticipated personnel restrictions were imposed. Nevertheless, the reduction in the staffs of the geographic bureaus which did take place (about 10 percent for all but NEA, which was already smaller than the others and absorbed a reduction of about 5 percent) presented problems to some CDs because their staffs, usually small to begin with, were reduced in size. It should be noted that the functional bureaus, in contrast to the geographic ones, were generally faced with only a 5 percent reduction, equal to that imposed on the entire department, and that critical seventh-floor units such as the Policy and Coordination Staff and the Executive Secretariat were left relatively untouched.[30]

Since State had already sustained sizable cuts in personnel under the earlier BALPA and OPRED (Operation Reduction) programs—one estimate was that by the end of

[30] The information in this paragraph is based on interviews conducted with several officers directly associated with the efforts to reduce positions. The generalizations are based on a composite of their opinions, as of mid-January 1972. Later results closely followed those indicated, as revealed by subsequent interviews in April 1973.

281

the current program there would be a total of 22 percent fewer people working in State than five years previously—the decisions as to where to cut were difficult, and assumed some significance as indications of how senior officials wanted to operate the department. For the first time in such exercises, the under secretary was actively involved in making substantive decisions on a position-by-position basis. They were apparently being made in a way that reflected the strong desire of those at the top to strengthen the seventh floor. Because of their felt need to be able to compete on more even terms with the White House, some suspicion of the career service, and, perhaps, an emerging belief (contested by many) that the day of bilateral relations essentially unaffected by broader considerations was passing, such centralization would no doubt have become a goal, even in the absence of the need for personnel reductions. It is instructive to contrast the histories of the Task Force VIII recommendations concerning the strengthening of the CD and geographic bureaus, which were essentially ignored, and those of Task Force XIII dealing with improving the management capabilities of the senior level, which were virtually all placed in effect. There was no inherent reason, of course, that a stronger seventh floor had to be developed at the expense of lower levels, but the simultaneous requirement for personnel cuts made it highly likely that such would be the net result.[31]

There was considerable dismay at this turn of events. One CD, part of the original sample, argued that "the country director system, which was an absolute success, is dead and will be buried, at great loss to the department." He strongly believed that such a move would further erode the position of State, since centralization in this fashion and consolidation of country directors into larger geographic groupings would once again drive country expertise back to the

[31] This paragraph based on approximately ten interviews with officials at various levels in January 1972.

desk officer (country officer) level, several steps removed from those attempting to make essential decisions. (CD #20) The clear assumption, several sources argued, was that the PARA documents would somehow give the senior officials enough detail to decide intelligently about complex matters. Even those developing PARA, however, agreed that in its current form it was too simplistic. Critics noted that while the CD did have some input and a chance to work directly with the under secretary on the PARA submissions, the fatal flaw was a misunderstanding of the worth of country planning documents, which were "of value only on the day written" due to continuously changing situations. In this view, the drive for centralization, coordination, and control at the top, while perhaps necessary, would be fulfilled only at the expense of reducing the weight and quality of State's input into the broader foreign policy-making process. This would be shortsighted, and would disrupt the department and would ultimately make corrective action in the opposite direction necessary.[32]

Later events indicated that the drive for centralization was subject to some of the same limitations that any attempts at innovation in State must confront. The PARA system, so highly touted at first, began to display some of the weaknesses that its early critics had predicted, and the critical link from the country level to the seventh floor, the biennial PARA review, had begun to be omitted in some cases by 1973. With the appointment of Henry A. Kissinger as Secretary of State in September 1973, the entire PARA apparatus came under close scrutiny, and additional modifications seemed almost inevitable. Moreover, the "seventh-floor collegium" (composed of the secretary, deputy secretary, under secretaries, counselor, and deputy under secretary for management), intended after its adoption under the "Diplomacy for the 70's" program to provide for joint direction and control from the top, did not function as

[32] Ibid.

283

well as hoped. Those at the top, because they were not individually directly responsible for specific activities to the degree common previously, tended to become isolated and at the mercy of what emerged from the bureaus and the seventh-floor staffs. Thus, the attempt at centralized control in some cases actually resulted in less substantive influence over decisions, since those at the collegium level were frequently reduced to saying yes or no to fully developed proposals sent up for their approval. A wholesale turnover in positions at the top (four of the seven) in the first part of 1973 left open the question of whether the collegium idea would even remain in force.[33] Additional changes after the arrival later in the year of a new secretary with his own distinct style left it even more in doubt. But while the threats to the CD system of consolidation and of centralization did not go as far as originally seemed possible, nothing was done to strengthen CDs either. Their influence remained essentially individual in origin; it could not be attributed to the strong support of their superiors.

But if the CD was not immediately threatened by events in State, the danger of declining CD influence still existed. Nowhere could it be seen more clearly than in the gradual tendency of the National Security Council staff to engage in more activities, even at the working level, as time passed. One former CD reinterviewed in the spring of 1973, for example, asserted that "the change over the past year has been a constant attempt to embrace more and more—they are biting off more and more and are unable to chew it." (CD #30) Paradoxically, since one of the avowed reasons a White House staff was deemed necessary was to prod a stodgy bureaucracy into action, this trend increasingly resulted in the overburdened NSC staff acting as a bottleneck, with slower reaction times than State. One 1973 CD, not part of the original sample, noted the proclivity of this staff to intrude itself into the operational responsibilities of indi-

[33] Information about developments regarding the "collegium" in this paragraph derived from interviews, April 1973.

vidual agencies in a haphazard way, weakening the coordination network at his level. There was neither sufficient staff to manage everything from the White House, nor any real interest in doing so, but these intermittent incursions began to accustom those in other agencies to expect "someone other than the CD to call," thus tending to weaken the latter's prestige and responsibilities. Because this complicated his attempts to provide leadership and to bring some order to the whole range of bilateral relationships, which he had found to be relatively easy until the "arrival of the NSC staff," this CD found the trend to be "frustrating and disturbing." He believed the NSC staff should work through the CD; this would allow the White House to follow important developments closely, while permitting the CD to exercise more systematic oversight.

Another former CD with intimate knowledge of NSC operations agreed substantially with these criticisms, and strongly believed the NSC staff would be better advised to keep out of anything except the most serious and sensitive matters. The biggest mistake in State-NSC relations, he suggested, and one partially responsible for the latter's expanded range of activities, had been the development of a confrontation relationship between the two. He had argued, futilely, he said, that State would function more effectively if a more cooperative tack were adopted by both sides. In his view, nobody involved was entirely without fault for these developments, and they had a negative impact on the government's ability to conduct foreign policy.

Of course, not all contacts between the NSC staff and CDs were abrasive or hostile. In several cases mentioned by 1973 interviewees, very close informal lateral relationships existed, usually because of personal compatibility and long experience working together. And as mentioned earlier, special circumstances surrounding Middle East policy allowed State to retain more influence for that region. In NEA, DASs and CDs as well as the assistant secretary were able to initiate new proposals, while NSC staffers usually

285

reacted to what they suggested, a reversal of the pattern usually found elsewhere.

Viewed from a broad perspective, however, it was indisputable that by mid-1973 the NSC staff and its peripatetic leader were even more ascendant than they had been in the early days of the Nixon administration. As one seventh-floor staffer wryly commented, NSC-State relationships "had been clarified," and there was "less fighting of city hall," since it was clear that it would have little effect.

In April 1973, reorganization of the NSC staff seemed likely to leave it even better staffed and organized to continue this dominance.[34] However, before the effect could be felt, the situation once again became ambiguous. In September, Dr. Kissinger became secretary of state, while retaining his former position as assistant to the president for national security affairs. It seemed inevitable that power would flow back to the Department of State, and that the NSC staff would find its own role reduced in some degree.

Whether this would benefit the country directors and other working-level officials in State was problematic. It appeared likely they would still be subject to close direction by Kissinger intimates, the only difference being that the latter would now be divided between the White House and the Department of State. Only a more decentralized system than seemed likely as long as Kissinger remained the prime mover of United States foreign policy would ulti-

---

[34] Under this realignment, five deputy advisors to the president for national security affairs were named, rather than one as previously. According to some in the administration the change was designed both to relieve the director of the staff of daily chores and to provide more recognition to some staff members who "chafed at the contrast between their anonymity and Mr. Kissinger's celebrity." If these reasons are reasonably accurate, the NSC staff might have been even more interested in intervening and in directing a wide range of activities than before, had the change become fully implemented. Quote and details reported in R. W. Apple, Jr., "Staff of the National Security Council is Reshuffled," *New York Times*, April 7, 1973.

mately redound to the benefit of those at the country director level.

There was thus a certain irony in the country director's prospects by late 1973. Acclaimed by many throughout his existence as at least a partial answer to the increasingly complex problems of managing the nation's bilateral relations, he seemed in some danger of losing his identity and a portion of the hard-won influence he had been able to build up since 1966. At the same time the Department of State was emphasizing the need for broad-gauged, activist, managerially inclined officers to meet new challenges, it appeared that a countertrend toward older forms of organization might blunt the impact of CDs with such skills and talents, and that NSC staff and seventh-floor operating procedures would make this even more likely.

Yet it would be a mistake to assume that the country director and the CD concept are likely to disappear. Old Washington hands realize that there is often a cyclical pattern to organizational change in government and that attempted innovations reflecting currently perceived needs are often countered by subsequent attempts at change when new needs appear, only to reemerge like the phoenix when the wheels turns again. The country director has demonstrated substantial powers of survival, and it is still possible that the country director concept of 1966 will come to be the operating principle by which the country's bilateral relations with all the diverse nations of the world are managed with expertise, flair, consistency, and a broad view of both domestic considerations and the requirements of modern international relations.

Chapter Nine

Conclusion

The quest for coordination is in many respects the twentieth-century equivalent of the medieval search for the philosopher's stone. If only we can find the right formula for coordination, we can reconcile the irreconcilable, harmonize competing and wholly divergent interests, overcome irrationalities in our government structures, and make hard policy choices to which no one will dissent. HAROLD SEIDMAN

THE country director system did not live up to the expectations of its architects. There was novelty in some areas, but CDs could hardly be said to have assumed "full responsibility . . . for all activities in the country or countries assigned to them."[1] The previous chapters, tracing the history of the CD from the conditions that led to creation of these new positions, through the way the role surrounding them developed to the part they came to play in the policy-making process, hopefully leave the reader with a reasonably complete picture of what the country director has been able to do and what has been beyond his reach. It has also been possible to indicate some of the uncertainties encountered in changing organizational structures to meet planned goals. Building on this material, some summary comments on the influence of the CD are now possible.

ROLE STRENGTH

At the heart of the question of the CD's importance in policy making was the strength of his overall role. If the policy process were essentially rational, it would be possible to conceive of situations where the force of the CD's analysis was such as to lead others to defer to his interpretation of

[1] See Introduction, n. 13.

288

the problems at hand and his suggested remedies, at least in the absence of other engaged interests. But in a process containing both intellectual and social elements, as has been argued to be the case, then differences of interpretation and prescription will arise from differing perceptions and goals. It is when such differences arise that the legitimacy and strength of individual roles come into play. If the CD were accepted as coordinator or *primus inter pares* and if he had the respect of his opposite numbers, he could be expected to have an important impact. He would not always prevail, simply because the collective policy and decision processes are weighted in favor of those participants who have predominant interest, but it is likely that under the conditions outlined the CD's position would always have to be taken into account. If on the other hand, as was clearly true in many instances, the CD was seen as merely one of many coequal participants, each advocating his agency's interests, his major input was likely to be limited to those issues accepted by others as "belonging" to State.

The CD's formal mandate from State to manage relations with his countries certainly did not give him preference or precedence over other participants from other agencies, or allow him to override their policy interests and organizational prerogatives. This weakness was compounded because the CD's superiors, nominally responsible for setting an overall foreign policy, had either abdicated or lost a substantial amount of control to other parts of government. The NSAM 341 system was intended to restore some of the secretary of state's authority, but failed to do so. The really important decisions continued to be made either on an ad hoc basis or by individuals or committees selected for a particular task, rather than by continuing institutional bodies. Thus, the CD's role was not strengthened by institutionalized prominence and prestige of his superiors, but only by the fleeting and less dependable assets and power of particular individuals. If anything, the weaknesses of State's

289

top leadership were even more pronounced between 1969 and 1973, and the consequences for CDs were essentially the same as during the Johnson period.

The relationship with one's superior was an important determinant of policy influence, because of the potential existing for shaping the thinking of those who could make important decisions. Although CDs would have preferred to have more contact with both the assistant secretary and the secretary, there was a general feeling that it was possible to influence them, particularly when one had strong area expertise. When this relationship was particularly close and intimate, the CD had greater potential influence with opposite numbers because he had easy access to a higher level. CDs worked to insure that their actions reflected superiors' thinking so that support would be forthcoming, and had few if any complaints about the backing they received. This is somewhat surprising, in view of bureaucrats' chronic complaints that their attempts to exert policy influence are undercut by failures of their superiors to support their initiatives. These responses may have been the result of the way questions were asked, and may also show a reluctance to criticize superiors openly, even in non-attributed interviews. However, other responses suggest that they may be due largely to limited role ambitions held by most CDs interviewed. If their vision was restricted to a minimal concept of their role, the amount of support perceived as necessary would of course be less than under a more all-encompassing orientation. Interviews previously cited also suggest that additional support might have been forthcoming from the assistant secretary level had most CDs been willing to risk attempting to play a larger part than most actually did.

On the other hand, support for the CD *concept* and what it implied for expanded leadership throughout government was clearly less satisfactory. This was of paramount importance, because an essential defining feature of the constantly shifting influence patterns in Washington is the predilections of those at the top about both their own roles and those of their subordinates, and the great impact those predilections have on what is possible at lower levels. The ability of working level officials like CDs to function effectively is not just a question of institutional or organizational arrangements; it is tied to what those higher up desire and are willing to fight for. But neither the secretary of state nor the president in either the Johnson or Nixon administrations made a continuing effort to emphasize the CD's prominence, although in each case lip service was given to his importance. The same was generally true for the geographic assistant secretaries, who were engaged in their own battles for policy influence. They perhaps would have given aggressive CDs more support if pressed to do so, but were unlikely to expend any of their limited political capital in such efforts of their own volition.

The presence or absence of conflicting role elements can also define an actor's influence in the policy process, for this will substantially determine his ability to take a strong and consistent policy line. If an actor is cross-pressured between two groups because he is charged with mediating between them, his influence depends on whether he is seen as being impartial, broad-gauged, and his own man, as well as upon his general power base and his recognized role in the issues being reconciled. If he is strong on these points, his opinion may be the deciding factor, making it worthwhile for others to cultivate his support. If not, then he may be almost irrelevant, serving only as a communications channel between two sides, each of which counts him as potentially hostile. As previously indicated, there was great doubt in other agencies about the CD's ability to be much besides the Washington representative of the U.S. embassy, and there were some complaints from embassies that he was not sufficiently aware of their problems. Such criticisms and suspicions weakened his influence.

Although difficult to document, it appears on balance that the CD had a greater authority to commit State to a proposed solution or agreement than most of his opposite numbers, because the latter were either more junior or agents of more centralized bureaucracies. Some CDs felt it was advantageous to work with more junior officials, since it might be easier to sell State's case to them. (CD #1) On the other hand, inability of the other participants to commit their organizations might lead to more senior officials of other agencies going higher in State, bypassing the CD. (CD #28) When this happened, the CD's power to decide for State and to issue instructions on his own authority was largely negated.

The CD's influence also depended upon two intertwined interpersonal factors: ability to be an agent for improved coordination (in the restricted sense of exchanging information and harmonizing the plans of the various parts of government), and success in developing continuing, amiable working relationships. The latter is more likely to be a function of personality than of role, but they are discussed in tandem because of their close relationship. Taken together, they could make the difference between an interaction pattern of hostile advocacy and one of cordial search for mutually acceptable solutions. Friendly working relations could facilitate agreement at the CD level, making it more likely that those with specific knowledge and expertise would shape a decision than if disagreement forced referral to a higher level. There was disagreement about the success of CD efforts to improve coordination. Where they were able to gain more comprehensive sharing of information, opposite numbers felt coordination was somewhat improved. But if the CD moved to tighten the whole process by pushing for control across agency lines, hostility and deteriorating communication was likely.

The factors just cited are part of the larger question of the utility of the CD role for others. The absence of strong support to impose the CD concept from the top might have been partially compensated for by CDs assuming such importance for the activities of the rest of the foreign affairs community that substantial influence accrued to them. However, as the CD role emerged, those aspects of it potentially most useful to others tended to be precisely the ones that received limited attention. Planning, initiating new ideas, and a broad emphasis on both worldwide ramifications and on all operating programs of all agencies all failed to develop to the degree envisioned by the CD system's major advocates. Instead, most CDs concentrated on performing the old geographic officer's job better, taking advantage of their increased rank compared to officers-in-charge and their more limited geographic area which allowed greater mastery of details compared to office directors. In short, they emphasized what have been called here residual role elements.[2] This was not entirely or perhaps even primarily the fault of initial country directors, but nevertheless the impact of the change was reduced, and the individual CD was forced to make his own way if he aspired to substantial influence. This occurred in a number of instances, but was far from being universal. When it did, it was when the CD was extremely knowledgeable, had a wide range of official and extraofficial contacts with other country experts, and in short, performed in a capable and active fashion. The slighting of those very role elements that would have enhanced their leadership of course raises some critical questions as to the viability of the CD reform, and the validity of some of the premises upon which it rested (see next section).

Before leaving the question of role strength, however, it is necessary to note that the CD system did make progress in some areas, even if it suffered from the weaknesses and limitations described above and throughout this study. Although his failure to assume a dominant role meant that the CD did not become *the* influential arbiter of policy affecting his countries of responsibility, he could not be ignored. Organizational practice within the Department of State, and to an increasing degree elsewhere, with the partial excep-

[2] Full discussion in Chapter III.

tion of the NSC staff, came to expect CD involvement with any matter concerning his countries. One CD noted, for example, that when the CD was not consulted, it was due to inadvertent omission and apologies and admissions of error were almost invariably forthcoming. (CD #7) This was hardly a manifestation of the CD's ability to decide policy on his own, but it did make it increasingly likely that the CD would be able by virtue of his role as the "central clearing point" to assert considerable influence, depending upon his own talents and the nature of the problem at issue. Without at least the beginnings of a powerful CD role, however, there was little likelihood of anything resembling control. Role strength is one of the cornerstones upon which the edifice of influence is built.

LEADERSHIP AND COORDINATION IN THE POLICY PROCESS: LARGER ISSUES

The record of the country director system raises basic questions about the amount of intra-agency coordination and leadership it is possible or desirable to attempt to assign to the working level in one department. Were the original statements about what was expected of country directors unrealistic or misguided, or could a strong and encompassing CD role have developed under different circumstances? If it could have, should it have? There are no definitive answers, but it is possible to highlight some relevant considerations bearing upon them.

Many in government would agree with Roger Hilsman's assertion that the assistant secretaries represent the lowest level at which wide political implications of proposed actions can effectively be taken into account.[3] This is not to reassert the old policy/administration dichotomy, but rather to introduce realism about what the senior working-level official can accomplish. For this and related reasons, some members of the Macomber Task Force on the Role of the

[3] Roger Hilsman, *The Politics of Policy Making*, p. 34.

Country Director argued that CDs should not play a major interagency policy role.[4] Such reasoning implies that it is extremely difficult, if not impossible, for any working level officials to operate on the basis of a broad "presidential viewpoint," as CDs were initially asked to do. Admittedly, there are great obstacles to forcing such a viewpoint downward, but the role played through the years by working-level analysts in the Bureau of the Budget/Office of Management and Budget shows that it may not be impossible under the right circumstances. They have been generally successful in claiming to speak for presidential rather than parochial interests, and in forcing acceptance of this interpretation. At the same time, it seems highly improbable that country directors can achieve anything approaching the same success as long as strong NSC staffers can claim to be "the president's men" with much greater plausibility. Practically, then, unless there is a fundamental organizational change in the foreign affairs community—which involves dismantling most of the NSC staff—those who assert the impossibility of a broad role for those like the country director at the working level may be correct.

Similarly, the CD's geographic responsibilities as a State Department official, as distinct from any government-wide role he might be assigned, inevitably caused him to be seen as one of many contending "advocates" representing specific viewpoints and therefore, in the minds of many, automatically disqualified from assuming a "judicial" role, mediating among many such contenders.[5] The conclusion that emerges, related to that above, is that as long as the "advocacy syndrome" is a key element of the policy process, a role such as that originally intended for the CD is unviable.

Another facet of the problem has to do with a basic premise of the CD system, that foreign affairs coordination among departments and agencies on the basis of individual country units is the most desirable way of insuring consistent policy. Several parts of State, most particularly the Bu-

[4] See Chapter VIII, n. 14.   [5] See Chapters III and IV.

reaus of Economic and Business Affairs and of Educational and Cultural Affairs, and virtually all other agencies with foreign affairs responsibilities in particular functional sectors, would argue that this premise is incorrect. Rather, the basis for coordination should reflect global needs and interests in particular subject areas. For example, the United States should look at trade questions not as an element in bilateral relations with each individual country (which presumably would lead to variations in the way they were approached), but instead in a more concentrated fashion, with as few deviations from a general policy line as feasible. Even in the geographic bureaus of State, signs began to appear in the late 1960s and early 1970s that the unit of policy analysis was increasingly becoming the geographic region, and not the individual country. Insofar as either functional problem areas or regions replaced individual countries as the focal point for American foreign policy, coordination such as the CD would presumably provide on a country basis will be increasingly seen as irrelevant, and be more resisted.

Yet as long as the basic unit of the international system continues to be the nation-state, many elements of U.S. foreign policy will of necessity be bilateral in nature, whatever the current vogue about the preferred base for policy development. As one 1973 Regional Affairs office director commented,

> Problems become regional largely because we force them into regional frameworks due to our bureaucratic arrangements, and this often conceals too much. For example, there really is no such thing as East Asia except as we choose to lump countries together.[6]

One skeptical 1973 CD added to this by expressing his doubts that State could deal effectively with other countries, especially smaller ones, on a primarily regional or functional basis. Personalities of key individuals in other

[6] Interview, April 1973.

governments had to be taken into account, he said, and this was much more likely to be done successfully by individuals who worked on a continuing basis with representatives of a given foreign government. He concluded that whatever else State tried to do, it would have to stay organized geographically.

As long as bilateral concerns remain prominent, a strong case can be made that coordination among all the programs and policies relating to each individual country will be required, and that repositories of country expertise will be essential. It is true that the country director concept was developed at the high point of the "New Diplomacy," when it was widely assumed that it was necessary for the United States to conduct a wide range of foreign activities and programs in order to protect United States' interests by influencing internal political-economic developments in a large number of foreign countries. At a time when at least in theory the emphasis on such activities has been strongly downplayed, it perhaps can be argued that part of the rationale for the CD system has disappeared, since to the degree that the theory of the Nixon Doctrine becomes practice, there will be fewer activities requiring coordination and rationalization. To expect all such programs to end does not seem realistic, however. Many parts of the United States government will continue to have foreign interests, even though new relationships and concerns will partially replace older forms of programs. If this is true, then there will be a continuing need for someone like the country director to serve as a focal point, whatever the variation in the precise nature of the duties assigned to him.

Another problem with working level coordination by officials in State, whether on a country, functional, or some other basis, has to do with the weakness of State compared to other contenders for power and influence. In recent years, whether the issue has been trade, monetary policy, agriculture, oil and energy, strategic arms limitation, the role of intelligence, national security, or important negotiations (e.g., China rapprochement, Vietnam ceasefire), it has been necessary to look beyond State to find the dominant individuals and organizations. This may well change under Kissinger, but insofar as the secretary of state cannot prevail on matters escalated to senior levels of government, there is no incentive for those in other agencies to agree against their own views lower down—after all, their views may yet carry the day. This increases the tendency to fight battles at successively higher levels. When this disparity between State and other parts of government exists, reform proposals which call for strengthening CDs, or for that matter other parts of the department, by additional grants of authority from State are likely at best to bring the CD's expertise into closer conjunction with policy making only on matters where State has the action. The effect on the broader foreign affairs community in all probability will be minimal. If, of course, the president elects to reemphasize State as the fulcrum for foreign policy, the CD would presumably find his own prospects enhanced, although some of the problems of working-level country coordination would still remain.[7]

But while a materially expanded role for the CD seems dependent on upgrading of the position of the Department of State, some improvements still seem possible even in the absence of any fundamental change in relationships in the broader foreign affairs community. The CD could be somewhat strengthened by more active and aggressive continuing support, as opposed to paper pronouncements, if the top levels of State and the assistant secretaries come to the realization that strong CDs are not necessarily a threat to their own influence and ability to guide policy. Indeed, discarding the expertise available at working levels (assuming the proper individuals have been assigned to jobs such as the country directors) may take away the one advantage assistant secretaries and those at the "political" level in State

[7] See on this argument William N. Turpin, "Foreign Relations, Yes; Foreign Policy, No," *Foreign Policy*, 8 (Fall 1972), 50-61.

have over their more strategically placed but less experienced and overburdened opposite numbers at the White House. More seriously, to base policy decisions on anything less than the best available advice garnered from all available sources is to court failure and perhaps disaster. If FSOs need to demonstrate broader viewpoints and a more managerial bent than has often been true heretofore, those at higher levels would be advised to adapt their own styles to delegate more rather than insisting on making all decisions themselves. With the proper linkage between levels, control of policy could still rest with senior officials, but decisions would be based on better information and those at the political level would avoid sinking in a morass of detail and be better able to give their attention to questions of general policy and to the major problems and decisions.

Such modifications in operating relationships might help alleviate some of the weakness of State by enabling it to perform better, and help overcome the resistance to a strong coordinating role for working-level officials, but the advocacy problem is likely to remain, unless the organizational structure of government is changed considerably. Even there, however, the right kind of CDs with continuing support could do better at gaining the confidence of others than has sometimes been the case to date. There will always be real substantive issues between different parts of the foreign affairs community, but broad-gauged individuals truly knowledgeable about all activities relating to their countries and sympathetic to the problems of their opposite numbers can at least help insure that differences reflect substantive issues rather than ignorance or parochialism. At times of course issues will have to be resolved higher up, but proper treatment by working level experts can sharpen the true issues and enable their superiors to make more informed choices among opposing goals and means.

In response to the questions posed earlier, then, it seems that a stronger role could have developed for the CDs, and that such a role does need to be played. While it was and is unrealistic to assume that CDs could or can dominate the rest of government, they have the potential to become more of a focal point, clearing house, and source of expertise and analysis for bilateral relations than they have been. This would require continuing support from higher officials, broader perspectives on their part, and a more general willingness to try seriously to make the system work. Such a role is needed as a means of better exploiting the expertise available in the bureaucracy, and of more successfully devolving some of the responsibilities and workloads of higher officials to the working level. Finally, country directors seem potentially better equipped to do this than anyone else, including NSC staffers at the White House.

There is, after all, a certain base of accomplishment which can be exploited, and there have been some pluses in the record of the country director innovation. The concept has partially survived, even when the "parent" NSAM 341 system was discarded in favor of a White House-centered national security system.[8] There is continuing support for modifications to the system to make it function in a way more congruent with original intentions, even if there have been some movements away from that concept in practice.[9] It has surmounted a change in national administration, and shown greater viability than its early opponents thought possible. The country director has become an established figure on the Washington scene, and has developed a modest measure of interdepartmental leadership. The system has provided some improvements, particularly within State and in the services provided to American embassies abroad and foreign embassies in Washington. Finally, experience gained with the system is available to be exploited for further progress in achieving better management of bilateral relations.

[8] Clark and Legere, pp. 14-21, provide a discussion on the differences between State-centered and White House-centered national security systems. The two terms are those used there.

[9] See Chapter VIII.

There are severe limits on what is possible, of course. No organizational change can be viewed entirely in its immediate context. Just as the policy process has open-system characteristics, so changes affecting the participants in that process cannot be treated as taking place in isolation. And the larger context of foreign policy has changed radically from the days when State could be dominant, while restricting its activities to traditional political and diplomatic concerns. The increased demands of the last quarter-century have resulted in a multifunctional pattern of U.S. foreign relations, in turn leading to uncertainty about State's role and to a multiple agency format for the conduct of those relations. The old concept of a diplomatic service supported by a foreign ministry responsible for all official contacts abroad has ceased to be viable, but no real solution has been found as to what is to replace it. One result has been the disjointed and incremental policy process described in this study.

In the absence of progress in establishing a cleancut role for State in the new era, the modest success of the country director system at the margins of the policy process represents a not inconsiderable achievement.

A Profile of Country Directors: Backgrounds and Experience

There are inherent dangers in attempting to impute performance or attitudes from an individual's inclusion in or exclusion from certain classes or categories on the basis of social origins, education, professional experience, or similar variables, but such information can be revealing as long as too much is not expected of it. The intent of this appendix is to present background information about the country directors, in order to show the experience and characteristics they brought to the tasks they faced. Where possible, they are compared with the entire Foreign Service. Some important items of social background (religion, father's occupation or income) were not available for individual CDs, but several profiles of the Foreign Service as a whole or of selected samples giving such information are available.[1] All data presented are for the entire group of 153 officers who had served or were serving as CDs from the beginning of the system in 1966 until September 1973.[2]

BIRTHPLACE, RACE, AND SEX

As was the case with the Foreign Service as a whole, CDs strongly overrepresented the northeastern section of the country, slightly underrepresented the Midwest, and

[1] See John E. Harr, *The Anatomy of the Foreign Service: A Statistical Profile*, Foreign Affairs Personnel Study, 4 (New York: Carnegie Endowment for International Peace, 1965): and a more inclusive version which forms the substance of Harr's *The Professional Diplomat* (Princeton, N.J.: Princeton University Press, 1969), esp. chaps. 4, 5.

[2] Country director information is taken from the *Department of State Biographic Register* (Washington, D.C.: GPO, 1966-1973), unless otherwise noted.

strongly underrepresented the South, the Pacific Coast, and the Southwest. The Mountain States were represented in about their proportion in the whole population. Table A-1 compares CDs with all FSOs at selected periods, and with the total population. Given the small number of CDs, variations from the entire Foreign Service are not significant, except for the overseas figures. Of the fourteen CDs in the foreign-born category, only two were not U.S. citizens from birth. Eleven were sons of American citizens abroad, generally diplomats or missionaries. One was from the Virgin Islands.

Turning to individual states, the concentration was even more striking. Seventy-three CDs (47.7 percent) were born in only five states: New York (29), Pennsylvania (12), Massachusetts (11), Ohio (11), and Illinois (10). While a total of thirty-five states was represented, only five others had as many as four each (Connecticut, Arkansas, Michigan, Montana, Texas), and eleven had only one.

With respect to race and sex, country directors, like the Foreign Service, were overwhelmingly white and male. While exact information on these points is not available, personal knowledge indicates that only two CDs were black, and only one female.

Although CDs were in some senses an elite group within the Foreign Service (see below), their state and region of birth, sex, and race were close to those of the entire service. Ultimately, they will become more representative only as does the service as a whole. An effort to broaden the service has been mounted in the past decade, but thus far the results have been unspectacular, particularly at the senior levels.

EDUCATION

Country directors attained an extraordinarily high level of education, even by comparison with the high standards of the rest of the Foreign Service. Only four of 153 did not

TABLE A-1

REGION OF BIRTH

Region	U.S. Population (By Residence)				Civilian Federal Executives	FSOs		CDs	
	1910	1930-40	1960	1970	1959	1925-49	1961-64	%	N
Northeast	28%	30%	24.9%	24.1%	30%	43%	44%	39.2	60
Midwest	33	31	28.8	27.9	35	25	23	26.4	40
South	22	23	21.2	21.4	19	13	12	11.1	17
Southwest	9	7	9.5	9.5	6	3	4	6.5	10
Mountain	3	2	3.9	4.1	5	3	3	3.9	6
Pacific	5	7	11.7	13.0	5	8	11	3.9	6
Overseas	–	–	–	–	–	5	3	9.1	14
Totals	100%	100%	100.0%	100.0%	100%	100%	100%	99.8	153

Notes: Population figures calculated from U.S. Census data.

Federal Civilian Executive data from L. Warner, *The American Federal Executive.*

FSO data reflects those entering the service during the period indicated. Taken from Harr, *The Professional Diplomat*, Table 19, p. 175 (developed by C. R. McKibbins, Department of Political Science, Drake University).

hold a bachelor's degree. The 97.4 percent with at least an undergraduate degree compare with 88 percent of military executives, and 85 percent of all career civil service executives and 90 percent of supergrades as reported in 1969,[3] and 85.8 percent of the Foreign Service reported by Harr in his 1962 study.[4] While the Foreign Service percentage has been climbing as former Wristonees leave (since by percentage far fewer of them had degrees, which new recruits almost invariably have),[5] the CD percentage is nevertheless impressive. Furthermore, three of the four CDs without college degrees had two or more years of college, and failed to complete a degree because of the intervention of wartime military service. Highest educational levels of the CDs were as follows:

High school diploma only	1
Some college	3
Bachelor's degree	65
Master's degree	64
LL.B.	4
LL.M.	1
Ph.D.	15

The content of this education was very likely to be in the fields traditionally favored by Foreign Service officers: international relations, history, and political science. Harr reports that, for the service as a whole, examination entrants are more likely than lateral entrants to specialize in these fields, while lateral entrants are much more likely to have studied public administration, economics, accounting, and business administration.[6] In this respect, the CDs reflected

[3] "Characteristics of the Federal Executive," *Public Administration Review*, 30 (March-April 1970), 172-173. Reprinted from a report of the same title issued by the Bureau of Executive Manpower, U.S. Civil Service Commission, November 1969.

[4] Harr, *Anatomy*, pp. 14, 39.

[5] Harr, *Professional Diplomat*, p. 168.

[6] Ibid. The Foreign Service has attempted to recruit more officers

the more traditional liberal education orientations of the diplomatically inclined officers of the past than the technical orientation of many of the "program managers" of the present, who most often entered the service via Wristonization or other lateral entry programs. Fields of academic specialization (final degree) were as follows:[7]

International relations	44
Political science	27
History	25
Economics	13
Modern languages	9
Law (including intl. law)	6
English	4
Business administration	3
Physical science, engineering	2
Philosophy	2
Journalism	2
Public administration	2
Literature	2
Mathematics	2
Public affairs	1
Social and technical asst.	1
Education	1
Architecture	1
	147
Unknown	6
Total	153

The colleges and universities attended by CDs were even more heavily concentrated in the Northeast than their

trained in fields such as economics and administration in recent years, but this has not yet affected the senior levels of the service.

[7] Information provided by the Analysis and Requirements Division, Office of the Deputy Director of Personnel for Management, Department of State.

birthplaces. Of the 153 CDs, 56.2 percent (86) attended colleges in that area. Socially, they cluster in a way reflecting the current Ivy League orientation of the Foreign Service, with more than a quarter (27.5 percent or 42) attending the Big Three, and 8.5 percent (13) more attending the other five Ivy League universities. An additional seventeen (11.1 percent) attended smaller equivalents of these schools, such as Amherst, Williams, and Wesleyan. Parenthetically, this concentration is changing for new entrants, but the overall balance of the service has not yet been appreciably affected. In other parts of the country, twenty-three (15.0 percent) attended schools with similarly high prestige, such as Chicago, Wisconsin, and Berkeley. Altogether, of 152 CDs who attended U.S. institutions, ninety-five (62.5 percent) attended prestige schools, while 37.5 percent (57) attended lesser known and/or less highly regarded institutions. One CD attended a foreign university. Eighty-one colleges and universities were attended, in the following rank order:

Harvard	19	Columbia	2
Princeton	12	Dartmouth	2
Yale	11	Duke	2
Chicago	8	George Washington	2
Georgetown	8	Haverford	2
Pennsylvania	5	Missouri	2
Wesleyan	5	North Carolina	2
C.C.N.Y.	4	Northwestern	2
U. Cal. (Berkeley)	3	Tufts	2
Wisconsin	3	Vanderbilt	2
Brown	3	59 with one each	

(Note: Three CDs without college degrees but with some college education included in the college totals where appropriate. List totals 157 because 4 CDs with two bachelor's degrees were counted twice.)

Schools at which higher degrees were taken reflected a substantial shift to those of particular interest to the Foreign Service by virtue of their programs and/or accessibility, such as the Fletcher School of Law and Diplomacy and George Washington University. These schools were as follows, with a total of 33 being represented, including three foreign universities:

Fletcher	18
Harvard	10
Columbia	9
George Washington, Johns Hopkins	6
Chicago	5
Syracuse, Yale	4
Pennsylvania	3
Wisconsin, N.Y.U., Virginia	2
21 with 1 each	

(Note: Those with 2 degrees from 2 schools listed twice; with 2 degrees from the same school, once.)

AGE, RANK, AND METHOD OF ENTRY

Several factors associated with career patterns provide information on the status of the CD within the service. Taken together, they indicate that the Foreign Service has attempted to place some of its most qualified officers in these positions. Rank is one indication of this. At the time they became CDs, 52 were 0-1s, 82 were 0-2s, and 22 were 0-3s. Compared with the needs of the entire service, the amount of senior manpower assigned to these positions was impressive. For example, in July 1970 there were 235 0-1s, or 9.3 percent of the whole service; 411 0-2s (13.3 percent); and 616 0-3s (20 percent). Only 7 Career Ambassadors and 55 Career Ministers ranked above the Class-One country directors.

Perhaps even more important as an indicator was the age of the CDs, compared with the average age of officers in the same ranks. As Harr has written,

309

The average-age-by-grade is widely viewed among FSOs as an important measure of career progress, and as the most tangible evidence of "success." An officer who is consistently younger than the average age for his grade obviously is moving ahead quickly and will enjoy greater rewards and probably better assignments than the officer who is consistently and significantly older than the average.[8]

Using 1966 as a base date, Table A-2 indicates that the CDs as a group were in this privileged category. Both the initial CDs and all 153 CDs as a group were younger than their counterparts, whether the latter were taken as a whole or subdivided into those who entered by examination and those who entered by lateral entry. This is particularly impressive, since a considerable number of CDs were lateral entrants, and might be expected statistically to raise the average age of the CD group (see below). Since the system started, the age of CDs has tended to remain approximately the same. While CDs at appointment have ranged from 34 to 57 years of age, the average age of the initial group of 49 was 46.7; of the January 1969 incumbents, 46.4; of the group of January 1972, 47.2; of the September 1973 incumbents, 46.8; and of all 153 CDs as a group, 46.8. This indicates that in the eyes of the department, the CD has not been downgraded since the system began. Such downgrading might have been shown by a tendency to assign either officers less senior by rank or those who were older than their colleagues of the same rank, and therefore considered to be "less successful" officers unlikely to advance further in the service.

[8] Harr, *Professional Diplomat*, p. 156. However, an even better measure would be "average-number-of-years-service-by-grade," since this would better reflect the rather wide difference in entrance ages from one period to another. This would be easy to calculate for CDs, but comparable figures are not currently available for the Foreign Service as a whole.

TABLE A-2
AGE BY GRADE, FSOS AND CDS

Grade	Foreign Service Officers				
	7/1/66	7/1 67	7/1 68	7/1 47	7/1/70
0-1	(277) 51.8	51.9	51.9	52.1	(285) 51.9
0-2	(414) 47.2	49.4	49.7	49.7	(411) 49.7
0-3	(632) 46.3	46.5	46.5	46.8	(616) 46.3

Country Directors				
Orig. CDs Mid-1966	1/1/69	1/1/72	9/1/73	All CDs
(18) 48.7	(15) 49.7	(13) 50.5	(11) 49.9	(52) 49.8
(26) 46.0	(28) 45.8	(26) 46.6	(22) 46.8	(82) 46.4
(5) 43.3	(5) 42.6	(4) 42.9	(4) 42.9	(22) 42.8

Notes: 1. All ages are averages.
2. FSO figures from DSNL, April 1971, No. 120, p. 44.
3. CD figures represent age and grade when assumed CD position.

When the CDs are compared with the entire Foreign Service by method of entry, few differences exist. Harr found that in 1966, 65.7 percent of the Foreign Service had entered by the examination method. Thirty-one of 49 (63.3 percent) original CDs who were FSOs entered the same way, with the remainder in each case coming in by the lateral method. By late 1968, 79.2 percent (38 of 48) of the FSO CDs in the interview group had come in through the examination method, and altogether 108 of 151 FSO CDs were exam entrants.[9] While comparable figures for the entire Foreign Service were not available, the percentage of those entering by the examination method has surely increased, given the retirement of many lateral entrants who

[9] Information provided by source indicated in note 7.

311

came in through the Wriston program, the increased number of junior officers taken into the service (all by examination), and the limited number of lateral entrants since 1958. What is clear is that those lateral entrants who have survived to reach the rank necessary to become CDs and who have been appointed to such positions are likely to be superior officers. In fact, the two CDs most often mentioned in the interviews by their colleagues and by opposite numbers as outstanding examples of what a CD should be and do were both lateral entrants.

PREPARATION FOR THE CD POST

Several indicators give some measure of the skills and experience which country directors brought to their jobs, some of which have been mentioned in other sections of this study. First, as one would expect from officials of their rank, they brought a long period of government and general foreign affairs experience to their positions. On the average, they had 20.5 years of experience as civilian government officials when they assumed their CD positions. The class-one officers had an average of 22.7 years; the class-twos 20.2 years; and the class-threes 17.2 years. Since these figures include lateral entrants who spent some portion of their careers in other endeavors, career officials would have had on the average even more federal civilian experience than indicated by these figures.

Of particular relevance for officials dealing with geographic areas, of course, was whether or not they had first-hand experience with the areas for which they were responsible. One hundred eight of 153 (70.5 percent) had served a tour in one or more of their countries of responsibility. An additional 26 (16.9 percent) had served in related or neighboring countries. Only 19 (12.4 percent) did not have direct experience in the immediate area for which they were responsible, and all but two of these had served at some field post, and usually one covered by the same geographic bureau of the State Department as the countries for which they held CD responsibilities. On this score, the CDs were carefully selected.

An item of more worry for those who held a broad concept of what a country director's range of concern should be was the nature of their career specializations. Although most CDs (98 of 138 for whom this information was available) were designated as having a "program direction" specialty by the time they assumed CD positions, jobs they had held previously having been so classified, this did not necessarily indicate competence in dealing with more than a few of the activities with which a wideranging country director would have to concern himself. It often meant that they had supervised a number of individuals who were working in the same functional area of specialization as their own.

CDs were overwhelmingly drawn from the traditional "glamor" specialty of the Foreign Service, the "political cone." As a group, political officers had had the greatest success in achieving the higher ranks of the Foreign Service, and were acknowledged, even by those having other specialties, to be the core upon which the rest of the service was built. Substantive specialties of CDs are listed on page 314, with "program directors" being classified by their prior function.[10]

While it is not surprising that officials dealing with geographic areas should be drawn from these fields in preference to others (administrative, consular, commercial, labor, intelligence and research, cultural affairs, public affairs), the heavy concentration on political affairs raised the potential danger that the operating programs of other agencies, for which the CD presumably has responsibilities of over-

[10] Because the categories of specialization under current Foreign Service personnel accounting procedures are to a degree self-assigned, and because there may be a "halo effect" around the political cone, specialties listed should be treated with some reservations. But in any event, the preponderance of the political officer among CDs still holds.

sight, would be beyond his experience, and therefore beyond his competence and/or interest. As indicated in the text, opposite numbers believed this to be a real weakness, and frequently faulted CDs for their lack of interest in and knowledge about nonpolitical matters.

Political	67	(43.8%)
Political/Economic	34	(22.2%)
Political/Politico-Military	16	(10.5%)
Economic	12	(7.8%)
Political/Consular	8	(5.2%)
Political/Economic (Development)	5	(3.2%)
Public Affairs/Information	3	(2.0%)
Political/Educational-Cultural Affairs	2	(1.3%)
Political/International Organization Affairs	1	(0.7%)
Economic/Politico-Military Affairs	1	(0.7%)
Political/Management	1	(0.7%)
Administrative/Management	1	(0.7%)
Political/Labor	1	(0.7%)
Unknown	1	(0.7%)
Totals	153	(100.2%)

(Note: Error in total percentage due to rounding)

Career Progression

Assignment patterns are relevant not only for consideration of a CD's preparation for his tasks but also as an indication of his status, and whether those who do well as CDs are marked for greater responsibilities in the future. During his average of two decades of foreign affairs experience, a CD had generally performed a variety of functions, whatever his career specialty, and had done so in several countries abroad, interspersed with tours in Washington in the various bureaus of the department.

While details of previous assignments are indicative of the amount of responsibility an officer had held, and therefore by implication of what was expected of a CD, such a recital can be misleading. A tabulation by job title does not precisely indicate the amount of responsibility held. A political officer in a large embassy, generally considered as being at the fourth level of the hierarchy (behind the ambassador, DCM, and political counselor) might be an FSO-2, while a DCM at the second level of a smaller post might actually be more junior, have had less experience, and hold the rank of 0-3. By the same token, the CD jobs themselves varied considerably in terms of the numbers of subordinates supervised, the number of countries of responsibility, and the importance of United States relations with those countries.

Nevertheless, the career progressions presented in Table A-3 do indicate the comparable level in a field post for the CD job, and whether or not the CD position is in the mainstream for those officers who aspire to higher positions. The data reveal that for an officer who does not retire directly from a CD job, that position can be equated roughly with a counselor (first secretary, i.e., third-ranking behind the ambassador and DCM) position at a large embassy, and a DCM or even ambassadorial position at a smaller one. Since these are all sought-after jobs, it is clear from the progression that having held CD responsibilities was in fact an important aid to an officer's career, providing of course that he performed well. This is buttressed by the number of CDs who either came to that position from year-long senior training experiences, or were assigned to them upon completion of a CD tour. Since attendance at one of these courses (National War College or equivalent, Senior Seminar in Foreign Policy given by the Foreign Service Institute) has become increasingly *de rigeur* for officers who hope to advance, the ability of CDs to gain assignment to them indicates that they are in most cases groomed for higher responsibility.

315

TABLE A-3

COUNTRY DIRECTOR CAREER PROGRESSION

SECOND PRIOR TOUR OF DUTY			PRIOR TOUR OF DUTY		
Abroad		84 (54.9%)	*Abroad*		59 (38.6%)
DCM	17		Ambassador	1	
Emb. Counselors	21		DCM	21	
Emb. Officers	27		Emb. Counselors	18	
Prin. Officers	13		Emb. Officers	9	
AID	4		Prin. Officers	4	
POL AD	1		AID	5	
Spec. Asst. (Amb.)	1		Spec. Asst. (Amb.)	1	
Washington (State)		62 (40.5%)	*Washington (State)*		85 (55.5%)
OD-Old System	1		Dy. Asst. Secy	1	
Dy. OD-Old System	5		OD-Old System	7	
Dy. OD-Functional	4		Dy. OD-Old System	10	
Int. Relations Officers	8		OD-Functional	7	
FSI-Staff	2		Dy. OD-Functional	4	
Public Affairs	1		Dy. CD	9	
Secretariats	4		Int. Relations Officers	12	
Personnel	2		Inspection Corps	4	
Spec. Asst.	3		Public Affairs	3	
Senior Training	32		Personnel	5	
			Policy Planning	1	
Miscellaneous (U.S.)		7 (4.6%)	Post Management	1	
AID	2		Spec. Coord.	1	
DOD	1		Spec. Asst.	3	
USIA	1		Senior Training	17	
NSC Staff	1				
Outside Govt.	1		*Miscellaneous (U.S.)*		9 (5.9%)
Visiting Prof.	1		AID	1	
(Civ. Univ.)			DOD	2	
			USIA	1	
		153 (100.0%)	NSC Staff	1	
			Diplomat in Residence	1	
			POL AD	2	
			Dept. of Trans.	1	

153 (100.0%)

LEGEND

DCM—Deputy Chief of Mission

Principal Officer—Consul General or other officer in charge of an independent post

Spec. Asst.—Special Assistant to a senior official in Washington, or to Ambassador in field

Embassy Officers/Counselors—includes Political, Economic, Politico-Military, and other categories

Functional—Office Directors or Deputies in nongeographic bureaus of State

FSI—Foreign Service Institute

COUNTRY	SUBSEQUENT TOUR OF DUTY			SECOND SUBSEQUENT TOUR OF DUTY		
DIRECTOR	*Abroad*		58 (50.4%)	*Abroad*		42 (54.5%)
	Ambassador	14		Ambassador	12	
	DCM	24		DCM	17	
TOUR	Emb. Counselors	8		Emb. Officers	2	
	Emb. Officers	1		Prin. Officers	7	
	Prin. Officers	8		AID	1	
	AID	3		Spec. Asst. (Amb.)	2	
				Mission Coord.	1	
(Ave. Length—	*Washington (State)*		40 (34.8%)	*Washington (State)*		20 (26.0%)
2.4 yrs. for	Dy. Asst. Secy.	5		Assistant Secy.	1	
Initial	OD-Functional	1		Dy. Asst. Secy.	3	
CDs,	Dy. CD	2		OD-Functional	4	
1.9 yrs. for	Inspection Corps	3		CD (2nd tour)	2	
all	FSI-Staff	2		Inspection Corps	3	
Completed	Personnel	2		Policy Planning	1	
Tours)	Policy Planning	2		Spec. Asst.	1	
	Spec. Asst.	5		Senior Training	5	
	Senior Training	18				
	Miscellaneous (U.S.)		7 (6.1%)	*Miscellaneous (U.S.)*		6 (7.8%)
	AID	1		Senior Adviser	1	
	NSC Staff	1		to UN Rep.		
	Nat. War Coll.	1		NSC Staff	1	
	(Faculty)			Diplomat in	2	
	ACDA (Asst. Dir.)	1		Residence		
	OEO	1		Nat. War Coll.	1	
	Fed. Regional	1		(Faculty)		
	Council			Dy. Exec. Dir.,	1	
	IASDI	1		Regional Bureau		
	Retired		10 (8.7%)	*Retired*		9 (11.7%)
			115 (100.0%)			77 (100.0%)

	Plus:			Plus:		
	Incumbents		38	Incumbents	38	
			153	On First		
				Subsequent Tour	28	
				Previously		
				Retired	10	
						76
						153

NOTES
1. Prior Tour percentages based on all 153 CDs; Subsequent Tour percentages based only on those in category.
2. Four CDs served two CD tours interrupted by one or more tours elsewhere. Tabulations above based on their first CD tour. Two are included in the last column as 2nd tour CDs; one became a CD again after two intervening tours; and one current incumbent is coded on the basis of his previous tour, reducing the number of incumbents shown above from 39 to 38.

One other aspect of career progression that deserves additional comment is the extent to which former CDs served subsequent tours in the country or area for which they had been CD. From the point of view of providing knowledgeable personnel to foreign posts, such tours were desirable. For career development purposes, however, an extended association with one country or area at a relatively senior stage of an officer's career ran counter to the desire to give those who would form the pool from which leadership positions would be filled broad experience in a variety of settings. Assignment decisions therefore tended to one choice or the other according to the perceived importance of current expertise for a given position, other available positions and the breadth of an officer's previous career experience. Of the total group of 153 CDs, 39 were still incumbents and 10 retired immediately after their CD tours, leaving 104 who served subsequent tours. Of this group, 83 (79.8 percent) served abroad at least once, while 21 (20.2 percent) did not. The eighty-three serving abroad included 27 (32.5 percent) who were assigned to a country for which they had been CD, 30 (36.2 percent) who served in the same general area, and 26 (31.3 percent) who while generally serving in a country covered by the same bureau could not be said to be serving in the same area. Thus, there was considerable direct exploitation of experience gained as CDs, although the trend was by no means universal.

PROMOTION

Perhaps the best indication of the regard in which CDs are held in the Foreign Service can be gained from examining the promotion record of officers assigned to CD positions. As is the case in most organizations (civilian and military) that assign ranks to their personnel, promotions and the "better" jobs tend to go hand in hand in the Foreign Service. A strong promotion record for CDs would indicate that the CD function was considered to be important, since it would show that valuable and highly regarded human resources were being allocated to fill those positions. To consider this subject, it is first necessary to disregard CDs who came to their jobs as class-one officers, since a further promotion to Career Minister was clearly not possible until a later stage of an individual's career, generally after one or two ambassadorial positions had been successfully held. Nevertheless, the fact that 49 of the 153 CDs were already class-one officers at the time they began their tours is a preliminary indication of the importance of these jobs in the eyes of the service. Of the remaining 104, 43 were promoted during their CD tours, and 17 after completing them. Further, given the requirements of minimum time between one promotion and the next, some CDs were effectively ineligible for promotion while CDs or immediately thereafter because they had gained a promotion before becoming CDs. Since the average time in rank for 0-3s before promotion to 0-2, and for 0-2s before promotion to 0-1 ranged from 3.9 years in each case in 1969, to as much as six years by 1973,[11] many CDs were effectively out of the selection pool for another promotion as of 1973. This should not be interpreted as meaning that their careers had been stymied, of course, since upon completion of the necessary time in rank, many if not most would receive another promotion. On this basis, another 24 CDs could be said to have a reasonable opportunity to gain another promotion, since they did not yet have as many years in their current grade as the average of those promoted in 1973. Another three had equaled the average time in grade of 1973 promotees but had not been promoted, and eleven more had exceeded it without being

[11] The exact figures are: 1969 promotees, 0-3s, 3.9; 0-2s, 3.9; 1970 promotees, 0-3s, 4.9; 0-2s, 4.5; 1971 promotees, 0-3s, 5.8; 0-2s, 4.3; 1972 promotees, 0-3s, 5.4; 0-2s, 5.0; 1973 promotees, 0-3s, 5.8; 0-2s, 6.0. Data on promotions of individual CDs from *Department of State Biographic Register*, 1973 and previous years; figures for average time in grade of promotees from U.S. *Department of State News Letter*, No. 120 (April 1971), p. 42; and from U.S. *Department of State News Letter*, No. 144 (April 1973), Special supplement, p. 10.

promoted. While this group of fourteen might still be promoted, their chances of it diminished as their time in grade increased.

With the adjustments indicated, 60 of 80 eligible CDs received a promotion, or 75 percent. The figures for the total group of CDs are as follows:

Class-one officers when assigned as CDs	49
Promoted during CD tour	43
Promoted after CD tour	17
Less than average time in grade for another promotion by 1973	24
Average or longer than average time in grade by 1973, but not promoted	14
Retired with longer than average time in grade and no promotion	6
Total	153

When ages of CDs at the time they were promoted to the grade they held when they assumed CD positions are compared to the ages at promotion of all recent FSO promotees,[12] the findings support the contention that some of the most promising FSOs are being assigned to these positions. There are some problems of comparability between the figures cited in Table A-4 for recent promotees and those for CDs in the various categories because average times in grade before promotions have been increasing in recent years, but the trend is clear: for all categories except January 1972 class-one incumbents, CDs were promoted at a younger age than FSOs as a whole. This coupled with the high percentage of CDs promoted indicates that most CDs were marked for higher responsibilities, paralleling what one would expect from their below-average age in rank and their assignment patterns.

[12] As is the case for the average-age-by-grade measure, a measure reflecting numbers of years service when promoted would be somewhat more revealing than chronological age. Unfortunately, such figures are not among those made public by the Department of State.

TABLE A-4

Average Ages of Recent Promotees and CDs When Promoted to Rank Held as CD

Pro-moted To:	Average Age—All Recent Promotees				
	1969	1970	1971	1972	1973
0-1	(38) 47.9	(35) 47.9	(27) 48.0	(23) 49.0	(37) 50.6
0-2	(54) 43.7	(69) 46.7	(47) 48.6	(45) 46.7	(51) 47.2
0-3	(91) 41.2	(86) 41.4	(54) 41.6	(60) 41.2	(78) 43.2
Totals	(183)	(190)	(128)	(128)	(166)

Grade	Average Age When Obtained Rank Held When Appointed CD				
	Original CDs	1/1/69 Incumbents	1/1/72 Incumbents	9/1/73 Incumbents	All CDs
0-1	44.4 (18)	45.6 (15)	48.0 (13)	47.5 (11)	46.3 (52)
0-2	43.7 (26)	43.2 (28)	43.4 (26)	43.4 (22)	43.0 (82)
0-3	39.1 (5)	38.7 (5)	40.3 (4)	38.7 (6)	39.5 (22)
	(49)	(48)	(43)	(39)	(156)

Notes:

1. Figures in parentheses for CDs indicate number in each category.

2. Total figures exclude one non-FSO CD, but include four FSOs counted twice, three having served one tour as an FSO-2 and one as an FSO-1, and one a tour as an FSO-3 and one as an FSO-2 (Total CDs = 153; Total FSO CDs = 152; Total CD tours = 157; Total FSO CD tours = 156).

CONCLUSION

As a broad generalization, it seems fair to conclude that the CDs as a group were among the most highly regarded FSOs of their ranks, and that a considerable effort had been made to staff these positions with the requisite talents, at least as the necessary skills and experiences were perceived. The major weakness appeared to many observers to have been too intense a concentration in making these assignments on the narrowly political and strictly diplomatic aspects of the CD role, with a consequent weakening of ability to deal with operating programs, the use of resources, and nontraditional areas of concern. Since the system was created in part to manage precisely these sorts of matters more effectively, this was of some importance. If the CD was to be something other than just a more senior officer-in-charge or an office director with a smaller area of responsibility, it was necessary for the functions and operations of the new officers to differ from those of their predecessors. A thrust in this direction was likely to be blunted as long as traditionally oriented officers, accustomed to the responsibilities of the old system, continued to be assigned to such positions, unless one assumed a radical shift in their attitudes with the advent of the country director system.

Appendix B

Country Director Areas of Responsibility
(Jan. 1, 1974)

Total Number   1966: 49   1972: 45   1973: 42

BUREAU OF AFRICAN AFFAIRS (5)

North African: Algeria, Libya, Morocco, Spanish Sahara, Tunisia, Sudan, Mauritania.

Central Africa: Congo (K), Congo (B), Rwanda, Burundi, Malagasy Republic, Mauritius, Gabon, Chad, Cameroon, Equitorial Guinea, Central African Republic.

East Africa: Ethiopia, Somalia, French Territory of Afars and Issas, Tanzania, Uganda, Kenya, Seychelles, Biot, Malawi, Zambia.

South Africa: Union of South Africa, South West Africa, Botswana, Lesotho, Swaziland, Portuguese Guinea, Angola, Mozambique, Southern Rhodesia.

West Africa: Dahomey, The Gambia, Ghana, Guinea, Ivory Coast, Liberia, Mali, Niger, Nigeria, Senegal, Sierra Leone, Togo, Upper Volta.

(Note: This is the structure after the Newsom Reorganization of 1969 [see Chapter VIII].)

BUREAU OF AFRICAN AFFAIRS (1966-1969) (9)

North Africa: Algeria, Libya, Morocco, Spanish Sahara, Tunisia.

North East Africa: Ethiopia, Somali Republic, Sudan.

Central Africa: Congo (K), Congo (B), Rwanda, Burundi, Malagasy Republic, Mauritius.

East Africa: Kenya, Tanzania, Seychelles, Uganda.

South East Africa: Southern Rhodesia, Malawi, Zambia, Angola, Mozambique, Portuguese Guinea.

South Africa: Union of South Africa, South West Africa, Lesotho, Botswana, Swaziland.

North West Africa: Guinea, The Gambia, Mali, Mauritania, Senegal.

West Africa: Ghana, Liberia, Nigeria, Sierra Leone.

West Central Africa: Ivory Coast, Niger, Upper Volta, Dahomey, Togo, Central African Republic, Cameroon, Chad, Gabon, Equatorial Guinea.

(Note: This is the structure of the original country director change, begun in mid-1966.)

Bureau of East Asian and Pacific Affairs (10)

Australia, New Zealand and Pacific Islands.

Republic of China.

Indonesia, Malaysia, Singapore.

Japan.

Korea.

Laos, Cambodia.

People's Republic of China, Hong Kong, Mongolia (formerly Asian Communist Affairs).

Philippines.

Thailand, Burma.

Vietnam.

(Notes: [1] Three original country directorates merged on January 1, 1968: Burma/Cambodia, Laos, and Thailand became Laos/Cambodia and Thailand/Burma. [2] Two original country directorates merged in fall, 1971: Indonesia and Malaysia/Singapore.)

Bureau of European Affairs (7)

Canada.

Central Europe: Germany, Austria, Switzerland.

Eastern Europe: Bulgaria, Rumania, Yugoslavia, Albania, Czechoslovakia, Hungary, Poland.

Iberia: Spain, Portugal.

Northern Europe: Scandinavia, Iceland, United Kingdom, Ireland, Malta.

Soviet Union.

Western Europe: France, Benelux, Italy.

Bureau of European Affairs (1966-1972) (10)

Canada.

Bulgaria, Rumania, Yugoslavia, Albania.

Czechoslovakia, Hungary, Poland, Baltic States.

France, Benelux.

Germany.

Austria, Italy, Switzerland.

Scandinavia and Iceland.

Soviet Union.

Spain, Portugal.

United Kingdom, Ireland, Malta.

(Note: All Eastern European countries, except Soviet Union, held by one country directorate 1966-1970.)

Bureau of Inter-American Affairs (10)

Argentina, Paraguay, Uruguay.

Bolivia, Chile.

Brazil.

Caribbean Countries.

Central America.

Coordinator of Cuban Affairs.

Ecuador, Peru.

Mexico.

North Coast (Colombia, Venezuela, Guyana).

Panama.

(Note: Country directorates for Bolivia/Chile and Ecuador/Peru merged briefly in 1970-1971, then separated again [original pattern] in the latter year.)

Bureau of Near Eastern and South Asian Affairs (10)

Cyprus.

Greece.

Turkey.

Iran.

India, Ceylon, Nepal, Maldive Islands.

Pakistan, Afghanistan, Bangladesh.

Israel and Arab-Israel Affairs.

Northern Arab Affairs (Lebanon, Jordan, Syria, Iraq.)

Arab Peninsula Affairs (Saudi Arabia, Kuwait,
   Yemen, Aden, Principalities).

Egypt (formerly United Arab Republic).

(Note: As this book went to press, further changes in areas of country director responsibility were in the offing. A long advocated shift of the Arab countries of northern Africa—Algeria, Libya, Morocco, Tunisia—from the Bureau of African Affairs to the Bureau of Near Eastern and South Asian Affairs seemed certain to occur, along with a switch of the country directorates for Greece, Turkey, and Cyprus from NEA to the Bureau of European Affairs. In neither case, however, had exact country directorate areas of responsibility in the new bureaus been determined, and it was not yet clear to which office the remaining countries in the former Office of North African Affairs would be assigned. One final modification in early 1974, of smaller importance, was the transfer of responsibility for Mauritius and the Malagasy Republic from the Office of Central African Affairs to the Office of East African Affairs.)

Appendix C
Methodology

The primary research tool employed in this study was the semistructured interview. This technique was selected over several other possible procedures because of the nature of the subject and of the respondents. A completely open-ended and nondirective technique would have made comparability extremely difficult, given the limited amount of time available for the interviews, while a more structured format would have resulted in loss of information. The total population of incumbent country directors was small enough that all could be interviewed, so sampling procedures were not necessary. Similarly, statistical techniques based on projecting from a sample to an entire population were inappropriate, since the population itself was available.

There were three basic categories of interviews, all of which were conducted by the author, for the most part between October 1968 and April 1969. First, 46 of 49 incumbent country directors were interviewed, using the schedule in Appendix C-2 as a guide. Because of time limitations, not all questions were asked of all CDs, which accounts for the disparities in the total numbers cited on particular points in the text. The schedule was designed to provide an interview approximately ninety minutes in length, and actual interviews lasted from fifty minutes to two and one-half hours, with most being between an hour and an hour and one-half. Whenever possible, these interviews were tape-recorded, but an initial decision was made not to insist upon this if the subject exhibited any reluctance. CDs were also guaranteed anonymity, and responses to certain ques-

tions were not taped if this additional safeguard was requested. Verbatim transcripts of tape-recorded interviews
were prepared, from which quotations in the text were
taken. Extensive notes were taken during those interviews
which were not recorded and expanded upon as necessary
immediately after the interview. Altogether, 26 CD interviews were tape-recorded, and 20 were not (2 because of
mechanical problems). A cross-check of responses between
recorded and nonrecorded interviews revealed no significant differences in responses which could be attributed to
the use of the tape recorder. Reasons for preferring that an
interview not be recorded included in a small number of
cases a concern for security, in others some sensitivity because specific individuals were being discussed, and in still
others some vanity about being quoted directly without a
chance to edit their remarks for grammar and consistency.
Of the three incumbent CDs who declined to be interviewed, two did so because of crowded schedules, while
one believed sufficient information had been obtained from
his ranking country officer, who had participated in one of
a series of pretest interviews.

The second category of interviews were those with opposite numbers in other parts of government, including the
functional bureaus of State. The schedule in Appendix C-3
was used for this purpose. Because these were relatively
short interviews, no attempt was made to record them. Responses were filled in on the interview schedule by the re-
searcher, and amplified as necessary immediately after the
interview. Here, some selection was necessary to determine
interviewees, since it would have been impossible to contact
all opposite numbers, even in the limited number of agencies consulted in this study. Those contacted were selected
from units of other agencies and departments having geographic responsibilities, or whose functional specializations
were such that they could be expected to have frequent
contact with the country directors. They were not selected

randomly, but rather to illuminate various arrangements and problems of interest. The numbers chosen in each agency varied, depending on the way that agency was organized and on the variation in responses obtained in the first few interviews. Where possible, opposite numbers were selected which the CD interviews indicated would be of particular interest. There were a total of 54 interviews of this type, averaging about thirty minutes in length.

The final major category of interviews were those that were primarily informational, being designed to provide details about events discussed in the study. Individuals having specific knowledge of relevant events were sought out, rather than officials holding specific positions. Because of the individualized nature of these interviews, which numbered 40 in all (30 in first wave, 10 additional in early 1971), no standard interview schedule was employed. Specific questions were developed for each interview based upon what was known about the subject's relationship to the CD system. Such information came primarily from other interviews, but was also obtained from press reports and from government documents and publications. These interviews were not recorded, but notes taken during them were transcribed shortly afterward.

After the interviews were completed, they were coded on the various topics discussed in the text, and gradations and positions were developed from the data rather than being imposed upon them. As has been mentioned at various points, the decision not to force answers into discrete choices predetermined by the interviewer meant that responses had to be interpreted, opening up the possibility of some error. At the same time, the chance to obtain more complete information and more subtle shadings of opinion was a compensating advantage, particularly since the total N was so small that hard categories on variables might have led to misleading results if they had been treated in a rigorously statistical fashion.

C-2: Country Director Interview Schedule

1. Could you briefly characterize the differences between the country director and office director positions?

2. What are the advantages and disadvantages of the change from your viewpoint? From the Department of State's point of view?

3. What contributions would you say that your efforts make to U.S. relations with your country of responsibility, and to the overall operations of the department?

4. Are there differences between prescribed country director activities and what you actually do?

5. What is the nature of the country director's relation with the SIG and the IRG? Under what circumstances do your problems reach these bodies?

6. Is the country director job basically an operating one? How much planning is possible? Desirable?

7. What types of decisions do country directors make at their level? What determines the level at which decisions are made?

8. How do most situations requiring decisions arise? How much room is there for country director initiative? Does the country director spend most of his time working on matters which are brought to him by others?

9. How do you differentiate situations calling for action? Is it meaningful to try to categorize such situations, and if so, according to what criteria?

10. Could you give me an example or two of recent matters you've been involved with, for example important decisions taken, recommendations made, or papers prepared?

11. With whom outside your own office do you have direct face-to-face contact? How often and about what?

12. What is the division of labor between deputy assistant secretary, country directors, desk officer? Where does the alternate (deputy) country director fit in? Do you have one? Why or why not?

13. Are some agencies/bureaus/individuals generally easier or harder to reach agreement with? For what reasons?

14. What is the nature of your working arrangements with the ambassador and the embassy overseas? How close is it, and what forms of contact are used? How could these relations be improved?

15. What is the nature of your relations with representatives of your country of responsibility in Washington? Is there a danger of finding yourself an advocate of their desires and wishes at the expense of U.S. positions? How do you keep a balance between the two?

16. Do you use an established committee or working group for interagency contact? What are the advantages and disadvantages?

17. What are the methods of coordination you use? How do you force a decision?

18. What are the best ways of selling your ideas in reaching decisions?

19. How important are personalities, timing, and moods in decision making?

20. What appeal procedures are used from country director decisions? How often? What is the usual outcome when a matter is carried higher up? Does the country director's point of view usually carry the day?

21. To what extent can country directors and their opposite numbers commit their agencies without additional clearance?

22. Are the resources available to the country director sufficient? How important is the trust of superiors, and how can it be developed?

23. In general terms, what use is made of intelligence information? Does the source of the information determine how much weight it carries?

24. How well accepted is the country director's position as coordinator? Does it differ from agency to agency, or from bureau to bureau within the department?

25. What are the limitations on your actions, and what are the sources of these limitations?

26. What qualities/styles/experience are needed for a country director to be able to perform effectively?

27. Are there differences in the way relations are seen by the country director, and the way the same man would see them while serving in an embassy? Is there a difference in perspective?

28. Is the amount of authority which can be exercised by the country director in part determined by such factors as the difficulty of relations with his country, the scale of U.S. commitments and programs there, and/or the geographic bureau in which he serves?

29. Is the country director job in general satisfying? What features are most (least) attractive? Is it good to have this job for career purposes? Are any other jobs that one might have at this stage of a career more attractive?

30. General opinions:

a. Should all foreign affairs be administered by one large department?

b. How useful are the programs often grouped under the term "New Diplomacy"?

c. What is the current nature of the "Communist Challenge"? Are we, as some claim, in a post-Cold War period?

d. Is the U.S. overcommitted or overextended with respect to your country of responsibility? In general? What changes are desirable?

e. What is the current caliber of the department and the Foreign Service? What has been the effect of Wristonization? Herter Report?

f. Can management programs and reorganization alter the department in substantial ways? Are they necessary?

g. What effect will BALPA have on U.S. foreign policy management?

h. Are PPBS and/or similar programming/planning/ budgeting innovations useful? Would a good system of this type help the country director? How?

31. What changes if any would you like to see in the country director operations? Are there some changes you feel are likely to be made in the future?

32. In general, is the organization of the department appropriate to its responsibilities? What changes would be desirable?

33. Are there any other significant matters which haven't been covered?

C-3: OPPOSITE NUMBER INTERVIEW SCHEDULE

1. How long have you been in this position?

2. How frequently do you work with CDs? Which ones (if not obvious)?

3. What methods do you frequently use in working with them? Do you participate in interagency staff meetings run by the CDs? How useful is this device?

4. What is the proper role that State in general and the country directors in particular should play in coordinating U.S. relations abroad? (If needed, follow up with: Should the CDs be seen as the overall coordination point, or as those who bring the diplomatic and political competence?)

5. How well do the CDs fill this role? How good are they, in terms of ability and knowledge of their countries?

6. Do they have a broad enough view, taking into account the problems and missions of other agencies?

7. What are the primary sorts of things that you deal with the CDs on?

8. How difficult are they to work out? Is it generally possible to work out most of your problems at the CD level, or do they have to be resolved higher up?

9. How useful were the SIG and the IRGs from your point of view? From what you know of it, is the new system better or worse for you?

10. Purely as a check on my own observations, I wonder if there are any CDs you have found to be particularly good (or bad, if you care to comment)?

11. Would there be any advantages in having all foreign affairs administered by one large department, formed out of State and the other existing ones?

12. On a related matter, should there be a combined personnel system for all (civilian) foreign affairs agencies?

13. Are there any other matters about the CD system that are important, from your point of view?

Select Bibliography

A. Books and Monographs

Argyris, Chris. *Some Causes of Organizational Ineffectiveness Within the Department of State*. Center for International Systems Research, Department of State, Occasional Paper, 2. Washington, D.C.: GPO, 1967.

Biddle, Bruce J., and Edwin J. Thomas, eds. *Role Theory: Concept and Research*. New York: John Wiley & Sons, 1966.

Braybrooke, David, and Charles E. Lindblom. *A Strategy of Decision: Policy Evaluation as a Social Process*. New York: Free Press, 1963.

Clark, Keith C., and Laurence J. Legere, eds. *The President and The Management of National Security*. A Report by the Institute of Defense Analyses. New York: Praeger, 1969.

Committee on Career Principles, American Foreign Service Association. *Toward a Modern Diplomacy*. Washington, D.C.: American Foreign Service Association, 1968.

Committee on Foreign Affairs Personnel (Herter Committee). *Personnel for the New Diplomacy*. New York: Carnegie Endowment for International Peace, 1962.

Cyert, Richard M., and James G. March. *A Behavioral Theory of the Firm*. Englewood Cliffs, N.J.: Prentice-Hall, 1963.

Downs, Anthony. *Inside Bureaucracy*. Boston: Little, Brown, 1967.

Elder, Robert Ellsworth. *The Policy Machine: The Department of State and American Foreign Policy*. Syracuse: Syracuse University Press, 1960.

Gross, Bertram M. *Organizations and Their Managing*. New York: Free Press, 1964.

Harr, John E. *The Anatomy of the Foreign Service: A Statistical Profile*. Foreign Affairs Personnel Study, 4. New York: Carnegie Endowment for International Peace, 1965.

————. *The Professional Diplomat*. Princeton, N.J.: Princeton University Press, 1969.

Leacacos, John P. *Fires in the In-Basket: The ABC's of the State Department*. Cleveland: World Publishing, 1968.

Lindblom, Charles E. *Intelligence of Democracy*. New York: Free Press, 1965.

————. *The Policy Making Process*. Englewood Cliffs, N.J.: Prentice-Hall, 1968.

Macmahon, Arthur W. *Administration in Foreign Affairs*. University, Ala.: University of Alabama Press, 1953.

March, James G., and Herbert A. Simon. *Organizations*. New York: John Wiley & Sons, 1957.

Mosher, Frederick C., and John E. Harr. *Programming Systems and Foreign Affairs Leadership: An Attempted Innovation*. New York: Oxford University Press, 1970.

Pruitt, Dean G. *Problem Solving in the Department of State*. Social Science Foundation and International Relations Department Monograph Series 2. Denver: University of Denver, 1964-1965.

Redford, Emmette S. *Democracy in the Administrative State*. New York: Oxford University Press, 1969.

Simon, Herbert A. *Administrative Behavior*. 2nd ed. New York: Free Press, 1965.

Snyder, Richard C., H. W. Bruck, and Burton M. Sapin, eds. *Foreign Policy Decision Making: An Approach to the Study of International Politics*. New York: Free Press, 1962.

Sorensen, Theodore C. *Decision-Making in the White House*. New York: Columbia University Press, 1963.

Wilensky, Harold L. *Organizational Intelligence: Knowledge and Policy in Government and Industry*. New York: Basic Books, 1967.

B. Essays and Articles in Collections

Argyris, Chris. "Organizations: Effectiveness and Planning of Change," *International Encyclopedia of the Social Sciences*, XI, 311-319. New York: Macmillan and Free Press, 1968.

Bauer, Raymond F. "The Study of Policy Formation: An Introduction," in Bauer and Kenneth J. Gergen, eds., *The Study of Policy Formation*. New York: Free Press, 1968.

Feldman, Julian, and Herschel E. Kanter. "Organizational Decision Making," in James G. March, ed., *Handbook of Organizations*. Chicago: Rand McNally, 1965.

Gouldner, Alvin K. "Organizational Analysis," in Robert K. Merton, ed., *Sociology Today*. New York: Basic Books, 1959.

Robinson, James A., and Richard C. Snyder. "Decision-Making in International Politics," in Herbert C. Kelman, ed., *International Behavior: A Social-Psychological Analysis*. New York: Holt, Rinehart and Winston, 1965.

Sarbin, Theodore R. "Role: Psychological Aspects," *International Encyclopedia of the Social Sciences*, XIII, 546-552. New York: Macmillan and Free Press, 1968.

Taylor, Donald W. "Decision Making and Problem Solving," in James G. March, ed., *Handbook of Organizations*. Chicago: Rand-McNally, 1965.

Turner, Ralph. "Role: Sociological Aspects," *International Encyclopedia of the Social Sciences*, XIII, 552-557. New York: Macmillan and Free Press, 1968.

C. Articles

Allison, Graham T. "Conceptual Models and the Cuban Missile Crisis," *American Political Science Review*, 63 (September 1969), 689-718.

Bowling, John W. "How We Do Our Thing: Policy Formulation," *Foreign Service Journal*, 47 (January 1970), 19-22, 48.

Johnson, U. Alexis. "Opportunity and Challenge," *Department of State News Letter*, No. 61 (May 1966), pp. 6-7. Reprinted from *Foreign Service Journal*, 43 (April 1966).

Macomber, William B., Jr. "Management Strategy: A Program for the 70's," *Department of State News Letter*, No. 105 (January 1970), 2-5. Originally delivered as speech to employees of State and other foreign affairs agencies, Washington, January 14, 1970.

Marrow, Alfred J. "Managerial Revolution in the State Department," *Department of State News Letter*, No. 68 (December 1966), 34-37.

Mays, Glenn R., Jr. "Companion Tools for Foreign Affairs Management: The PPBS and the SIG/IRG System," *Foreign Service Journal*, 43 (September 1966), Part I, 16-18; (October 1966), Part II, 25-26.

Rusk, Dean. "The Anatomy of Foreign Policy Decisions," *Department of State News Letter*, No. 54 (October 1965), 4-6. Originally delivered as speech to American Political Science Association Convention, September 7, 1965.

Smith, Rufus B. "Problems of the Foreign Service," *Foreign Service Journal*, 46 (June 1969), 28-30.

Spain, James W. "The Country Director: A Subjective Appraisal," *Foreign Service Journal*, 46 (March 1969), 35-36.

Taylor, Maxwell D. "New System for Coping with Our Overseas Problems," *Foreign Service Journal*, 43 (May 1966), 34-36. Originally delivered as speech to American Foreign Service Association Luncheon, Washington, D.C., March 31, 1966.

D. Government Publications and Documents

Crockett, William J. Letter to Country Directors, August 4, 1966. Reprinted as "What the Department Expects of the Country Director," *Department of State News Letter*, No. 67 (November 1966), 13, 69.

Rogers, William P. "Message on the Department of State's Responsibilities," February 7, 1969. Reprinted in U.S.

Congress, Senate Subcommittee on National Security and International Operations, Committee on Government Operations, *The National Security Council: New Role and Structure*. Washington, D.C.: GPO, 1969, pp. 3-4.

Rusk, Dean. "Message to His Colleagues in the Department of State," March 4, 1966. Reprinted in *Department of State News Letter*, No. 59 (March 1969), 3.

U.S. Commission on Organization of the Executive Branch of Government (Hoover Commission). *Foreign Affairs: A Report to the Congress*. Washington: GPO, 1949.

U.S. Congress, Senate Subcommittee on National Security and International Operations, Committee on Government Operations. *The National Security Council: Comment by Henry A. Kissinger*, March 3, 1970. Washington, D.C.: GPO, 1970.

―――. *Planning-Programming-Budgeting*. Washington, D.C.: GPO, 1968.

―――. *The Secretary of State and the Problem of Coordination: New Duties and Procedures of March 4, 1966*. Washington, D.C.: GPO, 1966.

U.S. Congress, Senate Subcommittee on National Security Staffing and Operations, Committee on Government Operations. *Administration of National Security: Staff Reports and Hearings*. Washington, D.C.: GPO, 1965.

U.S. Department of State. *Diplomacy for the 70's: A Program of Management Reform for the Department of State*. Department of State Publication 8593, Department and Foreign Service Series 1430. Washington, D.C.: GPO, 1970.

E. Unpublished Materials

Office of the Executive Director, Bureau of Inter-American Affairs, Department of State. "Organization of ARA/LA Geographic Area Offices." Memorandum prepared at request of deputy coordinator, Alliance for Progress, February 10, 1969. (Typescript.)

Office of Management, Department of State. "A Management Program for the Department of State." August 1966. Washington, D.C.: Department of State, 1966. (Privately circulated.)

Office of Management, Department of State. "Organizing for Action in the Regional Bureaus: A Study of the Role of the Country Desk Officer." Study prepared for the Deputy Under Secretary of State for Administration, March 6, 1963. (Privately circulated.)

Senior Interdepartmental Group Staff. Study on operating history of the Senior Interdepartmental Group, November 1968. (Privately circulated.)

Index

Acheson, Dean, 3n, 4n, 10n, 38-39, 45
ACORD, 54: and relation to country director change, 54. *See also* Crockett, William J.
action, collective nature of, 99
Action for Organizational Development, *see* ACORD
adjustment process, 198, 205
adjustment techniques: employed by country directors, 200-204; enumerated by Lindblom, 200-203
advocacy process, and country directors, 104-5, 295, 299
agency conflict, sources, 108-9
Agriculture, Department of, 84
Alliance for Progress, 58
Allison, Graham T., 11n
Allison, paradigms, 29-30
Alsop, Stewart, 52n
ambassadors: and country directors, 9, 68, 88; efforts to strengthen role, 48; Kennedy letter to, 48
ambiguity and role enactment, 79-80
American Foreign Service Association, 220: Committee on Career Principles, report of, 221, 241, 261; "Young Turks" in, 241-42, 251
Apple, R. W., Jr., 286n
Argyris, Chris, 235
assistant secretaries: use of country director system, 252-53; view of country director managerial competence, 226; view of country director system, 115

asymmetry in interagency relations, 266, 292
attachés: agricultural, 4; commercial, 4

Bachrach, Peter, 26
"backstopping," 186, 196
Ball, George W., 132, 243, 245. *See also* Senior Interdepartmental Group
BALPA (Balance of Payments), 133-34, 141, 281
Baratz, Morton S., 26
Barnard, Chester, 76
Barnes, William, 5n, 43n
Barrett, Richard, 54
Bauer, Raymond A., 24n
Bell, David E., 58-59
Bennis, Warren G., 234
bilateral relations, future of, 296-97
Blankenship, L. Vaughn, 187n
Blau, Peter M., 114
Bohlen, Charles E., 3n
"bounded rationality," 21
Bray, Charles W., III, 219n
Brazil, organizational experiment for, 50, 56
Briggs, Ellis, 48n
Brookings Institution, 237n
Bruce, David, 279
Brzezinski, Zbigniew, 93
Budget, Bureau of the, 54, 271, 295; organizational study by, 237n
Bundy, McGeorge, 6n, 141, 243

Campbell, John Franklin, 237n
CASP, *see* Country Analysis and Strategy Paper
Castro government, 58

341

develop, 246; failure to be operational when announced, 72-73; lack of ties to country director system in practice, 266; limitations of as agent for reducing interagency conflict, 109; operation of SIG under, 131-37; operations of IRGs under, 137, 141; potential of, 11; premises of, 7-8; rationale, 61-62; and relationship to State Department leadership, 85; relationship to Taylor experience, 73; replacement of, 300; structure, 64-65

occasion for action, 17, 178
office directors, in Department of State: duties of, 46; replacement by country directors, 8
Office of Management and Budget (OMB), 295
officers-in-charge: abolishment of positions of, 8; duties of, 47
"official-informal" letters, 165-66
Operation Reduction, 281
Operations Coordinating Board, of Eisenhower National Security Council, 62
opposite numbers, evaluations of country directors, 224-26
OPRED, see Operation Reduction
organizational activity, models of, 76
organizational change: concepts, 258-59; context of, 301; cyclical nature of, 287; distrust of in Department of State, 241; dynamics, 234; factors affecting, summary, 256-58; implementation of, factors affecting, summary, 240; initiation of, 236-37; initiation of vs. imple-

mentation of, 238-40; natural system model of, 234; planned, practicality of, 235; relationship to decision-making process, 259; requirements for, 233, 238; Weberian "rational" model of, 234
organizational climate, as problem for country director change, 242, 246, 257; attitude of Ball, 245; ineffectiveness of SIG, 245-46; limited attention change received, 243-44; loss of initial momentum, 244; relation to organizational change, 241-46; suspicion of as being administrative in nature, 242-43; unclear relationship of country director change to NSAM 341, 242
organizational milieu, of Department of State, 220-21
organizational theorists, human relations school of, 244n
organizations, change in, 12-14, 256-60

Paige, Glenn D., 10n
Palmer, Joseph, II, 279
PARA, see Policy Analysis and Resource Allocation
parochialism, risks of for country directors, 85, 100-101, 103-5, 174-75, 291
Parsons, Talcott, 77n, 234
"partisan analysis," 198
partisan mutual adjustment (PMA), 24-25, 180, 200-202. See also central coordination; Lindblom, Charles E.
Perry, Jack, 41n
personnel reduction, in Nixon administration, and effect on country director system, 280-83